The Rise of Moralism

The Rise of Moralism

THE PROCLAMATION OF THE GOSPEL FROM HOOKER TO BAXTER

C. F. Allison

Morehouse Barlow
Wilton

Morehouse Barlow Co., Inc.
78 Danbury Road
Wilton, Connecticut 06897

ISBN 0-8192-1353-5

Library of Congress Catalog Card Number 84-61194

Printed in the United States of America

Contents

Preface

If it is possible to acknowledge my profound debt to Canon V. A. Demant without implicating him in my interpretation I should like to do so. I pray I may exercise the same respect for *my* students' views that he accorded to mine.

I am indebted to the University of the South for a sabbatical leave, and to the American Association of Theological Schools for a research grant that provided the opportunity to put this together. Without the stimulus and support of The Very Reverend Richard Hooker Wilmer, Jr. this would never have been begun.

The discomfort inevitably concomitant with such an undertaking as this is involuntarily (or anyhow necessarily) shared by one's family. As secretary, proof-reader, adept critic both of grammar and theology, my wife has been as indispensable a part of this work as she is of my life.

Those readers who wish to ingest the essential argument presented here and avoid the detail of interest to specialists could omit, to my sorrow, chapters 2, 5, 6, 7, and 8.

Sewanee 1965   C.F.A.

Acknowledgements

Thanks are due to the following for permission to include material from copyright sources:

Abingdon Press: *"Arminianism in England"*, an article by W. O. Chadwick in *Religion in Life*.

Cambridge University Press: *The First Book of the Irenicon of John Forbes of Corse*, edited and translated by E. G. Selwyn.

Columbia University Press: *Liberty and Reformation in the Puritan Revolution*, by William Haller.

Oxford University Press: *Theology of Culture*, by Paul Tillich.

S.C.M. Press: *Christian Essays in Psychiatry*, by P. Mairet.

Introduction

The terms "orthodox" and "classical" employed in this study to characterize the early seventeenth-century period of Anglican theology may annoy some and perplex others. It will be helpful, then, here at the outset to explain what these terms mean in the pages that follow.

The early seventeenth-century divines—notably Hooker, Andrewes, Donne, and Davenant—established an Anglican theology: a theology that, before them, had been developing but had not come to fruition and was incomplete. Relying heavily upon the Councils of Nicaea and Chalcedon, and taking issue especially with the Council of Trent, those theologians defined the position of Anglicanism and distinguished it from that of Rome, on the one hand, and from the Reformed continental positions, on the other. Doing so, they incidentally accomplished a synthesis within Anglicanism that had not obtained previously and that became the basis upon which the best of Anglican thought builds: a synthesis of thought and sensibility (the special contribution of John Donne), of preaching and practice, of theology and devotion, and, most significantly, of doctrine and ethics. It is to this synthesis within Anglicanism that reference is made when the terms "orthodox" and "classical" are applied to the Anglican theology of the early seventeenth century. The representative figures of this period have never properly received the attention and respect they deserve. Neither the bitter polemic which characterized the sixteenth century nor the tendency toward Pelagianism and Socinianism which developed in the next half century can be found in the theology of this period. Only the uncritical tendency to sycophantic acquiescence in the Stuart concept of Divine Right seems distinctly embarrassing in the theology and sermons of the early seventeenth century.

This study has not, however, been undertaken primarily to argue that Anglican orthodoxy should be historically assigned to the early seventeenth century. Whether that theology be called orthodox or not, it will be argued here that the later Carolines—with powerful assistance from certain non-Anglicans—radically abridged the Anglican synthesis and prepared the way for a moralism that has afflicted English theology ever since and still afflicts it to-day, a moralism which is less than the full gospel. In making this argument, three points will emerge that depart importantly from the usual interpretation of seventeenth-century theology and history. Let us identify those points briefly in order to indicate the scope of the discussion that follows.

1. The question of the formal cause of justification, it will be demonstrated, is central to an understanding of seventeenth-century soteriology. Subsequent scholarship has been seriously distorted because it has been based upon an assumption that the issue of formal cause was not, in fact, crucial. Most scholars have blandly assumed, without evidence, that Hooker, Andrewes, Donne, and Bellarmine (Anglican and Roman Catholic) were all wrong when they explicitly stipulated that the question of formal cause *is* the fundamental issue posed to Christian soteriology. Careful examination of the evidence confirms that differences over formal cause basically divided Anglicanism from the teaching of the Council of Trent, and, furthermore, determined the direction of a new school of thought that arose during the Civil War in England, a school neither "orthodox" Anglican nor Tridentine. This latter school of thought grew in influence over the succeeding centuries until it became predominant within Anglicanism and English-speaking Christianity in general. A return to an emphasis upon the disputes over formal cause in Christian soteriology would go a long way towards clearing up other misunderstandings that have developed with respect to modern inadequate treatments of such terms as "infusion", "imparting", and "imputation".

2. The new school of thought which arose during the English

Civil War has never been adequately studied with due attention to its development, inconsistencies, moralistic tendencies, contrasts with "orthodox" Anglicanism, or its subsequent vast influence. It was represented, among others, by such disparate figures as Jeremy Taylor, Henry Hammond, Herbert Thorndike, George Bull, and Richard Baxter. Of subsequent students of the period, Samuel Taylor Coleridge alone affords a responsible criticism of the theology of Jeremy Taylor. It was Coleridge who acutely observed: "Socinianism is as inevitable a deduction from Taylor's scheme as Deism and Atheism are from Socinianism." This remark not only exposes the fatal flaw in Taylor's own theology but also sums up the trend from orthodoxy in the early Caroline period to a moralism and deism in the eighteenth century and on to the secularism of the nineteenth and twentieth centuries. Coleridge failed, however, to give the evidence for his dictum or to detect that his criticism of Taylor's theology as set forth in published works did not apply to the theology explicit in Taylor's prayers and devotions. The fact is, as we shall see, that Taylor held one position in his sermons and theology and another opposite theology in his prayers. It is important to inquire, as we shall, what led Taylor into this odd and embarrassing posture.

3. From the new school of thought, which might be called the new moralism, has issued the characteristically modern notion that deliberate sin is invariably more pernicious than sin founded in ignorance or grounded in the unconscious. This grotesque distinction, which inevitably puts premiums on ignorance and suppression, was first formally propounded at the fifth and sixth sessions of the Council of Trent, and was taken up by the later Carolines and by post-Civil War Protestants. It has come to be the prevalent theology of the whole Christian Church in the West with consequences disastrous for the Christian community. Lest it be supposed that this study will be an uncritical encomium to the genius of the early Carolines, let it be said that we shall seek to identify those weaknesses in the theology of Hooker, Andrewes, Donne, and Davenant that, as it were, gave an opening to Taylor and others for the development of their destructive doctrine. It

would also be negligent to ignore the traumatic impact of the English Civil War upon the Christian Church, upon both the Anglican and the Puritan traditions; and we shall seek to indicate how the "troubles" intruded into the realm of theology. Finally, that we may not be thought too provincial in our argument, we shall try to relate the tendency toward *dis*integration in seventeenth-century theology to the wider split that was occurring at the time in Western culture between thought and feeling, consciousness and unconsciousness, as has been pointed out, for example, by the late T. S. Eliot. That split, as it manifested itself in theology, is most painfully detectable as a radical seventeenth-century separation of ethics from doctrine.

Respect for seventeenth-century divines, early or late, has tended to be undiscriminating. There is indeed much to respect, but there is also much to deplore. And the longer the century went on, the more there came to be that was deplorable in theology. Surely no one, not even those recent scholars who have written so uncritically of Jeremy Taylor's theology, has ever approached Holy Communion having fulfilled the conditions Taylor established for a worthy communicant. One will search the sermons preached in England in the century after 1640 almost in vain if one looks for suggestions of the kerygma (possible exceptions will be noted in chapter 8). The later Carolines departed not only from the teaching of Hooker, Andrewes, and Donne but as well from the Prayer Book itself. It is an extraordinary fact that the "Arianism" of John Milton has been often discussed but (Coleridge excepted) the heretical inclinations of Jeremy Taylor have been ignored. The new moralism has achieved virtual dominion over theology, especially latterly, on account of its influence through the Latitudinarians, the Nonjurors and, less directly, the Wesleyans and the Tractarians. So great has been its influence that Church scholarship itself seems to have been effectively debilitated. A scholar to-day who ventures to criticize seriously either Taylor or Baxter would do well first to ponder another dictum of Coleridge: "Truth is a good dog; but beware of barking too close to the heels of an error, lest you get your brains kicked out."

1

Classical Anglicanism

We sometimes overlook how much agreement existed among Christians at the beginning of the seventeenth century. There was, for example, general acceptance of the dogmas of the Trinity and Christology, and the prevalent teaching on atonement was widely shared among Roman Catholic, Lutheran, Reformed, Anglican, and Puritan theologians. The end of the same century saw nothing like this agreement. A tradition of consistent and interrelated Christian teaching on creation, revelation, incarnation, and atonement had been largely undermined of its soteriological foundations. It is important to discover what happened to these foundations in the course of the seventeenth century. This requires that we first understand what the issues were as the century opened. The crucial argument, at that point, concerned the nature of the Gospel, and it was focused upon soteriology. The question posed itself this way: As recipients of the Gospel, what causes our new relationship with God to be what it is?

RICHARD HOOKER
1554-1600

Richard Hooker is one theologian who concerned himself with this problem, and his argument is typical of the position taken by Anglicans. He attempts, for one thing, to reassure those people who feared that if they had any doubt of their election, it meant they were, in fact, not of the elect. He points out that no man is "so enlightened in the knowledge, or so established in the love of that wherein his salvation standeth, as to be perfect, neither doubting nor shrinking at all".[1]

At the same time, however, Hooker points out the differences between the Anglican Church and the Council of Trent concerning the doctrine of justification. He notes the areas of agreement between them: they both teach that all have sin and are destitute of justice; that it is God who justifies; that no one has ever attained this justice except by Christ; and that this action of Christ must be applied to the sinner.

> Wherein then do we disagree? We disagree about the nature of the very essence of the medicine whereby Christ cureth our disease: about the manner of applying it, about the number and the power of means, which God requireth in us for the effectual applying thereof to our soul's comfort.[2]

The Council of Trent declared that the righteousness whereby a Christian man is justified is infused and inherent in the soul of man. As the body is warm by the heat which is in the body, so the regenerate person is righteous by his own infused, inherent grace.[3] Hooker argues that this position "doth pervert the truth of Christ"[4] and becomes the basis of other inevitable errors.

> Whether they [Roman Catholics] speak of the first or second justification, they make the essence of it a divine quality inherent, they make it righteousness which is in us. If it be in us, then it is ours, as our souls are ours, though we have them from God, and can hold them no longer than pleaseth him; for if he withdraw the breath of our nostrils, we fall to dust: but the righteousness wherein we must be found, if we will be justified, is not our own; therefore we cannot be justified by any inherent quality. Christ hath merited righteousness for as many as are found in him. In him God findeth us, if we be faithful; for by faith we are incorporated into him. Then, although in ourselves we be altogether sinful and unrighteous, yet even the man which in himself is impious, full of iniquity, full of sin; him being found in Christ through faith, and having his sin in hatred through repentance; him God beholdeth with a gracious eye, putteth away his sin by not imputing it, taketh quite away the punishment due thereunto, by pardoning it; and accepteth him in Jesus Christ, as perfectly righteous, as if he had fulfilled all that is commanded him in the law. . . .[5]

On the other hand, Hooker also argues that there *is* an inherent righteousness in sanctification.

Now concerning the righteousness of sanctification, we deny it not to be inherent; we grant, that unless we work, we have it not; only we distinguish it as a thing in nature different from the righteousness of justification.[6]

In other words: Christians are justified by the righteousness of Christ whereby they dwell in him and are thus acceptable to God, but this is not on account of any inherent righteousness of their own. The righteousness of sanctification is that whereby we grow in grace by virtue of being in Christ. It is a grateful response to a gratuitous justification.

The argument centred around a scholastic term: formal cause. The formal cause of a thing was that which made it to be what it is, as heat makes a thing hot. The Council of Trent held that the formal cause (*unica formalis causa*) of justification was the inherent righteousness of a regenerate person infused into him. Hooker insists that this righteousness of our own is the righteousness of sanctification, and, being imperfect, can never be that which makes our acceptance by God what it is. The righteousness whereby we are accepted by God is the righteousness of Christ *imputed* to us when we are incorporated in Christ.

Hooker was criticized by Walter Travers, the Puritan theologian, for using scholastic terms, and for suggesting that the English Church agreed in many respects with the Council of Trent. In reply, Hooker argues that Travers is unfair to the Roman Catholics when he states that they deny Christ's righteousness as the meritorious cause of taking away sin. Hooker further asserts that "no man doubteth but they (Roman Catholics) make another formal cause of justification than we do".[7] As to the use of scholastic terms he says that Travers' "opinion is no canon",[8] and goes on to argue that the question of formal cause is "the very essence"[9] of the problem, and is the basis of other, secondary disagreements with Roman Catholics.

His use of scholastic terms does not make Hooker's understanding of the Gospel dry or academic. His theological positions seem to have come from a pastoral understanding of sin and redemption. He insists, for example, that one essential emphasis of the Gospel is the initiative taken by God for our salvation.

> . . . it is no unnecessary thing that we note the way or method of the Holy Ghost in framing man's sinful heart to repentance. A work, the first foundation whereof is laid by opening and illuminating the eye of faith, because by faith are discovered the principles of this action, whereunto unless the understanding do first assent, there can follow in the will towards penitency no inclination at all. . . . For fear is impotent and unable to advise itself; yet this good it hath, that men are thereby made desirous to prevent, if possible they may, whatsoever evil they dread.[10]

Because fear *is* "impotent and unable to advise itself" the Christian Gospel consists of more than law and the threat of judgement. It also communicates the love of God to man. The Gospel is more than an exhortation to repentance. "Howbeit, when faith hath wrought a fear of the event of sin, yet repentance hereupon ensueth not, unless our belief conceive both the possibility and the means to avert evil. . . ."[11] Fear is thus powerless to effect repentance. It is the Gospel which provides the necessary good news of a merciful God. Hooker adds that we cannot "possibly forsake sin, unless we first begin again to love. . . . I therefore conclude, that fear worketh no man's inclination to repentance, till somewhat else have wrought in us love also."[12]

This may seem an obvious and pedestrian point, but in view of its absence among later Anglican theologians, it is important to take note of the emphasis Hooker gives to it. Even the calamities of judgement are seen by him in the context of God's prior love and action.

> So hard it is to cure a sore of such quality as pride is, inasmuch as that which rooteth out other vices, causeth this; and (which is even above all conceit) if we were clean from all spot and blemish both of other faults and of pride, the fall of angels doth make it almost a question, whether we might not need a preservative still, lest we should haply wax proud, that we are not proud. What is virtue but a medicine, and vice but a wound? Yet we have so often deeply wounded ourselves with medicines, that God hath been fain to make wounds medicinable; to cure by vice where virtue hath stricken; to

suffer the just man to fall, that, being raised, he may be taught what power it was which upheld him standing. I am not afraid to affirm it boldly, with St Augustine, that men puffed up through a proud opinion of their own sanctity and holiness, receive a benefit at the hands of God, and are assisted with his grace, when with his grace they are not assisted, but permitted, and that grievously, to transgress; whereby, as they were in over-great liking of themselves surplanted, so the dislike of that which did surplant them may establish them afterwards the surer. Ask the very soul of Peter, and it shall undoubtedly make you itself this answer: My eager protestations, made in the glory of my ghostly strength, I am ashamed of; but those crystal tears, wherewith my sin and weakness was bewailed, have procured my endless joy; my strength hath been my ruin, and my fall my stay.[13]

Hooker's understanding of the Gospel reflects an acute pastoral concern. He objects to any teaching of assurance and election that creates despair for the hearers on account of doubt or sin. He objects to the teaching of the Council of Trent that our inherent righteousness is the righteousness of our justification. He sees this teaching as the foundation of subsequent errors of the Church of Rome concerning merit[14] and works of supererogation.[15]

JOHN DAVENANT
1572-1641
Bishop of Salisbury

This crucial difference, discerned by Hooker, between Anglicanism and Roman Catholicism was explored more thoroughly by Davenant than by any other Anglican theologian. His work provides a detailed discussion of soteriology as it was commonly conceived by Anglicans prior to the Civil War (1640). In *A Treatise on Justification or the "Disputatio de Justitia Habituali et Actuali"*[16] (published in 1631) Davenant contrasts Anglican doctrine with the doctrine of justification proclaimed by the Council of Trent and defended by Robert Cardinal Bellarmine. Davenant does not attempt to discuss justification and works in its entirety, but by discussing certain aspects of it, he clarifies the total problem which confronted soteriology in the early seventeenth century.

His treatise is a two volume work, in reply to Cardinal Bellarmine, in which the principal arguments of Hooker are amplified in great detail.

Man's righteousness is from God and cannot be clothed with any semblance of merit or worthiness, nor can it be a causal condition for the free gift of justification. This righteousness, as Davenant construes it, involves two terms: *habitual* and *actual* righteousness. Habitual righteousness is, for Davenant, inherent righteousness, or "the supernatural gift of sanctifying grace opposed to Original Sin . . . both repairing and renewing that image of God which through Original Sin was defiled and lost".[17] Actual righteousness is the performance of good works.

Davenant agrees with Bellarmine that habitual righteousness is infused into the justified. He denies, however, Bellarmine's charge that Protestants hold sin to be covered up by God's acceptance in justification. On the contrary, he argues that Luther, Calvin, and the English Protestants hold that there is a real infusion of righteousness in justification. He insists that this habitual (or inherent) righteousness does not exclude original sin, nor does it formally justify believers in the sight of God. It is on these points that Davenant takes exception to Bellarmine's interpretation of the Council of Trent.

Formal cause was agreed upon by all sides as the central problem in a discussion of justification. The form—or formal cause—of a thing is "that by which a thing is what it is".[18] There was agreement that Christ's satisfaction was the meritorious cause ("on account of which") and faith was the instrumental cause ("with which") of our justification. It was, however, the formal cause ("by which") of justification that separated Roman Catholic from Reformed theologians. Bellarmine defends the argument of the Council of Trent that the sole formal cause of justification is the infusion of inherent righteousness.[19] That "which made our justification what it is", that "by which" we are justified, is an infusion of habitual (or inherent) righteousness into the soul of man. This infusion of inherent righteousness is, by its very nature, that "by which" we are justified.

The effect of infused love is, that it reconciles man to God, that is, makes him acceptable and a friend to God; and this effect follows absolutely, from the nature of the thing.[20]

For Bellarmine, this infusion accomplishes two things: washing and sanctification. Thus, justification is not merely forgiveness or remission of sins but also sanctification. It could not possibly be an *imputation* of righteousness. For anyone to be accounted righteous when only imputatively so would be fictitious, dishonest, and under anathema according to the Council of Trent.

Davenant does not deny that habitual righteousness is infused by God's grace, but he does deny that it is the formal cause of justification. He argues that it requires intolerable pride to assume that there is within us a righteousness of our own that makes us acceptable to God and righteous in his sight. He considers such an assumption a presumptuous infringement upon God's justice. Infused righteousness cannot perfectly and absolutely overcome the evil in man, and thus it is, in itself, an insufficient cause of justification. The difference on this question between Bellarmine and Davenant is reflected in their respective comments on Rom. 7.17-19: "For the good I would, I do not and the evil that I would not, that I do."

BELLARMINE
We learn hence that to be justified by Christ is not to be accounted or pronounced just, but truly to be made and constituted just by the obtaining of inherent righteousness absolute and perfect (*de Just.* lib. 2, cap. 3).

DAVENANT
We do not deny that inherent righteousness is infused into the justified by Christ . . . but we affirm that, whilst in this life it is inchoate and imperfect, and therefore not the cause of our justification, but the appendage.[21]

The Council of Trent held that concupiscence in the regenerate is not sin. Because grace and sin are mutually exclusive, the infusion of righteousness in justification has eradicated all that has the formal nature of sin, and there is nothing remaining in a justified person that is hateful to God.[22] It also held that:

Original sin is true death of the soul and constitutes man an enemy to God: but concupiscence remaining in the regenerate is by no means fatal, nor does it place them in a state of enmity with God; therefore, it has not the nature of sin.[23]

If concupiscence is sin, then has Christ not truly, but imputatively only redeemed us from sin; and the devil is more powerful than Christ; in as much as he has truly defiled us while Christ has not truly washed us.[24]

Davenant held, on the other hand, that, though real change takes place in justification,[25] there is nevertheless sin in justified persons. The infused righteousness, though real, is imperfect, and consequently is not, and cannot be, the formal cause of justification. He expresses this basic difference with Bellarmine and the Council of Trent in the following remarks:

Whether, by infusion or inherent grace, whatever hath the true nature and proper character of sin is forthwith eradicated and entirely taken away in the justified. We deny it, the Papists affirm it, . . . the questions involved in this one point lie at the foundation of all the other disputes concerning justification and works.[26]

For, according to our adversaries the formal cause of justification expels by inhesion whatsoever is in itself hateful to God, or worthy of punishment.[27]

Original sin has been "broken" and "hewn in pieces", but (despite the Roman Catholic assertion to the contrary) sin does exist in the regenerate along with infused grace. The justified must, therefore, continue to struggle against sin. There is no perfectionism for Davenant. No man fulfils the law and all men sin. He argues that Rom. 7.19 ("The evil I would not...") is a description of regenerate persons as much as it is of those still living under the old covenant.[28] Though justified, the regenerate still struggle against the "old Adam". He describes original sin as having infected the understanding, the will, and the affections. Concupiscence is seated, not in the sensual power alone, but in the will, and even in the soul itself, and it is always tainted with the residue of original sin. Bellarmine (following the Council of Trent) maintains that venial sin does not have the formal nature of sin. Davenant claims that the distinction between mortal and venial sin is an evasion. By making this distinction, and by denying that concupiscence is tainted with residual original sin, Bellarmine, in Davenant's opinion, attempts to avoid the inadequacy of inherent righteousness as the formal cause of justification. Davenant's argument that sin persists in the regenerate precludes any possibility that the infusion of inherent righteousness might suffice as the formal cause of justification.

The formal cause of justification, according to Davenant, is the *imputation* of Christ's righteousness.

> *To impute any thing, then, to any one* is the same, in this question, as *to reckon and account it in the number of those things which are his own and belong to him.* But not only our own peculiar passions, actions, or qualities may be imputed to us; but also certain external things, which neither flow from us nor inhere in us. . . . We grant the form of justification to be that, by which man is not only accounted and pronounced justified before God, but is made or constituted so. But . . . it is not absolutely necessary that this term be derived either from an inherent form, or that it should imply an inherent form.[29]

For instance: when a son is admitted into Royal favour in recognition of the loyalty and service of his father, it may be said that the qualities of the one are imputed to the other. The same may be said of a murderer who is pardoned in recognition of a favour or satisfaction made on his behalf by someone else.

Davenant's point, then, is that the quality of heat is the formal cause of a thing being hot, but moderate heat can make a thing only moderately hot.

> So imperfect and incipient righteousness renders a man just but imperfectly and inchoately; but not but that which is itself perfect and absolute can render him perfectly and absolutely so. And to such righteousness God has respect, when he either justifies the wicked at first, or, when regenerate, he esteems and accounts him *as* justified. Therefore let the former be the formal cause . . . (sanctification) but this latter alone will be the formal cause of this absolute and judiciary justification.[30]

Infusion of inherent righteousness, in other words, is the formal cause not of justification but of sanctification. For Davenant, salvation

> includes the cause of it and way to obtain it. The cause of human salvation is the free mercy of God putting away our sins, through the work of Christ and accepting us to life eternal on account of his obedience: and this gracious act of God we call *justification*. The way to salvation, or to the kingdom, is to serve God in holiness and righteousness all the days of our life. But that we may be able to enter upon this way of salvation God heals the weakness of our minds and restores and repairs his "image" in us; and this act we call *sanctification* or *regeneration*. God is said to save us by both acts.[31]

Justification is perfect and thus requires the imputation of Christ's righteousness as its formal cause. Sanctification is imperfect and requires the grace of God acting in our own lives.

Davenant does not deny the infusion of inherent righteousness, but he does deny that it is sufficient to be the formal cause of justification. Bellarmine did not consider it possible that God, by the righteousness and obedience of Christ alone, should reckon us as justified. The benefit of the imputation (which he did not deny) is restricted, in his view, to obtaining the effect of inherent righteousness. That is the substance of the difference between the Anglican view, represented by Davenant, and the view of the Council of Trent, represented by Bellarmine.

The question of formal cause is the basis of other differences between the two schools of thought. Works of supererogation are dismissed by Davenant, not only by appeal to Scripture and the Fathers, but equally by his argument that the regenerate, being yet imperfect, are unable perfectly to fulfil the law. Works over and above what is required by God seem, to Davenant, absurdly impossible.

He also denies, on the same basis, any merit of condignity (or claim by the regenerate on God's justice) on account of the supposed worthiness of good works. The regenerate is a child by adoption, a servant of God, and therefore can never claim a reward from God on the basis of justice. Furthermore, all the works of man are tainted with sin, and fall short of the righteousness of God. Nor will Davenant allow any claim on God's justice on account of his promise, because a promise does not confer parity between a good work and its reward. Our righteousness is acceptable to God only by virtue of his gracious mercy.

Good works may be said to be necessary to justification as concurrent or preliminary conditions only so long as they are not understood in a causal or meritorious sense. Good works are necessary, Davenant argues, in the sense of chronological conditions or order. They may even be considered as "the way appointed to eternal life"—but never in the sense of *cause*. He gives two illustrations:

1. A beggar must acknowledge his destitution, go to a place where alms are given, and hold out his hand; but he does not merit or *cause* the alms to be given by taking these necessary actions.

2. To be knighted a man must go and kneel before the sovereign as a necessary condition and act. It would be absurd to infer from this, however, that going to court and falling on his knees is the *cause* of his knighthood.

Davenant concedes, following the same argument, that good works are necessary to preserve a state of justification, but he insists that such works do not and cannot *cause* justification to be preserved. So concerned is he about possible confusion on this point, Davenant actually urges great restraint in saying that good works are necessary to justification. He fears that if the necessity is conceded, it will be construed as a concession that good works *cause* justification. He points out that the Church frequently refrains from certain expressions which, though true in themselves, lend themselves to false inferences in particular situations. Thus, though it is said with perfect truth that

the blessed Virgin is the Mother of Christ; yet the Holy Fathers were unwilling to use that expression, lest they should appear to make a concession to Nestorius, who denied her the title . . . Mother of God.[32]

For the same reason, he concludes, in discussions with Roman theologians great care should be taken when acknowledging the necessity of works not to permit any inference that works are the cause of justification.

Cardinal Bellarmine seeks to demonstrate the causal necessity of good works for salvation by the illustration of Matt. 25.34: "Come ye blessed of my Father, possess you the kingdom prepared for you from the beginning. For I was an hungered, and you gave me to eat. . . ." Davenant answers that the conjunction "for" does not imply meritorious cause but is only a sign of the cause. He illustrates his point by the example of a doctor who is told, "Come, take this place prepared for you for you are wearing the garb of a doctor". "For" here has reference, says Davenant, not to the cause of a situation but to a sign of that cause. In the same way, "for" in the text from Matthew represents not the *cause* of salvation but the *signs* or marks of a state of salvation. The Matthew text, and others like it, are descriptions not of the *means* of salvation but of the *way* of salvation, and thus are descriptive of the people who are to inherit the kingdom.

Davenant's understanding of the place of faith in justification as set forth in reply to Bellarmine's assertion that Protestants wrongly claim salvation is possible only by faith. Davenant argues that faith is not the formal cause of justification (any more than infused righteousness or good works). The function of faith is merely "to apprehend and apply to us the meritorious cause".[33] The question whether a man is justified by faith, even though he be a persistent sinner, is ridiculous and meaningless according to Davenant. Faith and works are, he asserts, separate but related. Faith is independent of good works with respect to efficacy, and can exist apart from good works with respect to operation. The very act of apprehending salvation, which is faith, necessarily issues in good works. Davenant draws an analogy to the act of the eye alone in perceiving colours. The neck, chest, and trunk are not necessary, except by presence, for this operation. Yet it would be wrong to infer that the eye alone would be able to see if a person were without neck, chest, and trunk. Though the eyes perform the operation of seeing, they cease to be able to do so without the presence of the other members. Similarly, faith can apprehend salvation without their [good works] concurring in the very act of apprehending it; yet it cannot, if they are separated as to their existence; for by such separation faith itself will be destroyed.[34]

Faith that justifies is not, then, the same for Bellarmine as it is for Davenant. Justifying faith for Bellarmine is general assent to the total revelation of God. Davenant concurs that justifying faith assents to total revelation, but insists that it is nevertheless principally grounded in Christ the mediator, and his (gratuitous) promises concerning the remission of sins. He quotes Aquinas, interestingly, to support his view that faith as justification does not subsume the total revelation of God, but only God in the action of remitting sins.

Davenant maintains, none the less, that his basic difference with Bellarmine concerning justification is not really on the level of faith and works at all. Good works, he says, are never perfect, are always tainted with sin, even in the regenerate. The basic difference, he insists, rests in the question of formal cause.

It rests with them [Roman Catholics] to endeavour to prove that wretched man, encompassed with this mortal and corruptible flesh, is nevertheless furnished with so perfect a righteousness, that he can present this his inherent righteousness, even before the scrutinising eye of God, for the purpose of receiving a plenary justification. Nay, more, they must also maintain this point, that from this infused righteousness flow works so purified from all defilement, so free from all stain of sin, that any regenerate person can say—truly to God—"If I have deserved it give me the kingdom of heaven; if my works do not deserve it on the principle of condignity, refuse me!" O intolerable pride! O desperate madness! . . . We have then to shew, that God imparts to the justified the first fruits of the Spirit and certain eminent gifts of sanctification, yet so that we are entirely dependent upon his mercy and the grace of our mediator; but that sin is not so entirely rooted out from this mortal body, as that we can derive from that infused and inherent righteousness, a ground for justification before God. This also we have to shew, that the works which flow from this inchoate righteousness, however pleasing and acceptable to God, are still not in themselves so absolutely perfect, as that life eternal should be, not the gift of God in Christ (Rom. 6.23), but a reward paid, on the principle of condignity, to these our works. . . . It is not therefore more difficult to shew that the doctrine of free justification is true, and to exhibit the deficiencies of man's righteousness, than it is to point to the light of the sun.[35] . . .

Davenant's whole thrust goes to the gratuitous nature of the Gospel. His conviction that sin is present in the regenerate is the foundation of his attack on the Tridentine formal cause of justification. It is significant that his emphasis on free grace is not motivated by antinomianism or belief that God makes fewer (or easier) demands under the new covenant. On the contrary, it is precisely his conviction that God's righteousness is absolute which leads him to insist that any righteousness of our own is wholly inadequate for salvation. He makes a penetrating point that some men think one way concerning justification in their public disputes and theological polemics, and quite another way in their private meditations and prayers.

> None of them speak of their own inherent righteousness before the Divine tribunal, but they fly full of fear to the mercy and acceptance of God in Christ. But if they were willing to stand by their doctrine, they must either depend upon this formal cause, or give up hope of salvation.[36]

This insight of Davenant is remarkably prophetic, as we shall see, of later developments in the treatment of the Gospel in the seventeenth century.

GEORGE DOWNAME
d. 1634

George Downame (sometimes Downham), Bishop of Derry, also wrote a work devoted to the doctrine of justification which was published in 1639. Its full title provides a summary of the contents:

> *A Treatise of Justification: Wherein is First Set Down the True Doctrine in the Causes, Effect, Fruits, and Consequences of it, according to the Word of God. And then all Objections and Cavils of the Adversaries to God's free Justification by Grace are answered and confuted, especially of Robert Bellarmine, Jesuite and Cardinall. Wherein also the Popish doctrine of merits is refuted and disproved, with many other waightie points of Christian Religion occasionally handled and discussed, and difficult places of holy Scriptures expounded, and vindicated.*

Bishop Downame's doctrine manifests the same concern as that of Davenant for the gratuitous nature of justification, and their views of the doctrine are similar in many other respects. Downame's understanding of the relationship of faith and justification is quite like that of Davenant and follows from the position taken by Hooker. The focus of justifying faith is Christ (as mediator), and this faith is essentially trust in Christ for the remission of sins. There are two senses in which it may be said that faith alone justifies. First, we are justified by the righteousness of Christ and not by any righteousness inherent in ourselves. Second, the righteousness of Christ may be apprehended by faith alone.

> Not that justifying faith is or can be alone : but because of there being many graces in the faithful which have their several commendations; yet none of them serveth to apprehend Christ's righteousness but faith onely and yet that faith which is alone severed from all inward graces and outward obediences, doth not justify either alone or at all; because it is not a true and lively, but a counterfeit and dead faith.[37]

For justification, therefore, "Good works are not necessary by necessity of Efficacie".[38]

God does, however, make and constitute righteous those whom he has justified. He does this in two ways: by the imputation of Christ's righteousness, and by actual infusion of righteousness. Downame agrees with Davenant that the former is the righteousness of justification, and the latter is the righteousness of sanctification. Justification, then, is the imputation of Christ's righteousness, which is an action of God *without* us. Sanctification is an infusion of righteousness, which is our own and *within* us. Justification is perfect. Sanctification, which is only begun in this life, will be perfected only in the life to come. There are degrees of sanctification whereby inherent righteousness is increased by the practice of good works, but there are no degrees of justification. Downame defines justification as that

> . . . whereby a faithful man is taught to believe and know, that hee being a sinner himselfe, and by sinne obnoxious to eternal damnation; is by the mercies of God, and merits of Christ through faith, not only freed from guilt of his sinnes and from everlasting damnation, but also

accepted as righteous before God in Christ, and made heire of eternal life.[39]

That righteousness by which we are justified must be perfect, and because our own righteousness is imperfect, only the righteousness of Christ is sufficient to effect our acquittal at the bar of God's justice. The presence of sin in the regenerate, Downame argues, makes it impossible to consider inherent righteousness as the formal cause of justification. Furthermore:

> Eternal life is not to bee had without perfect fulfilling of the Law, which is no where to be found but onely in Christ. And therefore, by the onely meritorious obedience of Christ . . . we are saved. But how should we be saved by his obedience, if it be not communicated unto us, and made ours for our selves? How can it bee made ours, but by imputation?[40]

Consequently, the formal cause of justification is the imputation of Christ's righteousness.

Cardinal Bellarmine argues that Christ's righteousness cannot be the formal cause of justification because it is the meritorious cause. Downame answers that the point is not that Christ's righteousness is the formal cause of justification, but rather that the *imputation* of it is. He goes on to describe the efficient, principal, moving, and instrumental causes of justification. The crucial issue, however, as with Davenant, is the formal cause.

Downame also rejects the attempt by some Protestants to make remission of sins the formal cause of justification. This is, in fact, the principal concern of his treatise. He concedes that justification is *both* remission of sins *and* imputation of righteousness, but he insists that only the latter can be the formal cause. He argues that if remission of sins be considered the entire formal cause, then the following errors will be necessary to maintain this "maine error": no righteousness will concur in justification with remission of sins; the righteousness by which we are justified will be solely the effect of Christ's righteousness (remission of sins); and, finally, the act of faith, not the righteousness of Christ, will be imputed for righteousness. This criticism of remission of sins as the formal cause of justification does not appear in Davenant's work, but his general theology would surely have led him to the same conclusions. Downame's discussion of works of condignity and supererogation is almost the same as that of Davenant. They share concern for the gratuitous nature of justification. They agree that *imputation* of Christ's righteousness is its formal cause. The conviction of sin in the regenerate is the common basis of their criticism of the Roman doctrine of merit and formal cause.

Downame's discussion of justification differs, however, from that of Davenant in one significant respect:

> We consider it [justification] not as a suddaine and momentary action, which is of no continuance, as if all our sinnes both past, present, and to come are remitted in an infant . . . for while we continue sinners, we have still need to be justified. And as we always have sinne in this life . . . we have need, that Christ's righteousness should be imputed unto us: and as we sinne daily so Christ our advocate should continually make "intercession for us". . . . But if justification should be wrought once and at once, . . . then must we erroneously conceive, that the sinnes which after the first moment of our justification we doe commit, are actually remitted before they bee committed; Whereas God forgiveth only sinnes past, Rom. 3.25. So shall we not only set open a gap to all licentiousness . . . but also shall open the mouthes of our adversaries. . . .[41]

Davenant, on the other hand, argues that justification cleanses us from the guilt of sin, uprooting it, and implanting within us the grace of Christ by the Spirit. This is done "in one moment, and perfectly; sanctification cleanses from the very indwelling contagion and filth of sin, little by little, and gradually".[42] Davenant seems to have involved himself in a difficulty on this point. If the imputation of Christ's righteousness is justification, and this is "in one moment", then how are subsequent sins forgiven? Since inherent righteousness (sanctification) is an imperfect basis for forgiveness of our sins, by what are we forgiven and accepted after our justification, or, for that matter, in the final judgement?

Downame's objection to the claim that justification is a "suddaine and momentary" action may well have been an implicit criticism of Davenant's position. There is little in Davenant that could be used to defend him from this criticism. It must be remembered, however, that Davenant specifically states that it is not his intention to discuss the *whole* doctrine of justification. His work is devoted almost entirely to justification in the sense of initial forgiveness and acceptance by God. Perhaps in a more complete discussion of justification his difficulty would have been overcome. It remains true, however, that his description of justification as an act "in one moment" raises problems that are not solved elsewhere in his work.

Downame discusses the relationship of justification and sanctification differently. The Bishop of Derry maintains that justification is a state as well as an act. It has made us a member in Christ. He distinguishes the righteousness of imputation, which is outside of us in Christ, from inherent righteousness which is within us. Inherent righteousness is infused "by the influence into them from Christ their heads".[43] The righteousness which is infused by this "influence" is the righteousness of sanctification. The relationship of imputed and inherent righteousness in Christ is explicated in his discussion of baptism.

> Thus in Baptisme we are incorporated into Christ, and in it we put on Christ, who is our righteousnesse and it is the Sacrament, not only of remission of sinne and of justification, but also of regeneration and sanctification, we being therein conformed to his death and resurrection.[44]

JOSEPH HALL
1574-1656

Joseph Hall, successively Bishop of Exeter and Norwich, shares with Jeremy Taylor and Robert Sanderson the distinction of leadership in Anglican moral theology in the seventeenth century. His views on the Gospel enjoy a considerable reputation. He does not discuss soteriology extensively as Davenant and Downame do, but his views parallel theirs. He, too, believes that inherent righteousness is infused by the Holy Ghost. God's justification of the wicked man does not leave him still wicked, but effects real change in him. Those whom he justifies he also sanctifies. The two acts are gratuitous and inseparable. However, the righteousness wrought in us by the Holy Ghost

. . . is not so perfect, as that it can bear us out before the tribunal of God. It must be only under the garment of our Elder Brother, that we dare come in for a blessing: his righteousness made ours by faith, is that, whereby we are justified in the sight of God: this doctrine is that, which is blasted with a Tridentine curse.[45]

He views the controversy not as conflict over the relation of faith to works but as a dispute about the formal cause of justification. The issue is

. . . what that is, whereby we stand acquitted before the Righteous Judge; whether our inherent justice, or Christ's imputed justice apprehended by faith. The Divines of Trent are for the former: all Antiquity, with us, for the latter. A just volume would scarce contain the pregnant testimonies of the Fathers, to this purpose.[46]

He mentions Chrysostom, Ambrose, Jerome, Gregory, Augustine, and Bernard. Hall asserts that no Reformed divine could more disparage our inherent righteousness, or more magnify the imputed righteousness of Christ than these Fathers did.

Like Davenant and Downame, his basic criticism of inherent righteousness as the formal cause of justification is based upon the claim that sin is present in the regenerate. He cites Rom. 7.19-25 as evidence of sin in a justified person. Righteousness infused by the Holy Spirit is imperfect and cannot be that by which we are absolved and accepted. Bellarmine's argument for such a formal cause is, Hall declares, not only unscriptural, unsupported by the Fathers, and an innovation, but is also contrary to reason.

To say now, that our actual justice, which is imperfect through the admixtion of venial sins, ceaseth not to be both true, and, in a sort, perfect justice (Bellarmine, de Justif. 1. ii. c. 14), is to say, there may be an unjust justice, or a just injustice; that even muddy water is clear, or a leprous face beautiful.[47]

Hall contrasts the imperfection of inherent righteousness with the perfect righteousness of Christ which is imputed to us in justification. Daily growth in grace and the increase of our renovation is accompanied to the very last by the prayer, "forgive us our trespasses". This daily reminder of the imperfection of our regeneration should convince us of "the impossibility of justification by such inherent righteousness".[48]

Hall vigorously dismisses the possibility that the dispute about justification is merely a misunderstanding. Like Hooker, he concedes that both sides agree on many important points, and that they both acknowledge inherent righteousness. Hall insists, however, that they do not conceive of inherent righteousness in the same manner nor for the same end. Inherent righteousness is the *cause* of justification for Bellarmine and the Romans; it is the *effect* of justification for Protestants. This distinction is of the utmost importance to Bishop Hall because he maintains, as does Hooker, that grave errors result from holding inherent righteousness as the formal cause of justification. The Roman doctrine, he argues, denies the disparity between our righteousness and God's, and breeds presumption in men while reducing the concept of God's righteousness to the level of imperfect righteousness found in the regenerate. Inherent righteousness cannot be considered to have satisfied God's justice. Who, he asks, can boast of perfect righteousness within himself? Only those who have lowered the concept of God's justice can do so.

> Perhaps some Isidore may say thus of himself, which voluntarily protested, that, for forty years' space, he found not in himself any sin; not so much as in his thought; not so much as any consent to anger or inordinate desire. Or perhaps, some Baronius or Bellarmine may report this of their late St. Gonzaga : or the offal of the Schools may say so of Bonaventure; in whom, if we believe them Adam sinned not : or Manicheus may say it of his elect masters : or, perhaps; Priscillian, Evagrius, Jovinian, the Messalians may brag thus of themselves . . . Otherwise, we shall come to that point, which Innocentius condemned in the Pelagians : "What need have we of God?"[49]

Hall argues vehemently that all such errors necessarily follow from the notion that inherent righteousness is the cause by which we are justified. He suggests :

> Let Bernard now, to conclude, shut up this stage. "Not to sin", saith he, "is God's justice; but the justice of man, is the pardon of God."[50]

JAMES USSHER
1582-1656

A similar view of justification is held by Archbishop Ussher. James Ussher's doctrine of justification is set forth briefly in a catechism entitled *The Method of Christian Religion,* written, he tells us in a preface, when he was still in his early twenties, and was published later to correct erroneous quotations which had been made from it over the years. The doctrine is more fully explicated in four sermons delivered in Oxford in 1640. Ussher takes a position much like that of Hooker, Davenant, Downame, and Hall. His emphasis, also, is upon the gratuitous nature of justification. He agrees that the imputation of Christ's righteousness is the formal cause of justification, and he asserts that Bellarmine and the Roman Church deny any "grace of justification" by proclaiming a doctrine of "infusion".[51]

Ussher himself argues that justification is forgiveness of sins *and* the imputation of Christ's righteousness. Forgiveness and imputation cannot be separated but are integral components of God's action in justification. As the darkness disappears when light is brought into a room, so our sins are forgiven when God imputes to us the righteousness of Christ.

> Now there is a double kind of righteousness, the one imputed, and the other inherent; the one is righteousness of Christ, an act atransient from another, which cannot be made mine but by imputation. Besides this, there is another which is inherent, a righteousness in us.[52]

The latter righteousness is sanctification. This is the point, he declares, of real difference "between us and Rome".[53] It is not a dispute about faith and works. It is rather that Bellarmine and the Romans deny God's initial acceptance by imputation of Christ's righteousness, and instead claim that we are justified by an inherent righteousness infused into us. Thus, Ussher argues, the Romans rule out any grace of justification. To see the difference as an argument about the relative efficacy of faith as against works is to miss the point completely.

Ussher agrees with Downame and Davenant that there is sin in the regenerate, noting, for example, that St Paul spoke of himself as a sinner.[54] Inherent righteousness (which is the grace of sanctification) grows throughout earthly life but is never perfect in earthly life. Gross sins may even be committed, but a truly regenerate man never finally and irrevocably falls from grace. Repentance, although it is not an "instrument of justification",[55] is necessary in the life of the regenerate because it "clears passages through which faith can act".[56]

The righteousness of Christ alone suffices for justification. It is imputed to us not "in one moment" (as for Davenant), but continuously throughout our sanctification. The difficulties which Davenant encountered holding justification to be "in one moment" Ussher avoids by holding that justification is a state as well as an act. Christ continually imputes his righteousness to us. Ussher also criticizes Bellarmine for arguing that it is infidelity to pray for justification *after* the remission of sins.[57] Ussher points out that justification is not only an act done, but an act continued.

> The point then is this: as long as we continue in the world, and by contrary acts of disobedience continue to provoke God to discontinue his former acts of mercy, and our sins being but covered, therefore so long must we pray for forgiveness.[58]

Ussher insists, in other words, that justification and sanctification operate simultaneously. There is grace of justification, the imputation of Christ's righteousness, which "is without me";[59] and there is grace of sanctification, the infusion of righteousness, which is

> . . . within me, the one receives degrees, the other not. As a man that is holy, may be more holy; but imputed righteousness doth not more forgive one man than another. Imputation is without augmentation or diminution . . . The contrary to justification is condemnation; but the contrary to sanctification is wickedness, and false dealing . . .[60]

Justification for Ussher is by faith *only*, but not by faith *alone* (apart from good works). He employs the illustration Davenant suggests: the eye alone sees but not as severed from the rest of the body. (Ussher also uses this illustration in another connection.[61]) There is, however, a difficulty implicit in the illustration which is not adequately disposed of in the works either of Davenant or Ussher. If the faith that justifies is accompanied by good works as the body is connected with the eye in seeing, this implies a body of good works present *before* justification and not, therefore, a consequence of justification. Davenant admits the necessity of certain actions (as in his example of a beggar stretching forth his hand to receive alms) before justification, but his major argument clearly requires that good works are possible only after God has justified. Justification is, in fact, a free act of God which brings sinners into the covenant where grace is then given to perform good works. Perhaps we may assume that (since Ussher considers justification a state as well as an act) faith and works, in this situation, refer to faith by which we are continuously justified and works which are the companion instruments of sanctification.

This assumption is consistent with Ussher's understanding of the relationship between justification and sanctification. Ussher does argue, fundamentally, that justification is a free act of God, apprehended through faith, and by which good works are in grace enabled. He makes this clear in his discussion of the apparent conflict between St James and St Paul on the nature of justification. When St Paul says we are justified by faith, and not by works, he is speaking, says Ussher, of the "first acceptation". When St James states that we are justified by works, and not by faith alone, he is speaking of justification in the "second acceptation".[62] The latter is, according to Ussher, sanctification. The works required by St James occur in sanctification, and demonstrate the validity of faith by which alone we are justified. He does not agree with those who attempt to resolve the conflict by arguing that St James is speaking of justification before men and St Paul of justification before God. Both are speaking of justification before God, Ussher insists, and the confusion arises from different uses of the terms "justification" and "sanctification". The same confusion, he adds, also afflicted the Fathers.

And so that which the Fathers call justification, is taken generally for sanctification; that which we call justification they call forgiveness of sins; that which we call sanctification, they call justification: so that the difference is only the terms.[63]

JOHN DONNE
1571?-1631

The writings of John Donne are different in style from those of the theologians already discussed, but his soteriology is nevertheless similar to that of the foregoing divines. We shall consider here the remarkable sermons of the great poet, sermons mostly composed during his service as Dean of St Paul's (1621-31).

Donne argues with Hooker and Davenant that there is sin in the regenerate. He asserts, for example, that though "St Paul speaks of himself in his best state, still he *was sold under sin*, because still, that concupiscence . . . remains in him. And that concupiscence is sin . . ."[64] He adds:

> . . . then wee shall meete the Apostle confessing himselfe to bee the greatest Sinner, not only with a *fui*, that hee was so whilest hee was a Persecutor, but with a present *sum*, that even now, after hee had received the faithful Word, the light of the Gospell, yet hee was still the greatest Sinner; of which [Sinners] I [though an Apostle] am [am still] the Chiefest.[65]

Like Davenant (and St Paul), he protests that, although he has been washed and forgiven, there is yet a residue of original sin in him. Donne expresses it this way:

> . . . though I have washed myselfe in the tears of Repentance, and in the blood of my Saviour, though I have no guiltinesse of any former sinnes upon me at the present, yet I have a sense of *root* of sinne, that is not grub'd up, of Originall Sinne that will cast me back again.[66]

Roman Catholics are "Puritans", he suggests, when they assert that there is sinlessness in the regenerate. By this doctrine, Donne argues,

> . . . a man may not only be empty of all sin, but he may be too full of God's presence, overfreighted with his grace, so far that (as they make Philip Nerius, the founder of their last order, their example) they shall be put to that exclamation, *Recede a me Domine*, O Lord

depart farther from me, and withdraw some of this grace, which thou pourest upon me.[67]

(St Philip le Neri was founder of the Order of the Priests of the Oratory in Italy. B. 1515, canonized in 1622.) To Donne, every sin is a violation and wounding of God, and the Roman distinction between venial and mortal sin is, therefore, a "frivolous and yet impious doctrine".[68]

Inherent righteousness, he argues, is infused into us by God, but it is imperfect and tainted with sin. We are neither worthy of the righteousness before God gives it to us, nor are we made worthy by receiving it. There is

> . . . no sparke of worth in us, before God call us; but that first grace of his, doth not presently make us worthy . . . If we love not Christ, more than all, and take our cross, and follow him, *non dignus sumus* we are not worthy of him. Nay all this doth not make us worthy really, but imputatively; they shall be counted worthy to enjoy the next world, and the resurrection, says Christ.[69]

That which makes us worthy in God's sight is that we are in Christ. Donne's emphasis upon our life in Christ, and the constant imputation of his righteousness to us, is even stronger than that of Downame.

> *Though mine iniquities be got over my head,* . . . my head is Christ; and [being] in *him* . . . all my sins shall no more hinder my ascending into heaven . . . then they hindered him . . .[70]

Reconciliation has already been accomplished by Christ for us while we were still in our sins. To become a member of Christ we need only accept the gift of reconciliation. The parable of the wedding garment illustrates that God accepts us only as we are covered with the righteousness of Christ.[71]

> And from this, from putting on Christ as a garment, we shall grow up to that perfection . . . He shall find in our bodies his wounds . . . in our hearts and actions his obedience. And . . . he shall do this by imputation . . .[72]

Donne is not hesitant to exhort good works. Salvation is achieved only by the will of man working in harmony with the will of God, and God saves no man without (or against) his will.

Till he have found faith and beliefe in God, he never calls upon good works, he never calls them good; but when we have Faith, he would not have us stop nor determine there, but to proceed to works too.[73]

There are reservations, Donne says, in regard to the new covenant, but they are in respect only of the possibility of falling away. His emphasis is upon the necessity of prevenient grace for entrance into the new covenant, since only then are we enabled to do good works.[74]

Man, in a state of nature, is in such a predicament that he is not of himself able to help himself, and must depend wholly upon the free gift of reconciliation. This gift cannot be acquired; it can only be accepted. Donne's numerous exhortations to righteousness, repentance, and good works are directed at those in the process of sanctification. Justification is by God's grace, and we are unable of ourselves to do anything but accept it. God does not, however, sanctify us without our participation. Justification is by faith, but this faith must issue in good works if sanctification is to occur. Just as

> God gave a reformation to his church, in prospering that doctrine, that justification was by faith only: so God gave us a unity to his church, in this doctrine that no man is justified, that works not.[75] Furthermore, howsoever our adversaries slander us, with a doctrine of ease, and a religion of liberty we require . . . more exactness, and severity, than they do.[76]

Donne agrees with Davenant on the place of good works in the accomplishment of salvation. Salvation is essentially by grace through faith. Good works declare and testify that salvation is being worked out, but they cannot be the means of salvation. Donne's comment on the problem of assurance illustrates his view of *fides formata* (whether faith itself contains the righteousness of obedience).

> This assurance (so far as they will confess it may be had) the Roman Church places in faith, and so far, well; but then In *fides Formata;* and so far well enough too; In those works which declare and testifie that faith; for though this good work do nothing toward my Salvation, it does much towards the neerness, that is, towards my assurance of this Salvation; but herein they lead us out of the way, that they call these works the soul, the form of faith: for though a good tree cannot be without good fruits, yet it were a strange manner of speech to call that good fruit, the life or the soul, or the form of that tree; so is

it, to call works which are the fruits of faith, the life or soul, or form of faith: for that is proper to grace only which infuses faith.[77]

Donne's soteriology has two strong foundations: the depth of sin and the freedom of man. The depth of sin makes necessary God's action in justification, and man can do no more than accept the gift of reconciliation. The emphasis, therefore is on justification as a free gift. On the other hand, grace never destroys nature nor does it compromise the essential freedom of man. God will not save man except through man's freedom. Donne, therefore, also places emphasis upon repentance and exhortation to good works as necessary for sanctification.

Donne strongly insists that sin goes much deeper than mere transgressions: "Wee have sinne upon us, sinne to condemnation, original *sinne* before we *know sinne,* before we have committed any sinne."[78] Sin is separation from God, and our transgressions are merely symptoms or expressions of that separation. This interrelation of sin has direct bearing on Donne's doctrine of justification. Christ's righteousness is imputed to us as not only satisfaction for our transgressions, but also in order to establish in us a new state or condition of being. The justified person becomes a member of Christ, and his separation from God is overcome.

Donne clearly advocates a soteriology shared by Hooker, Davenant, Downame, Hall, and Ussher. They are agreed on the following crucial points: their concern to proclaim the gratuitous nature of justification; their conviction of the presence of sin in the regenerate; their criticism of the Tridentine doctrine of inherent righteousness; their insistence that we are justified by the righteousness of Christ imputed to us; and their understanding of justification as that by which we are begun to be made righteous.

LANCELOT ANDREWES
1555-1626

We come last (but certainly not least) to the soteriology of Lancelot Andrewes, successively Bishop of Chichester, Ely, and Winchester. He, too, was critical of the Tridentine doctrine of inherent righteousness as the formal cause of justification. "For it is not in question whether we have an inherent righteousness or no, or whether God will accept it or reward it";[79] but whether it is that by which we are justified. He asserts that Bellarmine and the Schoolmen are "nipping at the name of Christ" when they claim that the formal cause of justification is our inherent righteousness.

> All which I put you in mind of to this end, that you may mark that this nipping at the Name of Christ is for no other reason but that we may have some honour ourselves out of our righteousness.[80]

There are two forms of righteousness, "one ours by influence or infusion, the other by account or imputation. That both these are, there is no question."[81] It is only by the latter, however, that we are acceptable to God. Andrewes makes the same point as Davenant when he argues that the

> . . . very schoolmen themselves, take them from their questions, quodlibets, and comments on the sentences, let them be in their soliloquie, meditations, or devotions, and especially in directing how to deal with men in their last agony . . . you would not wish to find *Jehova justitia nostra* better or more pregnantly acknowledged than in them you shall find it.[82]

He suggests that the way to settle this controversy is to consider which righteousness will adequately serve us in the final judgement, our own inherent righteousness or that of Christ imputed to us.

> But let us once be brought and arraigned *coram Rege justo sedente in solio,* let us set ourselves there, we shall then see that all our former conceit will vanish straight, and righteousness in that sense will not abide the trial.[83]

In the sight of God no man's inherent righteousness is sufficient. This is what Andrewes takes to be the meaning of "justification by faith only".

> The Papists ask where we find "only" in justification by faith? Indeed we do not find it, but we do find that "by faith" and nothing else we are "justified", and so we may well collect it by faith only. "By grace we are saved through Faith; and that not of ourselves, it is the gift of God." And on this warrent have many of the ancient Fathers been bold to add the word "only"; as Origen upon Romans

3.28 . . . Hilary upon Matthew 9 and divers others say, "Faith only justifieth".[84]

The theme of Andrewes' argument against the Romans is that they wrongly credit eternal life to inherent righteousness. He grants that there is an inherent righteousness, and that good works are truly worthy in themselves. However, in comparison with God's righteousness, judgement, and final reward, none of our works is worthy—"it is neither our fear, nor our works, all is but God's gracious acceptation".[85] He quotes St Augustine and St Chrysostom to support his contention that God accepts even the very best of good works only by his gracious mercy, and never because of their inherent merit or condignity.

Although Andrewes criticizes the doctrine of inherent righteousness primarily in the context of the last judgement, his views are those of Hooker and Davenant on the other issues of soteriology. He discusses the phrase, "make you perfect in all good works" (Heb. 13.21) in a sermon prepared to be preached on Easter Day, 1624. He suggests that the verb καταρτίσαι means "to set you in joint". That our nature "is not right in joint is so evident that the very heathen . . . have confessed it. And by a fall of things come out of joint, and indeed so they did . . ."[86] He goes on to say that good works are impossible to be willed, much less to be done, until we are "put in joint".

Good works are possible only by the Holy Spirit, which is freely given to all who hear the Gospel and receive the Sacrament. Andrewes not only argues that the presence of sin in the regenerate makes their inherent righteousness imperfect, but he also contends that the Romans are seriously in error when they suppose that infused righteousness absolutely replaces sin. The Lord's Prayer does not make sense unless we understand the daily necessity to ask forgiveness of sins. Andrewes' emphasis in discussing the doctrine of justification is upon the inadequacy of inherent righteousness before God, and the consequent necessity of the imputed righteousness of Christ, especially in the context of the last judgement. He stresses the absolute nature of God's righteousness, and the gratuitous nature of grace.

Anglican soteriology in early seventeenth-century England was marked, then, by emphasis upon God's initiative and forgiveness, and man's initial, continual, and final necessity to rely upon his relationship with Christ as that which makes him acceptable to God. Perhaps the best summary of this position is found in the later hymn of William Bright.

> Look, Father, look on his anointed face,
> And only look on us as found in him;
> Look not on our misusings of thy grace,
> Our prayer so languid, and our faith so dim;
> For lo! between our sins and their reward,
> We set the passion of thy Son our Lord.

The theology of the divines in this chapter represents a soteriology that we shall call the classical Anglican position.

2

Other Views

WILLIAM FORBES
1585-1634[1]
First Bishop of Edinburgh

Forbes published nothing during his lifetime, but in 1658 a post-humous work, *Considerationes Modestae et Pacificae Controversiarum de Justificatione, Purgatorio, Invocatione Sanctorum, Christo Mediatore, et Eucharistia* was published from his manuscripts by "T. G." (Thomas Sydserf, Bishop of Galloway). Although this work is scarcely a polished document, it is impressive in its scholarship and learned familiarity with other relevant theological works. It was not unusual to find divines of the period who were familiar with the Fathers, but Forbes, in his work on justification, quotes or refers to works of twenty Anglicans, twenty-nine Roman Catholics, and thirty-seven Protestants, all of whom were contemporary or slightly earlier.

Forbes' motive is irenic. His method usually takes the following form: he rejects the positions of "the more rigid" Protestants and Roman Catholics in a specific controversy; then he quotes Protestants ("the more learned") who disagree with the "more rigid" Protestants and Roman Catholics who contradict "the more rigid Romanists"; he then states his own view of the controversy, which is seldom for one or the other but for some third position in between; finally, in most cases, he adds that the whole matter is, for the most part, a difference of words, or that it is not treated with sufficient charity by either side "in this age which is marked by more contentions than Christian piety". It must be said, however, that in his concern for peace he does not gloss over differences. He may describe the differences as unimportant, but he points them out, not only differences between the Anglicans and the Roman Catholics, but also differences among the various protagonists on either side.

Forbes begins his first book, a work on justification, by calling attention to the "common Protestant division" of faith into four types: historical, miracle working, temporary, and justifying faith. He proceeds to distinguish justifying faith from assurance and defines the former as

> . . . nothing else than a firm assent of the mind, produced by the Holy Ghost from the word, by which we acknowledge all things revealed by God in the Scriptures, and especially those concerning the mystery of our redemption and salvation, wrought by Christ, to be most true, by reason of the authority of God who has revealed them.[2]

The question of whether or not this faith *alone* justifies occupies Forbes for two chapters. He notes that those who teach that faith alone justifies refer not to a dead but a living faith. The Roman Catholics are unfair, he says, in claiming that the Protestants deny the necessity of good works, although he admits that some of "the more rigid" Protestants do indeed teach incorrectly on the subject. Even they, however, when "interpreted charitably", do not deny the "indivisible connection of good works with justifying faith".[3] The "more rigid" Protestants are wrong, however, when they interpret St Augustine to the effect that no good works precede justification. Scripture shows, Forbes points out, that there are "predisposing acts" which, though they do not merit justification ("as many Romanists own"), do influence justification. He joins what he calls the Protestant view (that faith justifies as an instrument) and the Roman Catholic view (that faith justifies as a disposition) by arguing that faith justifies as both instrument and disposition.

Forbes acknowledges that Scripture contains expressions quite close to "justification by faith alone", but it nowhere expressly states it, and, on the other hand, it contains many passages in which works do apprehend righteousness. These works include, he says, repentance, good works, and participation in the sacraments. The reason Scripture especially mentions faith is twofold: faith is the root and foundation of all our righteousness, and it clearly demonstrates that our salvation is from Christ. Thus, although both faith and good works are causes of our justification, Forbes assigns the chief place to faith.

The Protestants err, according to Forbes, in thinking that St Paul excludes all good works from justification when actually he excludes only those works done outside the grace of God. The Roman Catholics err, on the other hand, in their excessive emphasis upon human merit. The works excluded from justification by St Paul are those done by man's unaided powers and the ceremonial works of the Law. Forbes argues that if all works are excluded from justification, faith itself must also be excluded, since it is itself a work. (Protestants who insist that faith is not a work are "impertinently subtle".) Forbes says that the Fathers who affirm that we are justified by faith alone (Origen, St Hilary, St Basil, St Ambrose, St Augustine, St Cyril, St Chrysostom) meant by "alone" to exclude works of natural and Mosaic law, works done in our own strength, any false faith or heresy, the absolute necessity of *external* works (when the power or opportunity to do such works is not present), and all vain assurance and boasting of our works of whatever sort. They did not intend to exclude the internal works of good affections, penitence, and love. Forbes' conclusion is that both the more rigid Protestants and the extreme Roman Catholics are wrong. Even many of the former, he adds, would agree that the word "alone" might be abandoned. The solution for Forbes is relatively simple : faith which justifies is that which is united to love.

Forbes' second book is a discussion of the formal cause of justification. The Roman Catholics, he notes, maintain that the formal cause is the infusion of inherent righteousness; if it were not so, God's pronouncing someone righteous when he is not "actually" righteous would be a legal fiction. The act of justification must, therefore, have a "true basis"—a formal cause—consisting of the internal righteousness of the justified, or inherent righteousness. The Protestants, on the other hand, argue that the formal cause is the forgiveness of sins, or the imputation of Christ's righteousness, or both. That man's righteousness might be the formal cause seems to most Protestants a spiritual pretension and destructive of the gratuitous nature of atonement.

Forbes himself argues that too much stress has been placed on the question of formal cause by both Protestants and Roman Catholics. Incorrect opinions are advanced on both sides, he claims, and some members on each side seem to agree with some of their opposite numbers. Forbes' position is that the formal cause of justification is twofold, consisting of both the forgiveness of sins and inherent righteousness. He denies that faith can be the formal cause because it is, he says, the efficient cause. He considers that the Council of Trent was "too severe" in anathematizing any who hold the imputation of Christ's righteousness to be the formal cause of justification. There were, he notes, many Roman Catholics before and after the Council who did so argue. It is nearer the truth, none the less, according to Forbes, to hold that the imputation of Christ's righteousness is the meritorious rather than the formal cause of justification. The imputation of Christ's righteousness as the formal cause is untenable for these reasons: it would make us as righteous as Christ in God's sight; it would make all the justified equally justified; and it would make the justified more righteous (in God's sight) in this world than in the next. Those Protestants who claim that inherent righteousness which is infused into us by God is not the formal cause of justification, confuse the cause *by* which and the cause *on account of* which. The formal cause is denoted by the former, but not the latter. We are justified *on account of* the obedience of Christ and *by* the justice that God infuses into us, and not by the merits of Christ imputed to us.

The Council of Trent erred, Forbes says, when it held that there is but one, single formal cause of justification (infusion of inherent righteousness). Even Bellarmine, he notes, acknowledges that the formal cause of justification must include the remission of sins as well as the infusion of inherent righteousness. Bellarmine fails, however, in his attempt to gloss over the error of the Council. The formal cause of justification is, therefore, both the infusion of inherent righteousness and the remission of sins, although Forbes admits that the latter is more important. God's justifying must include, however, a "making just".[4] Forbes believes the Protestants err when they deny that sanctification is a part of justification (even though they strongly hold that the two are always joined). He does not, however, attach great importance to this difference, and describes it as verbal rather than real. The Council of Trent was in error when it held that "God hates nothing in the regenerate".[5] Forbes believes, for example, that concupiscence which remains in the regenerate is in itself evil. Thus, Forbes is clearly neither Roman Catholic nor typically Protestant in his views on the formal cause of justification.

His third book is concerned with the uncertainty, changeableness, and inequality of righteousness. He notes that the Roman Catholics, in general, deny the faithful have the assurance and certainty of justification, and, in general, the Protestants assert that all true believers do have this assurance. Forbes points out that some Roman Catholics agree with the "more rigid Protestants" and some Protestants, in fact, deny the certainty of justification. He notes also that the Roman Catholics, in general, do not question the certainty of final preservation or forgiveness, but only the *moral* certainty of election. He criticizes those Protestants who maintain that this required certainty is a comfortable doctrine. On the contrary, he says, doubt should be encouraged by the promise of the Gospel, and the necessity for certainty should not be pressed on any, lest "those who are afraid should grow more afraid and that others should lose even their filial fear of God". And he adds, that all divines should avoid too curious a measuring of the amount of this certainty.[6]

The fourth book contains Forbes' discussion of the righteousness of works. Luther and many of his followers said many "harsh things" about the necessity of good works for salvation, but most other Protestants hold that good works are necessary to salvation in some way, whether by necessity of presence or even, perhaps, of efficiency and cause. Forbes claims that Scripture, the Fathers, and St Bernard, in addition to many Protestants, agree that there is a causal relation between good works and salvation. Forbes agrees with Bellarmine

that good works are necessary to salvation not only by way of presence, but also of some sort of efficiency, and that works not less than
faith conduce to salvation, each after their own manner

and he deems this dispute "altogether vain and useless, nay in great
measure a mere contest about words".[7]

Forbes thereupon proceeds to a discussion of the relation between
the Law and the Gospel. He believes that Christ is a lawgiver, and
that the Gospel is therefore a true law. The "rigid Protestants"
disagree, but other Protestant divines support his view. The difference between the Law and the Gospel is that the Law merely commands, whereas the Gospel commands and gives help. Discussing
the possibility of fulfilling the Law under the Gospel dispensation,
Forbes notes that it would be unjust for God to condemn anyone for
not accomplishing that which it is impossible to accomplish, so that
in one sense the regenerate can and do fulfil the demands of the
Gospel when it is

. . . considered not rigidly, but according to mercy . . . and according to that degree of performance of the law which God by the Gospel
covenant rigorously exacts from us in order to our becoming partakers
of the promised forgiveness of sins and eternal salvation.[8]

Forbes defends "the sounder Protestants" from the charge of the
Roman Catholics, denying that the former hold every work of the
righteous to be a mortal sin or that all our works done even in grace
are not "unmixedly good". However, he thinks those Protestants go
too far who say that even the best works of the righteous are defiled
by sin and worthy of eternal death. The text of Isaiah (64.6) stating
all our righteousness to be as "filthy rags" is wrongly held by many
Protestants as a description of the righteous works of holy men
under the Gospel. It is more precisely a description of the works
of the Jews during the exile. He insists St Bernard did not mean *all*
our works when discussing this text, and he condemns Davenant
as "extravagant" for holding that even the best works of the righteous are not wholly free from some evil concupiscence. Forbes
concludes the matter by asserting that no one should boast of his
works as if they could stand under God's strict jujdgement, but

neither can we say that man is unable by the grace of God to do anything that is not defiled by sin.

The problem of election and the possibility of the faithful falling from grace is dealt with in Bishop Forbes' usual irenic manner. After quoting favourably the "less rigid" of both parties, he states that the problem of election (or predestination) arises when it is looked at from two different perspectives: *a priori* (from a certain absolute decree of God), and *a posteriori* (from a final perseverance in faith and grace). Concerning the possibility of falling from grace, he bids "the more rigid" to acknowledge that many reprobates do believe and are justified for a time, yet fall away later from their faith and justice. The elect, he says, always retain a spark, or seed, of faith which may later be kindled, or itself grow, so that it is always a living faith that justifies them.

Such a living faith must be joined by good works for justification, as St James makes clear. Forbes contends that the Protestants are wrong when they reject the common distinction of first and second justification. However, he denies that the apparent discrepancy between St James and St Paul is resolved by arguing that St Paul speaks of a first justification and St James of a second. To refute this argument he quotes Jackson, Piscator, and Estius against the Protestants, and Vasquez and Suarez against Bellarmine (who also taught that St Paul was speaking of the first and St James of the second justification). Forbes cites a quotation from Cornelius a Lapide to demonstrate that each apostle used the example of Abraham to illustrate both the first and second justification. He also points out that the example of Rahab used by St James exemplifies the first justification (since she was impious and a harlot); therefore, St James cannot be said to have spoken only of the second justification. Forbes concludes that each apostle is speaking of both justifications, and that faith without works is useless to the office of justification. Useless, also, are works without faith.

Forbes' last book (Book 5) is concerned with the merit of good works. He finds nothing wrong with the word "merit", and quarrels only with the way some Roman Catholics use the word. He quotes Davenant to support his view. Those Protestants who argue that eternal life is rendered to works only as they are signs of faith contradict Scripture. He differs from those Protestants who claim that the words in Scripture relating good works to eternal life, such as "because", "for", "therefore" ("for I was an hungred and you gave me to drink"—Matt. 25.35) are merely indicative of order, progression, or the way of obtaining salvation. Forbes insists that such words also indicate the causal relation of works to salvation. He explicitly takes exception to Davenant's argument that "good works are not the causes of our right to eternal life, but only (of our introduction into it)".[9] Davenant, however, is favourably quoted shortly thereafter as saying, in effect, that eternal life is not given to believers who perform good works according to justice as usually understood: that would imply an equality between the work and the wages, and would suggest merit of condignity.

"Merit of condignity" as held by "Vasquez and other Romanists"—that good works of themselves merit eternal life without any covenant or favour of acceptance—is rightly rejected, says Forbes, not only by the Protestants but also by many learned Roman Catholics (including Bellarmine and Suarez).[10] But Bellarmine errs when he goes on to argue that good works, by condignity, merit eternal life on the ground of merit of works themselves *and* the covenant, conjointly. Forbes himself believes that the whole dissension could be cleared up (at least "between all moderate men") if the Roman Catholics would drop altogether the word "condignity" (the merit or worth of the works in themselves), and instead ascribe the merit of works altogether to God's gratuitous promise and his gracious acceptance.

Forbes' work is informed by a commendable spirit of peace and charity, and is indicative of careful (if not profound) thought. His work is not, however, carefully or clearly written. As has been pointed out, the work existed only in manuscript form, and was published twenty-four years after his death. The following passage is not untypical.

> To conclude this consideration. Since it is nowhere expressly said in Holy Scripture (and none contend more vehemently than the Protestants that in matters of faith we must both think and speak as it does),

that "we are justified by faith alone"; and since the Fathers, who certainly have often used this expression, never understood it in the sense in which it is universally taken now-a-days by Protestants; and since the explanations and conciliations which have been lately devised are altogether futile; and since, finally, very learned men of both parties have accounted, and even now account, this question to be by no means necessary; we, therefore, being led by the desire of truth and of the unity of the Church to agree with them, deem it right that it be no longer pertinaciously contended for; and therefore that the opinion of all the more rigid Protestants is opposed as well to truth as to Christian charity, who contend that the assertion commonly defended by the Romanists, "that faith alone does not justify", apart from every definition either of faith itself, or of the merit, even improperly so called, of the other works or acts which concur with faith towards justification—that this assertion of Romanists is not only diametrically repugnant to Holy Scripture, and the pious Fathers, but also that it (besides innumerable other things) has afforded and does still afford to Protestants a just cause for seceding from the Roman Church.[11]

Forbes' writing is often difficult to follow, and it is frequently difficult to distinguish between quotations and his own statements. These problems may help to explain why Forbes' work is ignored by later theologians who discuss the same issues. Bull, for example, does not refer to Forbes (even though Forbes' work had been published several years before Bull began to write). Yet Forbes would have been more congenial to Bull than Davenant whom he does quote. J. H. Newman,[12] who was thoroughly familiar with Taylor, Andrewes, Hooker, Jackson, Barrow, and especially Davenant and Bull does not appear to have known that Forbes' work existed. Several secondary writers of the history of doctrine or of systematic theologies mention Bull, Davenant, and Forbes with short descriptions of the positions of the first two but only the comment "see also Bishop William Forbes" concerning the latter.[13] Few have ventured a description of Forbes' position.[14] There has been suspicion that Forbes' work was tampered with and doctrinal changes made in the text. There was certainly ample opportunity to do this, but on careful examination of the internal evidence it seems doubtful. There exists a copy of the manuscript with marginal notes, which John Cosin had with him in France during his exile a decade before it was published, indicating that if there was any tampering it was done before Cosin obtained his copy. There are discrepancies, but there is a consistent theme on essential matters running throughout the work. It would have meant rewriting the whole work to change appreciably the fundamental position that Forbes sets forth. The confusing style appears to be due more to the unfinished state of the manuscripts than to doctrinal tampering.

Bishop Forbes' arguments concerning the meaning of major terms embraced in the doctrine of justification can be condensed as follows. "Faith" is limited to a mental operation alone. "Justifying faith . . . is nothing else than a firm and sure assent of the mind, . . ."[15] Nor is it knowledge. "Justifying faith is not knowledge, but this is its antecedent; for faith is properly assent."[16] Disagreeing with Peter Baroe because the latter held that the love of God belongs to the nature of justifying faith, Forbes states, ". . . as we have above largely proved faith is situated in the intellect only".[17] This brings us to an apparent contradiction within Forbes' argument. Denying that justifying faith is the assurance of obtaining forgiveness, he states, "For not only does this assurance spring from faith, but also it is seated in the will, while faith is seated in the intellect."[18] Thus faith is assent "seated in the intellect" and not in the will. Faith is in the intellect but is not knowledge; it is assent but not will. Forbes does not explain how it is possible for faith to be an assent of the mind yet no matter of the will. He also insists that trust is not a part but an effect of faith and is reducible to hope not faith.[19] Furthermore, he argues that

> Those Protestants are foolishly subtle who would exclude faith in itself, in so far as it is a work, from the business of justification, but not in so far as it is an instrument apprehending justice. For faith is an instrument or medium of our justification, only as it is a work . . .[20]

Thus to justify means to make righteous.

> Nay, that whenever the Scripture makes mention of the justification of the sinner before God (as blessed Paul speaks, and after him St Augustine very often, besides others), the word "to justify" neces-

sarily signifies not only to pronounce just, after the forensic manner, but also truly and inherently to make just . . .[21]

At times Forbes speaks of justification and sanctification as synonymous. In answering the objection that Scripture sometimes distinguishes justification from sanctification he replies that it is not right to

> . . . confine the word and whole essence of justification to the forgiveness of sins alone, on account of one or two passages where justification is distinguished from sanctification, contrary to the whole tenor of Scriptures in almost all places, and to the unvarying teaching of the Fathers.[22]

In all the places in Scripture where justification and sanctification are mentioned together Forbes claims they have the same meaning, and are used interchangeably for emphasis. Yet it is apparent that, for Forbes, justification embraces the forgiveness of sins as well as sanctification.

> It may also be proved by many arguments taken from Scripture, that sanctification, and not merely the forgiveness of sins, pertains to justification.[23]

Occasionally, Forbes simply equates the two terms (see above, extract 21), but more frequently he includes in justification forgiveness as well as "making righteous". Sanctification is the "making righteous" part of justification. The two terms are of the same nature for Forbes because the justice of each is the same justice. "The distinction between the justice of justification and that of sanctification, which is wont to be here used . . . is not solid."[24] This argument is developed in Forbes' long discussion of the formal cause of justification as consisting of forgiveness of sins and inherent righteousness (Book 2).

Forbes is by no means ignorant of the opposing view. He explicitly disagrees on the issue of the formal cause with Lancelot Andrewes among others.[25] He writes,

> . . . very many Protestants wrongly separate inherent justice, not indeed from those who are justified, but from the formal cause of justification, and call it not justifying but sanctifying justice.[26]

Also,

> Protestants . . . admit that the infusion of inherent justice . . . is
> necessarily and invariably joined to our gratuitous justification; but
> they in general do not admit that it is any part of our justification,
> or that it pertains to its essential form, but hold that it is, and is to be
> called, sanctification, which they say must be accurately and neces-
> sarily distinguished from our justification, since it is merely a conse-
> quence of it.[27]

> Many Protestants indeed teach that all true believers are formally or
> quasi-formally as they speak, justified before God by the one and the
> same justice of Christ apprehended by faith, and imputed by God:
> many more teach that by hope, love and the other virtues, no one is
> justified, but merely that those who believe and have been justified,
> are by them sanctified. But of both these errors we have said enough
> and more than enough above.[28]

Forbes disappointingly fails to give a cogent argument or to submit
evidence against this position, but contents himself with such
phrases as "is not solid".[29] These quotations demonstrate, however, that Forbes shows a real measure of responsibility in describing the arguments of his adversaries in an age notorious for dis-
torting opposing positions in theological polemics.

Forbes' doctrine of justification can be briefly stated as follows:
justifying faith is simply an assent of the mind; to justify is to make
righteous; the meritorious cause of justification is Christ's obedience; the efficient cause ("is merely external as all allow"[30]) is
faith; the formal cause ("is internal, and that which expresses the
essence or being of a thing"[31]) is both forgiveness of sins and the
infusion of inherent righteousness. It is surprising, in the light of
his doctrine, that Forbes suggests the "unscriptural" word "alone"
be given up, merely "for the sake of peace".[32] Given the above
definitions it would seem that justification ("made righteous") by
only an "external" "assent of the mind" (faith) should be denied
on logical rather than irenic grounds.

The method Forbes uses to expound his view of the Gospel seems
to be influenced considerably by his desire to make peace and bring
to an end the fruitless quarrels of "this contentious age". His work
abounds in such phrases as "a great lover of peace" by which he

describes men with whom he is in sympathy in contrast to the "more rigid Protestants" (or Roman Catholics). Likewise, he frequently uses such phrases as "if charitably interpreted" to describe positions he is seeking to reconcile. His method of discussing each point in conflict develops, as we have noted, into a pattern in which he describes the disagreement and cites members on both sides who agree with their opposite numbers and/or disagree in part amongst themselves. His irenic method indicates the wide knowledge and the charitable disposition of the author. But it neither proves nor disproves any position to demonstrate that a particular school of thought is itself divided on the subject. It is worth noting that there are Roman Catholics who disagree with Bellarmine that the "disposing acts done by faith and preventing grace merit justification in any way, even in that of congruity; . . .",[33] but it does not, of itself, prove that Bellarmine is wrong. Similarly, he quotes with approval Theodore Beza,

> We need not use the slightest labour to determine whether this one or that [justification or sanctification] precedes in order, since we never received the one without the other . . .

and comments,

> Would that this moderation were religiously followed by . . . theologians of both parties, who now-a-days excite so many and so great disturbances in the church about the mode and order of the divine operations.[34]

The fact that Beza wishes to terminate the quarrel over the chronology of soteriology is no evidence that Forbes' position is correct.

This very quotation of Beza (which Forbes describes as "much to be approved of") actually includes two statements manifestly divergent from Forbes' belief. The first: "If you take justification . . . for the gift of imputed justice . . . then sanctification will be another gift, which always follows . . ." Previously Forbes has denied that justification can be taken for the gift of imputed justice. It is wrong to hold "that all our justice whereby we are justified before God is external, to wit, the very justice of Christ, who becomes ours by God's gratuitously imputing it to us . . ."[35] The other statement in this "approved" quotation from Beza claims that the Council of Trent erred by confounding justification with sanctification. True or not in itself, this criticism is as applicable to Forbes as to the Council, for on this point both agree. Apparently, because of Beza's peaceable statement that we need not "contend much which of the two precedes in order" Forbes takes no adverse notice of the two statements contrary to major points in his own position and recommends the quotation with approval. The motive of peace that is the obvious theme of Forbes' work is perhaps commendable, but too often his solutions lack the evidence or cogent argument necessary to form solid ground for agreement.

Forbes does not admit that he differs from St Augustine in the matter of justification. The Bishop of Hippo had stated,

> Our justice also, although it be true, because of the end to which it is referred, viz., the true God, yet in this life is such as to consist rather in the forgiveness of sins, than in the perfection of virtues.[36]

Forbes argues that

> in which words this most holy and learned Father teaches these two things: 1. that our justice consists (that is, that we are just) both in the forgiveness of sins and in the perfection of virtues, such perfection, namely, as befits the state of this life, 2. but that forgiveness of sins is much to be preferred to the perfection of virtues.[37]

Because Forbes holds that "to justify" means "to make righteous" the words "justice", righteousness", and "justification" are almost interchangeable. Hence, what St Augustine says about "our justice" in this life is inferred by Forbes to pertain to justification. This claim that Augustine's statement, in reality, means that our righteousness consists both in forgiveness and in the perfection of virtues is offered as evidence that the formal cause of justification embraces both the forgiveness of sins and the infusion of inherent righteousness. Actually, in this quotation the Bishop of Hippo is not speaking about justification. The whole of the twenty-seventh chapter (from which this is taken) consists of a description of the imperfect nature of righteousness and the gross inadequacy of the virtues of those in the City of God in its present pilgrim state—"for it cries to God by the mouth of all its members, 'Forgive us our debts as we forgive our debtors' ".[38] Forbes' definition of the verb "justify" thus leads him consistently to include all that is said of justice and of righteousness under his doctrine of justification.

Forbes explains St Augustine's statement, that "good works follow a justified person, but do not precede in one about to be justified", to mean that only those good works which do not come from grace are denied to precede justification.[39] This description by St Augustine of sinfulness and unworthiness in the regenerate had generally been used by Protestants as evidence that the imperfection of inherent righteousness prevents it from being the formal cause of justification. Since our inherent righteousness, in other words, is manifestly inadequate and sinful, only Christ's righteousness imputed to us is sufficient to be the very "form" of our justification. The problem of sin in the regenerate indeed appears to be a serious problem for those holding inherent righteousness to be the formal cause. Some hold that the regenerate do not really sin. The Council of Trent held that God hates nothing in the regenerate.[40] Bellarmine maintains that only venial—not mortal—sins are committed by the regenerate. In one instance Forbes acknowledges sin in the justified but is quite ambiguous about it in a following statement.

Although the guilt of habitual concupiscence or passion is by the power of baptism altogether destroyed and taken away, and it is itself broken and weakened in its powers; yet there remains, even in the justified, some remains of it which occasionally show themselves in them, and even in themselves are morally bad, vicious and hateful to God . . . but they cannot hurt those who do not consent, but manfully resist through Christ's grace; nor . . . [are they] any longer reckoned as sins.[41]

He deals with this difficulty by holding that the imperfection or sins of the regenerate pertain to *actual* justice "(i.e., that of our works)" and not to *habitual* justice which is "not our work but the work of God".[42] He does not explain this distinction more fully nor does he explain how this "habitual justice" which is "not *our* work but the work of God" differs from the imputation of Christ's righteousness. However, he defends his position on the grounds of what he considers to be the nature of the Gospel.

. . . the works of the regenerate, although they are not done here in that measure of faith and love which might be justly required of them, if God willed to deal rigidly with them, as has been said above, yet they are not therefore all of them defiled with sin, because in the question about the performance of the law, we must always look to the meaning of God who enjoins it. Since therefore He does not require from us an observance of the law rigid and in the highest degree of perfection, but merely according to clemency, and in the proportion to the powers of grace which have been granted to us, as we have shown at length in the preceding chapters, therefore the works which are here performed by the regenerate in that measure of faith and love which is prescribed by the covenant of grace, and which is possible to us, and with which God is graciously satisfied, are altogether free from the stain and guilt of sin; whence it will easily appear what is to be answered to that saying of St Augustine, "it is a sin, when either love is not [present] which ought to be; or when it [love] is less than it ought to be," and to a few other passages in favour of the same opinion which are commonly objected from St Augustine as well as from some others of the Fathers. Love which is less than it ought to be, would certainly be a sin, and even properly so, if God willed to deal with us according to strict justice: but since God, who is merciful to the human race, now for Christ's sake deals graciously and lovingly with us, it is not sin at all, if we speak strictly, but only in the wide acceptation of the word sin, when it is taken for a defect or imperfection . . .[43]

The Protestants, in general, object to inherent righteousness as the formal cause on the grounds that it is imperfect and mixed with many sins. It is on this question that the most significant difference of Forbes with the Council of Trent arises. Forbes grants that the righteousness given in justification is imperfect but

the opinion which we have supported is not thereby injured, since we have always joined forgiveness of sins with the donation of justice, and contended that we are and are called formally just before God, not by the latter only but by the former also, nay by it principally, as St Augustine has already said.[44]

Forbes is comparatively lenient toward the regenerate who must perform only those works required "according to clemency" and not by the "observance of the law rigid", and who are not expected to attain the "highest degree of perfection". He is much more strict and exacting toward those who have not yet been justified. He insists that ". . . forgiveness of sins is never conferred without internal sanctification of the soul . . ."[45] but this statement can be taken in two ways. It could mean that an act of forgiveness effects a sanctification of the soul, or it could mean that an "internal sanctification of the soul" is a prerequisite for forgiveness. Forbes comes quite close to the latter meaning in the following statement.

> And as to what the Apostle [St Paul] there says that "God justifieth the ungodly," God Forbid that you should understand it as some of the more rigid Protestants do, of a man who is simply ungodly in the very act of justification, (for this would be diametrically repugnant to almost every word of Scripture) but of him who a little before was such, but now seriously deploring his own ungodliness, and flying for refuge to the throne of grace, is justified gratis by faith in Christ.[46]

The ungodly must not be ungodly only in the very act of justification; in fact, he must cease to be ungodly "a little before" justification. Similarly, he states that the regenerate can fulfil

> that degree of performance of the law which God exacts from us *in order to our becoming partakers of the promised forgiveness of sins* and eternal salvation.[47]

Forbes consistently, if not altogether clearly, maintains that good works as well as faith are required in order to be justified. These works are necessary not only by way of presence but also by way of causal relation.[48] St Paul in discounting works as prerequisites for justification is merely disallowing "legal and Judaical" works.[49] Forbes does deny that works earn or merit justification. of themselves, yet he insists that they must be performed before God forgives and before he makes righteous. Hence, it would appear that righteousness is required in order to be made righteous. Forbes' doctrine of justification cannot, therefore, be a description of God's acceptance of the ungodly nor can the forgiveness of a sinner be truly gratuitous.

Does this demand by Forbes, that the unregenerate must produce good works before the infusion of the grace of justification, mean that he was Pelagian? His work contains little that could be used to defend him from this accusation. It is certain that, for Forbes, works must precede the grace of inherent righteousness. Yet he implies that these works before justification must be works of grace. However, nowhere does he explain how or from whence this grace comes.

Bishop Forbes should not be too severely or finally judged on the basis of the *Considerationes Modestae*, his only published work. Besides his wide familiarity with so many writers on the subject and his commendable accuracy in describing beliefs contrary to his own, Forbes was living at a time when there was, possibly, a need for a more peaceful uniformity in theology. It must also be considered that his work was only in manuscript form, and was not published until twenty-four years after his death. There is abundant internal evidence that it was not ready for publication even if publication was intended. It might have changed considerably in editing. However, there is great doubt that the major theme could have been fundamentally altered merely by clarifying and rewriting.

Forbes' doctrine of justification is not a description of the way in which a sinner enters into the way of salvation. Justification for him presupposes a goodness sufficient to be acceptable under the Gospel covenant. That covenant demands both works of love and faith for acceptance. If Bishop Forbes had other ways to explain how the unrighteous sinner is initially brought into the covenant, they do not appear in his published work.

THOMAS JACKSON
1579-1640

Thomas Jackson, like Bishop Forbes, attempts to reconcile the two opposing positions concerning the doctrine of justification. The title of Jackson's work explains his general approach to the subject: *Justifying Faith* or *The Faith By Which The Just Do Live*, "A Treatise containing a Description of the Nature, Properties, and Conditions of Christian Faith With a Discovery of Mispersuasions Breeding Presumption or Hypocrisy; and Means How Faith May be Planted in Unbelievers." Jackson endeavours to steer a course between "Presumption" and "Hypocrisy" in his discussion of justification. He identifies the Council of Trent with "Hypocrisy", and many Protestants with "Presumption".

> As the Trent Council's doctrine, which upon penalty of damnation exacts a measure of inherent righteousness, whereof mortality is not capable, nurseth final doubting or despair; so others, in opposition to it, minister occasion of carelessness or presumption, either by not urging such a measure of perfection as God's word requires, or by deeming that sufficient enough to salvation, although it be subsequent to justification.[50]

Jackson appears to disagree with those who require works for sanctification but not for justification. "That it [works] should be more necessary to one of these than to another implies a contradiction . . ."[51] Nor can it be claimed that works are more necessary after justification than before. A justified man is the immediate heir of salvation, and if he dies the moment after justification, then he gains entrance into the kingdom of heaven without the righteousness of the scribes and Pharisees, which our Lord expressly said must be exceeded (Matt. 5.20). Thus, it is equally important for works to precede justification as it is for them to follow.[52] Jackson has difficulty in explaining his view of soteriology in the light of the Articles and the statement of St Augustine that good works only follow justification.

> If we be not justified (as all agree) without some operation or works of Faith, and all other good works subsequent to justification . . . [we must then] take justification (as St Austen, also Article XII doth) for the first infusion of that grace whereby we are justified and enabled to bring forth works truly good . . .[53]

Jackson argues, then, on the one hand, that works are as necessary to justification as to sanctification, but, on the other hand, when he attempts to reconcile this with the doctrine that works can only follow justification, he argues that justification means "the first infusion of grace whereby we are justified and enabled to bring forth works truly good". Much of the confusion within Jackson's works derives from his inconsistent and often contradictory use of the term "justification". In most cases he means final absolution,

but sometimes he gives it two additional meanings: the initial forgiveness of sins and the perpetual remission of sins. He uses the
word in all three senses without explaining in any given instance
the particular meaning he intends. He does finally explain this

> . . . threefold justification: one, radical or fundamental, which is
> the infusion of habitual grace or faith; and this is never but one: an-
> other, actual, which I account actual supplications made in faith for
> the remission of sins committed . . . the third is, justification virtual,
> which consists in the performance of that and the like precepts,
> watch and pray continually; . . . In this perpetuity of virtual prayer
> consists the permanent duration of justification, which yet hath many
> interruptions.[54]

This tardy explanation does not yet set the matter straight, however, because he neglects to include his most general meaning of
justification: final absolution. Previously Jackson explains that

> . . . there is another acceptation of justification yet behind, most fre-
> quent with St Paul, to wit, the actual acquittance of the parties so
> qualified as St James requires. And so this final sentence . . . is appre-
> hended by faith alone; although . . . it cannot be by parties desti-
> tute of works.[55]

Again,

> Thus when the Apostle speaks . . . of justification . . . , his mean-
> ing can be no other than this, that all of them have received
> undoubted pledges of God's mercy, and need not doubt of justifica-
> tion actual, or final absolution, so they walk worthy of their calling.[56]

In yet another instance he has still another meaning for "actual"
justification:

> . . . albeit in this life we be actually justified, that is actually acquitted
> from the guilt of sins past by belief in Christ's death and resurrection;
> and freed likewise from the rage and tyranny of sin by participation
> of his grace, and inhabitation of his Spirit in us . . .[57]

Such differing uses of the term justification are confusing throughout Jackson's work.

His discussion of the apparent conflict between St Paul and St
James suffers from the same confusion. He asserts that St Paul
speaks of a working faith, and includes works in faith, and St
James, so he says, speaks of works and faith by which we are justi-

fied. This assertion comes at the beginning of a chapter, yet only ten pages further into the problem he makes this observation:

> If the works required by St James be not truly good without presupposal of faith, nor justification possible without presupposal of such works; the more operative we make St Paul's faith, the more we rather draw than loose this former knot, whose solution in this respect must be sought by unfolding the divers acceptation of justification.[58]

He proceeds to solve the dilemma in a way that differs markedly from his original claim that Paul's faith included works and, therefore, did not, in fact, differ from James.

> St James, affirming we are just by works, and not by faith alone, speaks of the passive qualification in the subject or party to be justified, or made capable of absolute approbation, or final absolution; this qualification supposed, St Paul speaks of the application of the sentence, or the ground of our plea for absolution . . .[59]

Whatever this means, and it is no easy thing to say what it does mean, it is surely not what he claimed at the outset of the chapter. He becomes somewhat more clear when he writes,

> Faith then makes him just, and justifies him in that sense St James meant, as it is operative; but he lives by it as it unites him to the Lord of life; yea by it alone, inasmuch as by it alone, not by it and other parts of grace as joint supporters, he trusts in God's mercies offered in Christ . . .[60]

Jackson is using justification in the sense of final absolution in the beginning of the chapter. He denies that Paul ever affirmed that a man could be saved or justified without works, and he reconciles the Apostles by insisting that St Paul, like St James, included works in faith. Later, however, he uses justification to mean the initial forgiveness of sin, and he reconciles the two Apostles by arguing that St Paul is referring to the first infusion of grace whereby we are enabled to bring forth good works.

At the beginning of the same chapter, furthermore, Jackson takes another position which he later contradicts.

> Seeing then both faith and the righteousness it works are inherent in us, how are we not justified by inherent righteousness . . . ? . . . our

Saviour's doctrine seems to put it out of all controversy; "Except your righteousness exceed the righteousness of the Scribes and Pharisees, ye shall in no case enter into the kingdom of heaven." What righteousness doth he here mean? Inherent questionless . . .[61]

He continues by denying that obedience to the commandments is more necessary to sanctification or salvation than to justification. It is a contradiction, he says, to argue that such righteousness is more necessary to sanctification than to justification, or that works are less necessary before justification than after it. This definition of justification by inherent righteousness is contradicted countless times in other places. His most consistent argument against the Church of Rome is that by this doctrine it exacts a degree of righteousness of which mortals are incapable, it destroys the relevancy of the Lord's Prayer,[62] and most important of all, it denies the eternal priesthood of Christ.[63]

Thus in the opening pages of this one chapter Jackson takes three positions which he later contradicts: 1. Paul and James are reconciled on the grounds that Paul's faith includes works; later they are reconciled by "unfolding the divers acceptations of justification,"[64] —St Paul means justification in the sense of the initial infusion of grace and remission of sins. 2. Justification is by inherent righteousness; subsequently he insists on the

> utter insufficiency of works, or righteousness inherent, to justification in the sight of God . . . the only complement of all inherent righteousness possible in this life is the perpetual unfeigned acknowledgement of our unrighteousness . . .[65]

3. On pages 286-7 he is clearly using justification to mean final absolution, whereas, on page 314, its meaning seems to be the initial beginning of salvation, and when, finally, he comes to define his uses of the term on page 357 he gives three definitions, none of which, however, includes his preliminary assumption.

It is difficult to account for these discrepancies, but we may have some clue in a sentence found in the preface to the chapter:

> And unto the use and measure of faith, and other graces inherent, I reduce the controversy of justification, here inserted, *contrary to my first intent*, lest otherwise I might have ministered some offence unto

the church wherein I live, or left some scruple in the reader's mind, how faith should justify without works . . .[66]

This may indicate some change of mind. It is possible, judging from the contradictions and the other confusions in his writing, that Jackson changed his mind about justification while he was writing this chapter. He nowhere clears up the semantic difficulties, but his doctrine of justification can be clarified by taking into consideration his various uses of the term justification. He seems to argue that the works and inherent righteousness required by St James are necessary to justification in the sense of final salvation. They are necessary, then, only by way of "passive qualifications",[67] or by way of "presence but not efficacie".[68] But faith alone justifies in the sense of justification as being united to Christ,

> yea, by it alone, inasmuch as by it alone, not by it and other parts of grace as joint supporters, he trusts in God's mercies offered in Christ, wholly relying on them not partly on them, and partly on righteousness inherent.[69]

One of Jackson's principal concerns, as has been noted, is to deny the Roman Catholic claim of inherent righteousness as the formal cause of justification. The first infusion of grace is,

> by their doctrine, partly of grace, (because the foundation of it was mere grace precedent) partly of debt (Canon 32, Sess. 6, Council of Trent), because they merit these additions by right use of their freewill.[70]

Jackson further disagrees with Bellarmine's discussion of Abraham's justification.

> Abraham all this while unfeignedly believed himself to be a sinner, no way justified in himself, but seeking to be justified by him, who if he shew not mercy unto sinners while they are sinners, all mankind should utterly perish. Against this poisonous leaven, wherewith the Pharisee first, and the Romanist his successor since, hath infected the bread of life, and tainted the first fruits of God's Spirit . . .[71]

Also:

> But would to God they [Roman Catholics] would learn at length to speak as consequently to the truth here, Rom. 6.23, by our apostle, as they do to their own tenets, or to the canon of the Trent Council, con-

cerning justification; which tenet or canon neither Calvin nor Chemnitius . . . could more punctually have crossed after it was made, than our apostle here in this verse did almost 1500 years before it was made . . .[72]

In contrast to the Council of Trent (and to Forbes), Jackson does not consider that the regenerate are sinless. Original sin is not entirely removed by baptism,[73] and "Christ doth not cease to execute the office of an Advocate for the regenerate, so long as they live on earth".[74] In this life we are not "Freed from all relics of sin inherent . . ."[75] Jackson's doctrine is thus explicitly opposite to that of the Council of Trent and markedly different from that of Forbes. Jackson does have some of the same concerns as later appear in the works of Taylor, Thorndike, and Hammond. As we have noticed, Jackson, at the beginning of his work, wished to correct those who "minister occasion of carelessness or presumption . . . by not urging such a measure of perfection as God's word requires . . ." He is careful to emphasize the importance of good works and holy living, but he is exceedingly inconsistent in stating how works are related to salvation.

> The immediate qualification for remission of sins, is not the habit or inherence, but the right use of grace, or perseverance in prayers conceived by that faith which unites us unto Christ.[76]

Here he speaks of a qualification for remission of sins which is the right use of grace, but maintains that this grace itself is "conceived by that faith which unites us unto Christ". However, elsewhere he has claimed that forgiveness of sins is gained by this same grace solely on the external merits of Christ.[77] He does not represent the new covenant as a more lenient one purchased by Christ's obedience and granted only upon certain conditions.

In contrast to the doctrine that appeared later, Jackson argues

> . . . that no man can do those works which are capable of the promises before he be enabled by God to do them; and that this ability to do them is from the gift of justifying faith.[78]

His stated purpose, at the outset, is to discover the "mispersuasions" that do not urge "such a measure of perfection as God's word requires". However, it is apparent that where he insists upon this perfection and righteousness as necessary for justification he is speaking of justification in the sense of final absolution.

> Nor is it possible for any man not thus far justified by working grace, to make the right plea of faith, whereby justification properly taken, that is, final absolution, is attained.[79]

Jackson resolutely asserts that it is faith alone which unites us to Christ. Does Jackson then agree with Hooker, Andrewes, Davenant, Ussher, and Hall concerning justification and the imputation of Christ's righteousness as the formal cause? He certainly agrees with them in denying the doctrine of Trent, but he curiously (and uniquely) denies that there is any formal cause at all. Jackson claims that it is a "school-trick" to demand a formal cause of justification. The Roman Catholic speaks of a formal cause of justification because he holds us to be formally just. But in reality justification

> is a form or entity as simple as any formal cause can be, and simple or uncompounded entities can neither have formal causes, or ought in proportion answering to them. Wherefore . . . it is either the folly or knavery of our adversaries to demand a formal cause of their justification, that deny themselves to be formally just in the sight of God. For so to be just, and to be just only by acceptance, or non-imputation of unjustice, are terms as opposite as can be imagined. He alone is formally just which hath that form inherent in himself, by which he is denominated just, and so accepted with God . . .[80]

This statement is central to Jackson's entire doctrine, and is a strange but important mixture of agreement and disagreement with the other points of view. He denies the possibility of a formal cause of justification on the grounds that to be just only by acceptance and non-imputation of sin is not to be actually just. He is so firmly cognizant of the relics of sin in the regenerate that he cannot bring himself to hold that those who live by justifying faith are *formally* righteous or just. Jackson obviously assumes that the formal cause of justification implies that the justified person is formally just. Since we are not just, the meaning of justification for Jackson swings toward "final absolution" as a compass needle swings towards north. But what is the formal cause of the first "acceptation", when "the Lord imputeth not that sin unto him which he still unfeignedly acknowledgeth to be in him . . ."?[81] What *is* the formal cause of justification understood in this sense?

According to the usually accepted definition of formal cause it is difficult to see how anything that is can be without a formal cause. Jackson's denial of any formal cause is not less than a denial that anyone is formally righteous. What he says about justification implies the same formal cause as that of the "imputation" divines. Justification is "not by inherent righteousness, or aught within us immediately incompatible with them, but *by the external merits of Christ* . . .[82] Also, in differing with Bellarmine:

> The point then in which will he nill he, we must join issue, is, what should be the true immediate and next cause of this final absolution, aught within us, or somewhat without us?[83]

The external merits of Christ for Jackson are clearly the "true immediate and next cause", and the *cause by which* we are not only initially forgiven and accepted but also finally absolved. With the actual content the "imputation" (Caroline) divines assigned to the imputation of Christ's righteousness as the formal cause, Jackson is clearly in agreement. His attempts to deny a formal cause seems to be based upon two assumptions: a tendency to assign justification to final absolution so that there often is no "actual" justification in this life; and a tendency to assume that to admit a formal cause of justification is the same as to admit that the justified are formally righteous.

The essential content of Jackson's doctrine, thus, does not differ appreciably from that of the "gratuitous justification" school. He is equally insistent in denying the Tridentine doctrine; he definitely believes that sin remains in the regenerate; and, in fact, he agrees with Hooker and Davenant as to "that which makes our justification to be what it is".

THE CONFERENCE
CONCERNING MONTAGUE'S BOOKS
1626

A controversy at the opening of the Caroline period presents us with a slightly different view of justification from that of the "imputation" divines. In 1624 Richard Montague (1577-1641) in the course of a dispute with a Roman Catholic, published a book called *A Gagg for the Gospell? No: A New Gagg for an Old Goose*. On the petition of two ministers Montague was accused before Parliament of popery and Arminianism. Montague defended himself in a book published the next year addressed to the King and entitled *Appello Caesarem*. Although the doctrine of justification was not extensively discussed in either book, it became one of the issues argued by his critics and defenders.

A statement about justification which seems to have provoked great criticism appears in the first work.

> A sinner is then justified when he is made just: that is, translated from state of Nature, to state of Grace . . . which . . . consisteth in forgiveness of sinnes primarily; and Grace infused secondarily: Both the act of God's Spirit in man, but applyed, or rather obtained through Faith . . .[84]

Montague argues that justification is by faith alone, instrumentally, and by God alone, causally. He goes on to say that "beside God and Faith, wee yeeld to Hope, and Holinesse, and Sanctification, and the fruits of the Spirit in good works". However, he immediately adds, "But both these are not justification: rather fruits, and consequencies and effects, and appendants of justification; then justification, which is a solitary act."[85]

In the second work Montague defends himself from the charge of having included sanctification and good works in justification. He insists that God will not call anyone righteous who is unholy and unsanctified. The person must first be made acceptable and then accepted. He claims, however, that his critics overlook the important qualification that justification is primarily remission of sins and only secondarily grace infused. He asserts that justification can be understood in two ways.

> *Stricte magis,* and *extensive*: Precisely, for remission of sinnes, by the onely merits and satisfaction of Christ, accepted for us, and imputed to us. And enlargedly, for that Act of God, and the necessary and immediate concomitants unto, and consequents upon that, the whole and entire state and quality and condition of man regenerate, changed; by which a sinner guilty of death, is acquitted, cleansed, made just in himselfe, reconciled unto God, appointed to walke and beginning to walke in holinesse and in newnesse of life.[86]

Montague argues, then, that justification in the first sense is the action of God whereby we are pardoned of our sins, accounted righteous, and accepted by him in Christ. The second meaning of justification includes regeneration and sanctification. This

> second justification (for why contend wee about words, that agree upon the point?) is distinct from Remission of our sins by God, and imputation of Christ's righteousness unto us; wherein is our Acceptance and Justification.[87]

St Paul and St James do not, he maintains, contradict each other because the former is speaking of attaining justification and the latter is speaking of justification already attained. Thus, faith alone is necessary for attaining justification but justification is not without works. Good works can no more be separated from justification than light from the sun. He asserts that he was referring to such good works when he argued that the justified were made just. He points out that even the Reformed Churches acknowledge such a change in justified persons "by the grace of sanctification".[88]

Almost immediately some anonymous critics replied to Montague in *A Dangerous Plot Discovered by A Discourse Wherein is proved, That, Mr Richard Montague . . . Laboureth to bring in the Faith of Rome, and Arminius; under the name and pretence of the doctrine and faith of the Church of England.* Montague is not criticized in regard to justification for what he wrote in the second book. It is claimed, however, that if he really believed that justification in its strict sense did not include sanctification he would have said so in his first book. "You did not beleeve that Justification is as now you pretend, for if you had so beleeved, you would have expressed that beleefe . . ." [89]

Another attack on Montague came from George Carleton, Bishop of Chichester, in *An Examination of those things wherein the Author of the late Appeale holdeth the Doctrines of the Pelagians and Arminians to be the Doctrine of the Church of England*. Carleton is not particularly concerned with the matter of justification, but he objects strenuously to Montague's assertion that the regenerate can fall from grace. The whole affair achieved such proportions that a conference was called to discuss the orthodoxy of Montague's books.

JOHN COSIN
1594-1672

One of the few passages that gives any indication of John Cosin's attitude toward justification occurs in his discussion of the events of the conference: *The Sum and Substance of the Conference concerning Mr Montague's Books, which it pleased the Duke of Buckingham to appoint at the request of the Earl of Warwick and my Lord Say, in York House, Febr 11, 1625*. John Buckeridge, Bishop of Rochester, and Francis White (1564?-1638), Dean (and later Bishop) of Carlisle, were Montague's principal defenders. Thomas Morton (1564-1659), Bishop of Lichfield, and John Preston were the principal critics. Cosin attended the conference at the urging of White. The matter of justification was not extensively discussed, but there was some criticism that Montague included sanctification in his description of justification. Morton asked White what he might answer to this objection.

"Nothing," quoth the Dean; "for Mr Cosin hath the place here ready, where Mr Montague answers you himself at large, and it is in that very period which your lordship hath cited. His words are these: 'In the strict acceptance of the word justification, we acknowledge instrumentally faith alone, and causally God alone. In a second and third sense, besides God and faith we yield to hope, and holiness, and sanctification, and the fruits of the Spirit in good works. But these are rather fruits, and consequencies, and effects, or appendants of justification, then justification itself (as it signifieth remission of sins and imputation of Christ's merits), which is a solitary act.' "[90]

Cosin defends Montague by insisting that he adheres to the doctrine of Article 11, that justification is by faith alone, and that even in the first work Montague demonstrates that good works are the fruits and consequences of justification. John Cosin does not discuss justification himself, and we get only this slight indication of his views as a part of his defence of Montague. Whatever Cosin believed about justification, it is important to note that his defence of Montague follows the argument of the "gratuitous justification" doctrine. Montague is defended from the accusation that his doctrine is "papal" by a counter-argument that he holds sanctification and good works to be subsequent to justification, and that he argues that it is the imputation of Christ's righteousness by which a sinner is justified.

WILLIAM LAUD
1573-1645

William Laud, later Archbishop, was himself indirectly involved in the Montague affair, but the only indication we have of his views is expressed in two letters addressed to the Duke of Buckingham and signed by several bishops including Laud. The second letter seems to express Laud's general attitude toward such doctrinal matters.

> Now, may it please your Grace, the opinions which at this time trouble many men in the late work of Mr Montague, are, some of them, such as are expressly the resolved doctrine of the Church of England, and these he is bound to maintain. Some of them, such as are fit only for schools, and to be left at more liberty for learned men to abound in their own sense, so they keep themselves peaceable and distract not the church.[91]

On the other hand, however, it is significant that neither Cosin nor Laud seemed to have considered the matter of soteriology as an important difference between the Church of England and the Church of Rome. In a conference with Cyril, the Archbishop of Trapezond, Cosin discusses the "Romish or Tridentine new and additional articles of faith".[92] They discuss papal supremacy, transubstantiation, invocation of saints, purgatory, and prayers for the dead, but they do not mention justification. Similarly, in his *Conference with Fisher the Jesuit*, Laud does not once bring up the subject of justification.

Be it noted that Montague's position tended slightly towards that of the Council of Trent, and he did not see justification in the way that Jeremy Taylor, Henry Hammond, and Herbert Thorndike were later to describe it.

WILLIAM CHILLINGWORTH
1602-44

William Chillingworth, however, does represent in this period a foretaste of the way in which the later Caroline divines were to interpret the doctrine of justification. Chillingworth, writing in 1637, insists that Protestants require repentance as a condition of remission of sins

> and therefore, Protestants requiring this to remission of sins, and remission of sins to justification, cannot with candour be pretended to believe, that they are justified before any good work.[93]

He maintains, also, that a Christian must place his hope of justification and salvation "not in the perfection of his own righteousness . . . but in the mercies of God through Christ's satisfaction".[94] However, charity is a necessary disposition in anyone who is to be justified, and although it cannot be perfect, no one can be justified without charity. In this emphasis upon charity as a condition of justification, Chillingworth is an early representative of a point of view that later on was to consider justification as a central concern of holy living. This approach, which was to become increasingly popular in the seventeenth century, is expressed by Chillingworth thus:

> For my part, I do heartily wish, that, by public authority, it were so ordered, that no man should ever preach or print this doctrine,—that "faith alone justifies", unless he joins this together with it,—that "uni-

versal obedience is necessary to salvation": and besides, that those
chapters of St Paul which entreat of justification by faith without
works of the law, were never read in the Church but when the thir-
teenth chapter of the First Epistle to the Corinthians, concerning the
absolute necessity of charity, should be to prevent misprision, read
together with them.[95]

3

The Theology of Jeremy Taylor

Bishop Jeremy Taylor stands out in the history of the Anglican Church as one of the most significant and influential divines. Few have written so much or been read by so many as he. His works comprise fifteen volumes in the Heber edition. His devotional works, *Holy Living* and *Holy Dying*, were avidly read not only by the Wesleys and the Evangelicals of the eighteenth century and by the Tractarians of the nineteenth, but also by countless English speaking Christians until the twentieth century.

In *Ductor Dubitantium* (1660) Taylor's avowed aim was to produce a work of moral theology which would help fill the gap left by the repudiation of "jesuitical" casuistry and by the prevalent reluctance to deal with "middle axioms" of Christian behaviour. But even earlier Taylor saw that his casuistry would have to be grounded on soteriology. The *Unum Necessarium* or *The Doctrine And Practice Of Repentance* (1655) was written to establish the doctrinal basis for Christian ethics. It was Taylor's conviction that the doctrine of repentance there set forth would restore the balance of the distorted soteriology of the time, and thereby prepare the way for the moral theology of his *Ductor Dubitantium*. His work on repentance, however, attracted so much criticism from both Anglicans and Presbyterians, including questions as to his orthodoxy, that he became involved in extensive correspondence, and found it necessary to write a defence of his position, *Deus Justificatus* (1658).

It is ironical, if not surprising, that the *Ductor Dubitantium*, his *opus magnum*, is probably his least read work, and that the substance of his reputation and influence rests primarily upon his devotional works, especially *Holy Living* and *Holy Dying*. The theological works leading up to the *Ductor Dubitantium*, especially those which describe the nature of repentance, are primarily important for elucidating Taylor's understanding and teaching about the Gospel. He is not so concerned as his predecessors were about the use of traditional terms, or so insistent on particular doctrinal expressions. He is largely concerned with the practical effect of his doctrine on holy living, and much less concerned with argument involving careful theological distinctions. Taylor rarely discusses the problems of "imputation" or "infusion". This is not to say, however, that he is indifferent to the reality represented by such terms. On the contrary, as we shall see, he is constantly wrestling with the steps he considers necessary for justification and forgiveness and for admission to the covenant and eternal life. This fundamental concern abounds in his sermons, devotional works, doctrinal writings, and in his prayers.

THE DUBLIN SERMONS
JUSTIFICATION, FORGIVENESS, RIGHTEOUSNESS

Three sermons preached in Christ Church, Dublin (1662), after the Restoration demonstrate admirably Jeremy Taylor's method of expounding the nature of the Gospel. He argues that, "whatsoever is said of the efficacy of faith for justification is not to be taken in such a sense as will weaken the necessity and our carefulness of a good life".[1] Good works, though necessary, cannot be meritorious conditions of justification. Good works in this life are never altogether free of sin, nor can they be such as require no repentance. When St Paul says we are justified without works of the law, he refers, according to Taylor, to meritorious good works or to good works so good that there need be no repentance.

Taylor asserts that no man "is justified in the least sense of justification, that is, when it means nothing but pardon of sins, but when his sin is mortified and destroyed".[2] A man's sins are pardoned only to the extent that they are mortified and removed by repentance. Our faith must obliterate our sinful nature or it can never procure our pardon. Faith that does not cure sin will not justify. No one is justified except as he is in some measure sanctified.

Taylor seems to argue that sanctification must precede justification, but he is somewhat ambiguous in discussing this point. "So that no man is justified, that is, so as to signify salvation, but sanctification must be precedent to it."[3] But in other passages Taylor is very careful to insist upon prevenient grace as necessary to empower the works upon which the conditions of the new covenant are based. This point of view leads him to an elastic understanding of justification which is difficult to distinguish from salvation. It is not so important, however, what Taylor says about justification, or how he uses the terms of soteriology. What does concern us is how he understands the nature of the Gospel, and what he considers to be the necessary conditions of initial acceptance and forgiveness by God. He discusses these issues in a sermon entitled "The Miracles of Divine Mercy".

> God is so ready to forgive, that himself works our dispositions towards it, and either must, in some degree, pardon us before we are capable of pardon, by his grace making way for his mercy, or else we can never hope for pardon. For unless God, by his preventing grace, should first work the first part of our pardon, even without any dispositions of our own to receive it, we could not desire a pardon, nor hope for it, nor work towards it, nor ask it, nor receive it. This giving of preventing grace is a mercy of forgiveness contrary to that severity, by which some desperate persons are given over to a reprobate sense; that is, a leaving of men to themselves, so that they can not pray effectually, nor desire holily, nor repent truly, nor receive any of those mercies which God designed so plenteously, and the Son of God purchased so dearly for us.[4]

This is as close as Taylor comes to an explication of the gratuitous forgiveness involved in the Gospel, or of the initiative God takes in reaching out to sinners who cannot help themselves. It is an exception to his pervasive argument that God acts only when and after man has by his works of repentance fulfilled his part of the new covenant. The predominant emphasis of Taylor's sermons is that a sinner must root out his sin, and the habit of it, and obtain some measure of the opposite virtue, before he can expect pardon. He explains his view of the controversy in the following terms:

> They say that Christ's righteousness is imputed to us for justification, do it upon this account; because they know all we do is imperfect, therefore they think themselves constrained to fly to Christ's righteousness, and think it must be imputed to us, or we perish. The other side, considering that this way would destroy the necessity of holy living; and that in order to our justification, there were conditions required on our parts, think it necessary to say, that we are justified by inherent righteousness. Between these the truth is plain enough to be read. Thus:
>
> Christ's righteousness is not imputed to us for justification directly and immediately; neither can we be justified by our own righteousness: but our faith and sincere endeavours are, through Christ, accepted instead of legal righteousness: that is we are justified through Christ, by imputation not of Christ's, nor our own righteousness, but of our faith and endeavours of righteousness, as if they were perfect: and we are justified by a non-imputation, viz., of our past sins, and present unavoidable imperfections: that is, we are handled as if we were just persons and no sinners. So faith was imputed to Abraham for righteousness; not that it made him so legally, but evangelically, that is, by grace and imputation.[5]

Our imperfect services and sincere endeavours of obedience are imputed to us ("as if they were perfect") for the righteousness of justification.

Taylor categorically denies, in his sermons, that Romans 7 is a description of a regenerate person, let alone a description of St Paul unless when he was living under the law. In fact, every Christian is called to arrive at a state of righteousness in which no habit of sin remains in him. "Now if this (Rom. 7.19-25) be a state of regeneration, I wonder what is, or can be, a state of reprobation!"[6] "He that commits any one sin by choice and deliberation is an enemy to God, and is under the dominion of the flesh."[7] "In short, he is not a child of God, that knowingly and deliberately chooses anything that God hates."[8]

> It is necessary that all sin, great and little, should be mortified and dead in us, and that we no longer abide in that state of slavery, as to

say, "the good that I would, I do not; but the evil that I would not, that I do".[9]

Taylor acknowledges that righteousness need not be perfect, but he does not explain how much stain of sin will be accepted by God's mercy. Clearly, if there is too much stain of sin then the sinner is in a difficult situation. If we are not good men, our prayers will do us no good, Taylor says, and we shall be in the condition of them that never pray at all. Throughout the sermons there is a consistent exhortation to behave and live a holy life. He uses every argument he can muster to encourage obedience and good works, but there is no declaration of what God has himself already done to elicit a grateful response and a holy life from the faithful. Taylor stresses, instead, God's pardon and eternal life as rewards for and incentives towards obedience and holy living.

REPENTANCE AND THE HOLY LIFE

The works of popular devotion, *Holy Living* and *Holy Dying*, have the same emphasis and content with respect to justification as do his sermons. Here, too, the key to the doctrine is repentance and the holy life. Repentance itself must include the holy life. A bare contrition or feeling of sorrow, without corresponding works of charity, cannot be accepted as a complete repentance.

> Repentance of all things in the world makes the greatest change: it changes things in heaven and earth; for it changes the whole man from sin to grace, from vicious habits to holy customs, from unchaste bodies to angelical souls, from swine to philosophers, from drunkenness to sober counsels . . . but repentance is a conjugation and society of many duties; and it contains in it all the parts of a holy life from the time of our return to the day of our death inclusively . . .[10]

Also:

> True repentance must reduce to act all its holy purposes, and enter into and run through the state of holy living . . . For to resolve to do it and yet not to do it is to break our resolution and our faith . . . and to make our pardon hopeless and our hope fruitless.[11]

Taylor's understanding of baptism and justification centres, for the most part, upon our agreement to the new covenant, whereby we contract to live a holy life. Upon the fulfilment of these conditions only are the rewards of heaven given. He proclaims that the rewards of heaven are so great and glorious, and Christ's burden so light and his yoke so easy, that it is shameful impudence to expect so much "at a lower rate than a holy life".[12]

> But our hopes of pardon are just as in the repentance; which if it be timely, hearty, industrious, and effective, God accepts, not by weighing grains or scruples, but by estimating the great proportions of our life. A hearty endeavour, and an effectual general change shall get the pardon . . .[13]

In the covenant of repentance Christ has purchased a leniency whereby God accepts "a hearty endeavour". Though there be slight imperfections and short interruptions in the holy life, our imperfections will be paid for by Christ provided that we watch, pray, and strive. The new covenant is precisely this state and condition of repentance.[14] Despite the leniency of the covenant there are, nevertheless, necessary conditions which must be fulfilled before God's "gratuitous" forgiveness and pardon are granted. Taylor argues that sin and grace always maintain a balance of increase and decrease. As sin grows, grace decays. The more need we have of grace, the less we shall be able to have. The "greatness of our sins which makes the need hath lessened the grace of God, which should help us, into nothing."[15] The devotional works, *Holy Living* and *Holy Dying*, represent the Good News as essentially a gospel of repentance.

A state of grace and favour with God are never on account of justification or baptism. Favour with God is a consequence of repentance within the covenant.

> No man, therefore, can be in a state of grace and actual favour by resolutions and holy purposes [this for Taylor seems to be the real function of justification and baptism]; these are but the gate and portal towards pardon: a holy life is the only perfection of repentance, and the firm ground upon which we can cast the anchor of hope in the mercies of God through Jesus Christ.[16]

Not only does Taylor argue, as we have seen from the sermons, that obedience precedes justification, but also that justification and baptism are but the gate and portal towards pardon. Thus, if one "strives", "sincerely endeavours", obeys, and engages in works of charity, he will be initially accepted into the covenant of leniency whereby, in turn, his slight imperfections and short interruptions will be accepted, provisionally, on "account of the cross". Full pardon is deferred until final completion of a holy life and a holy death. Man must take the initiative, and then only God will act.

> For a holy life being the condition of the covenant on our part, as we return to God, so God returns to us, and our state returns to the probabilities of pardon.[17]

It would seem that Taylor's soteriology, as developed in these works, assumes not that God first loves us but that we must first love God.

There is, however, an inconsistent emphasis within these devotional works as to the question of severity in dealing with post-baptismal sins. For the most part, Taylor says, they come under the "leniency" of the new covenant provided there is sufficient endeavour and striving. This *is* consistent with Taylor's insistence upon the tenuous and provisional nature of justification and baptism. However, he also states that:

> We are but once to change our whole state of life, from the power of the devil and his entire possession, from the state of sin and death, from the body of corruption, to the life of grace, etc. . . . : and this is done in the baptism of water, or in the baptism of the Spirit . . . After this change if ever we fall into the contrary state . . . God hath made no more covenant of restitution to us; there is no place left for any more repentance . . . or new birth: a man can be regenerated but once . . .[18]

This discrepancy in Taylor's discussion of sin in the regenerate occurs also in his theological discussion of repentance. As has already been noted, he sees clearly the need for basing his casuistry upon a doctrinal description of the relation of atonement to the sinner. He develops this in his doctrine of repentance. There is a lengthy section on repentance in *The Great Exemplar* (1649), and repentance is the subject of his *Unum Necessarium* (1655). (In fact, much of the latter is a restatement of what he first propounds in *The Great Exemplar*.)

DOCTRINE OF REPENTANCE IN
TAYLOR'S THEOLOGICAL WORKS

His theological works on repentance give a more complete indication of Taylor's thought in regard to justification than do his sermons or his devotional writings. In his theological works we find less strict requirements for forgiveness and more qualified descriptions of righteousness in the regenerate. Righteousness is considered to be commensurate with the more lenient requirements of the evangelical covenant. In that covenant of mercy sins are forgiven in the regenerate provided they sincerely endeavour to lead a holy life.

Although Taylor plainly differs seriously from the teaching of Hooker and Andrewes, he does not by any means agree with those who argue for the infusion of inherent righteousness, nor does he agree with the position of the Council of Trent. He does not accept that the regenerate are made righteous in justification by infused grace or that this grace satisfies the demands of God. Taylor's position is rather that our faith and sincere endeavours before justification are accepted as the required righteousness on account of Christ. The covenant, in other words, is a relationship of mutual responsibility.

> Upon that we entertained the mercies of redemption; and God established it upon such an obedience, which is a constant, perpetual, and universal sincerity and endeavour; and as we perform our part, so God verifies his, and not only gives a great assistance by the perpetual influences of his Holy Spirit, by which we are consigned to the day of redemption, but also takes an account of obedience, not according to the standard of the law and an exact scrutiny, but by an evangelical proportion . . .[19]

This passage does not make clear whether Taylor refers to the initial acceptance by God into the covenant relationship or to its continuation. He does, however, describe baptism as the first step towards salvation.

> But baptism is a new birth, and by it we are . . . "renewed unto repentance", unto that state of life which supposes holiness and imperfection, and consequently needs mercy all the way: according to that saying, "justus ex fide vivet", "the just shall live by faith": that is, all our righteousness, all our hopes, all our spiritual life, is conserved by, and is relying upon, this covenant of mercy, the covenant of faith, or repentance: all his life-time the just shall need pardon, and find it, if he perseveres in it,—that is, endeavours to obey according to the righteousness of faith, that is, sincerely, diligently, and by the measures of a man.[20]

It is clear, then, that obedience is necessary before entering the covenant that Christ has provided. Taylor maintains that it is God's purpose to bring us to himself by Christ. Christ is the medium to God but obedience is the medium to Christ. We are accepted by Christ on the condition of our sincere endeavours before entering the covenant, and we remain in the covenant subject to our subsequent holy life. Both baptism and justification are conditional, depending for their efficacy upon previous obedience and the subsequent holy life of the regenerate. They do not depend upon any infusion of righteousness when they occur.

> And, therefore, in the present condition of things, our pardon was properly expressed by David, and St Paul, by "a covering" and "a not imputing". For because the body of sin dies divisibly, and fights perpetually, and disputes with hopes of victory, and may also prevail, all this life is a condition of suspense; our sin is rather covered, than properly pardoned; God's wrath is suspended, not satisfied; the sin is not to all purposes of anger imputed, but yet is in some sense remanent, or at least lies ready at the door.[21]

Furthermore, covering does not mean acceptance and forgiveness by God in spite of our own unworthiness as it does for Hooker, Andrewes, and Donne, but rather a tenuous and conditional acceptance that is contrasted with being "properly pardoned".

> Now let a prudent person imagine what infirmities and oversights can consist with a state thus described, and all that does no violence to the covenant; God pities us, and calls us not to an account for what

morally cannot, or certainly will not, with great industry, be prevented.[22]

Such statements about a regenerate person within the covenant of repentance differ markedly from what Taylor says on the same subject in his sermons and in his popular devotional writings. However, there is, at the same time, a similar emphasis upon the necessity for obedience and holy living. This emphasis is qualified only by a reminder that the covenant is also a covenant of mercy.

The lenient note of mercy which Taylor finds in the new covenant does not, however, eliminate the condition required for it. God will do his part only when we do ours.

> But then we having received so great a favour, enter into covenant to correspond with a proportionable endeavour; . . . That is the condition on our part: and if we prevaricate that, the mercy shewn to the blessed thief is no argument of hope to us, because he was saved by the mercies of the first access, which corresponds to the remission of sins we receive in baptism; and we shall perish, by breaking our own promises and obligations, which Christ passed upon us when he made with us the covenant of an entire and gracious pardon. For in the precise covenant there is nothing else described, but pardon so given and ascertained upon an obedience persevering to the end.[23]

The problem of the "blessed" thief on the cross is a particularly difficult one for Taylor because it could, of course, easily be used as an argument for deferring repentance and the holy life. He recalls the example of the thief, not to stress the importance of God's love and mercy, but essentially to preclude the use of the example as any encouragement to delay repentance. He argues that the thief had the same relationship to Christ as a Turk or other heathen who has just been converted to Christianity.[24] The forgiveness granted "the blessed thief" is, in other words, the same as that granted a Christian upon entrance into the covenant through baptism and/or justification.

Taylor develops this point further, arguing that it is much more grievous to sin after the initial acceptance into the covenant than it was previously, and that subsequent sins are much more harshly dealt with once one has entered the covenant.

But after we are once reconciled in baptism . . . if we then fall away into sin . . . Never must we expect to be so again justified, and upon 'such terms as formerly . . . not that God will never forgive them that sin after baptism, and recover by repentance; but that restitution by repentance after baptism is another thing than the first redemption.[25]

This explication of the example of "the blessed thief" involves Taylor in some contradiction of his emphasis upon the lenient aspects of the covenant of mercy, and corresponds more closely to the tenor of his sermons. He even suggests, at one point, that perhaps the sin of a regenerate person is the very sin against the Holy Ghost.

And this might not be improperly said to be the meaning of those words of our blessed Saviour, "He that speaks a word against the Son of Man, it shall be forgiven him; but he that speaks a word against the Holy Ghost, it shall not be forgiven him": that is those sins which were committed in infidelity, before we became disciples of the Holy Jesus, are to be remitted in baptism and our first profession of the religion; but the sins committed after baptism and confirmation, in which we receive the Holy Ghost, and by which the Holy Spirit is grieved, are to be accounted for with more severity.[26]

Despite this lapse into severity the basic thrust of Taylor's theological works on repentance differs from his sermons and popular devotional works in that more allowance is made for the imperfect nature of the regenerate. His discussion of "the blessed thief" is the only instance in the theological works where he departs from the general emphasis upon the covenant of mercy, and he uses it only to stress that there can be no deferment of the holy life for the members of the new covenant. Otherwise, Taylor's theological works focus upon God's willingness to accept our striving and endeavour even though sometimes we fail or fall short of achievement.

ATONEMENT AND COVENANT IN TAYLOR'S THEOLOGICAL WORKS

The theological works also introduce a new and strange doctrine of the atonement and of the new covenant. The new covenant differs from the old in that the latter provided no forgiveness for failings or shortcomings. The new covenant is indeed a covenant of works and holy living, but there is a leniency, not provided in the old, which was purchased by Christ to provide for the acceptance by God of imperfect works in the regenerate.

> . . . for the whole Gospel is nothing else but that glad tidings which Christ brought to all mankind, that the covenant of works, or exact measures, should not now be exacted, but men should be saved by second thoughts, that is, by repentance and amendment of life, through faith in the Lord Jesus. That is, if we become disciples (for that is the condition of the covenant), we shall find mercy, our sins shall be blotted out, and we shall be saved if we obey heartily and diligently, though not exactly.[27]

> Under the first covenant, the covenant of works, no endeavour was sufficient, because there was no allowance made for infirmities, no abatements for ignorance, no deductions of exact measures, no consideration of surprises, passions, folly and inadvertency; but under the new covenant, our hearty endeavour is accepted . . .[28]

Taylor's overruling preoccupation with holy living confronts him with another difficulty not unlike that of the thief on the cross, and he handles it in much the same way. If a man lives an habitually vicious and sinful life, refuses to repent, produces no works of charity, and at the last moment before death repents and is forgiven, his example is, of course, dangerous and threatening to people struggling with temptations and endeavouring to lead a holy life. Death-bed confession is one of the prime objects of Taylor's attack on the Roman Church.

> A repentance upon our death-bed is like washing the corpse: it is cleanly and civil; but makes no change deeper than the skin . . . God intended we should live a holy life: he contracted with us in Jesus Christ for a holy life: he made no abatements of the strictest sense of it, but such as did necessarily comply with human infirmities or possibilities; that is, he understood it in the sense of repentance, which still is so to renew our duty, that it may be a holy life in the second sense; that is, some great portion of our life to be spent in living as Christians should.[29]

His doctrine of repentance includes not only contrition but the actual "acting out" of virtues opposite to the sins which have been confessed. This must first be performed on our part before God on his part will pardon us. Pardon obtained in baptism, or justification, or initial acceptance into the covenant is partial, conditional, and provisional. Final pardon and complete forgiveness, or washing away of guilt, is granted only upon our fulfilment of all the conditions of the covenant.

> Our sins are not pardoned easily and quickly; and the longer and the greater hath been the iniquity, the harder and more difficult and uncertain is the pardon; it is a great progress to return from all the degrees of death to life, to motion, to quickness, to purity, to acceptation, to grace, to contention, and growth in grace, to perseverance, and so to pardon: for pardon stands no where, but at the gates of heaven.[30]
>
> This is the sum total of repentance: we must not only have overcome sin, but we must after great diligence have acquired the habits of all those Christian graces, which are necessary in the transaction of our affairs, in all relations to God and our neighbour, and our own persons.[31]

THE WORTHY COMMUNICANT

Jeremy Taylor's understanding of the Gospel is nowhere better set forth than in *The Worthy Communicant* (1660) in which he describes the conditions necessary for attendance at Holy Communion. A man need not be perfect to take Communion but he cannot be in the habit or state of desiring anything sinful.

> He that hath resolved against all sin, and yet falls into it regularly at the next temptation, is yet in a state of evil, and unworthiness to communicate . . . But if, having resolved against all sin, he delights in none, deliberately chooses none, is not so often surprised, grows stronger in grace, and is mistaken but seldom, and repents when he is . . . whatever imperfection is still adherent to the man unwillingly, does indeed allay his condition, and is fit to humble and cast him down; but it does not make him unworthy to communicate . . . and the holy sacrament, if it have any effect at all, is certainly an instrument or a sign in the hands of God to help his servants, to enlarge his grace, to give more strengths, and to promote them to perfection.[32]

Such imperfections or sins as are allowable to the state of regeneration are non-deliberate or are those of ignorance. No one may

> . . . approach to the holy sacrament upon the account of his mere resolution to leave sin until he hath broken the habit, until he hath cast away his fetters, until he be at liberty from sin, and hath shaken off its laws and dominion . . . till then he may do well to stand in the outward courts, lest . . . he . . . bring away from thence the intolerable sentence of condemnation.[33]

Indeed, it is a crucial matter to determine whether or not one is worthy before coming to receive the sacrament because he who does so unworthily eats and drinks at the very peril of his soul.

> . . . if you receive it worthily, it will do you good; if unworthily, it will be your death and your destruction. Here the penitent can be cleansed, and here the impenitent are consumed: here they that are justified, shall be justified still; and they that are unholy become more unholy and accursed: here they that have shall have more abundantly; and they that have not, shall lose what they have already; here the living are made strong and happy, and the dead do die again.[34]
>
> I do not say that persons unprepared may come, for they ought not; and if they do, they die for it: but I say, if they will come, it is at their peril, and to no man's prejudice, but their own . . .[35]

It is, in other words, exceedingly important to inquire carefully into the qualifications necessary to be prepared and to be a worthy communicant and not a damned one. The essential qualification is, of course, faith but it must be a faith that corresponds with the special definitions Taylor assigns to this virtue. Faith

> . . . is not understood only [as] "the act" of faith but "the body" of faith, not only believing the articles, but the dedication of our persons; not only a yielding up of our understanding, but the engaging of our services; nor the hallowing of one faculty but the sanctification of the whole man. That faith, which is necessary to the worthy receiving this divine sacrament, is all that which is necessary to the susception of baptism and all that which is produced by hearing the word of God, and all that which is exercised in every single grace; and all that by which we live the life of grace, and all that which works by charity, and makes a new creature, and justifies a sinner, and is a keeping of the commandments of God.[36]

Without such a faith "they eat and drink damnation to themselves".[37] How far must this faith which is "the sanctification of the whole man" be completed and accomplished? Taylor tells us that those parts of repentance which must be finished before one approaches the blessed sacrament are the resolve never to commit any sin, "concerning which he can deliberate . . . And . . . he must resolve so to stand upon his guard, that he may not frequently be surprised . . ."[38] This is consistent with Taylor's argument that the new covenant allows repentance and the holy life to be inadequate only in ignorance, surprises, and non-deliberate sins. Hence, these are inadequacies which do not necessarily render a person unworthy to communicate. Yet,

> . . . he that comes, must have repented first . . . he is to be examined . . . whether he have so washed, that he is indeed clean from any foul and polluting principle.[39]

There must, then, be a complete extirpation of any known sin or desire for sin, and there must be such a cleansing in repentance that a man truly believes he shall never any more commit that sin for which he is repentant. He must inquire diligently to be sure that his resolution is not "one only of satiated appetite and shame of sin handled and will it still be there when the appetite returns?"[40] If a man does not possess such repentance he is unworthy to communicate.

> It is nothing to dispise a cheap sin and a common temptation; but art thou strong enough to overcome the strongest arguments that thy sin hath?[41]

For ". . . by faith in Christ we are admitted to the pardon of our sins, if we repent and forsake them utterly".[42] A man must be quite sure that his repentance is stronger than any temptation and "examine whether there be in thee any good principle stronger than all the arguments and flatteries of thy sin . . ."[43] In fact, the best test of whether a man is a worthy communicant is to ask himself whether he is ready to die. One not prepared for death is not prepared for Holy Communion. Men "must not communicate till they be in that condition, that if they did die, it would go well with them".[44]

The idea of sacrifice in the Eucharist seems for Taylor to imply the offering of a pure and spotless soul on the part of the communicant.

> For if an unclean man brings a clean sacrifice, the sacrifice shall not cleanse the man, but the man will pollute the sacrifice; let them bring to God a soul pure and spotless, lest God espying a soul humbly lying before the altar, and finding it to be polluted with a remaining filthiness, or the reproaches of a sin, he turns away his head and hates the sacrifice.[45]

Taylor is saying here that if an unclean person comes to Communion, the sacrifice of Christ will not cleanse him, but rather his impurity will pollute the sacrifice of Christ, and God will turn "away his head and hate the sacrifice". The cleansing, in any case, must be done prior to Communion.

> For he that is in that state of things, that he is to examine how many actions of uncleanness, or intemperance, or slander, he hath committed since the last communion, is not fit to come to another; but must change his life, and repent greatly before he comes hither.[46]

If we do what we should in repentance to be worthy communicants we thereby change our lives before we come and then

> . . . we should find that, upon the day of our communion, we should have nothing to do but the 3rd particular, that is, "The Offices of Prayer and Eucharist", and to renew our graces by prayer and exercises of devotion.[47]

To be worthy communicants we must present our souls as "pure and spotless" sacrifices, we must be so strong that we are certain of overcoming the strongest of future temptations. There must be "complete extirpation" of all known sins and sinful desires, and a faith that is the "sanctification of the whole man". We must be in such a state that if we should die we should be confident that "it would go well" with us. These severe conditions of holiness that must be accomplished before coming to Holy Communion at the risk of our damnation might seem to make it unnecessary to partake, one being already so clean from sin, righteous, and ready to die. What then did Taylor see as the advantage of receiving Holy Communion? Spiritual graces are more like corn than grass, and one must therefore weed out the sins so that the Holy Communion becomes a "blessing upon our endeavours".[48]

This "blessing upon our endeavours" is the main purpose of Holy Communion because ". . . he that comes to redeem our souls from sin and death, from shame and reproach, would have our souls brought to him as he loves them".[49] Thus, we should cleanse ourselves and come to Christ in the Eucharist in order to secure a blessing upon our endeavours. How, then, does Taylor understand the scriptural passages where Christ receives and confers his love upon sinners before they have repented?

> For although it be true that God loves us first, yet he will not continue to love us, or proceed in the methods of his kindness, unless we become like unto him in love.[50]

Once in the covenant, in other words, if we fail to be like Christ, there is no longer any dealing with us in "the methods of his kindness", and here the wicked hope in vain for pardon, ". . . because God accepts no breakers of their vows".[51] Taylor quotes Ambrose as to the necessity of coming to the sacrament clothed in the "wedding garment". But, whereas Hooker, Andrewes, and John Donne had seen the "wedding garment" as the righteousness of Christ and a covering by our "elder brother", Taylor suggests that the "wedding garment" is the whole conjugation of our works of charity by which "we are fitted to this heavenly supper of the king".[52] "Faith working by charity is the wedding garment",[53] and we must not presume to come to the Lord's table except we be "clothed with white garments, the righteousness and justification of the saints".[54]

Taylor also has some advice for those who are reluctant to receive Holy Communion with too great a frequency for fear of falling "into lukewarmness and indevotion". He rebukes them, saying that their "consideration is good: and such persons, indeed, may not receive it often, but not for that reason; but because they are not fit to receive it at all".[55]

CONCLUSION

The Gospel as expounded in Taylor's sermons, in his devotional literature, in his theological works, and in his preparations for Holy Communion, may be concisely summed up as the willingness of God to accept us tentatively on account of his more lenient covenant. Thereafter, however, our hope depends upon our sincere endeavours in the life of repentance. The sole inconsistency is that point, discussed above, where he gives contradictory emphasis to the seriousness and the forgivableness of sins committed by the regenerate. There is more than a hint of legalism in Taylor's concept of the new covenant—for example, "Every deadly sin destroys the rewards of seven years' piety".[56] Also, despite his explicit denial of the possibility of works of supererogation in *Dissuasive from Popery*, his doctrine of the covenant forces him to maintain that "there is a 'minimum religionis' ",[57] a least measure of religion, a lowest degree of acceptability, that is a condition of entering and remaining in the new covenant. He does not explain how he regards works done over and above the required minimum. It must also be said that the Gospel according to Taylor puts the sinner in an almost inextricable plight. He insists that anyone who is in the habit or state of any one sin whatsoever provokes God to anger in every prayer he makes and without a holy life he cannot have the effect of one prayer.[58] Furthermore,

> [When] the will loves it [lust], and so long as it does, God cannot love the man; for God is the prince of purities, and the Son of God is the king of virgins . . . God can never accept an unholy prayer, and a wicked man can never send forth any other; the waters pass through impure aqueducts and channels of brimstone, and therefore may end in brimstone and fire, but never in forgiveness, and the blessings of an eternal charity.[59]

Christianity is, for Jeremy Taylor, an enterprise only for those capable of helping themselves. There is no indication as to how Christianity applies to the helpless, nor as to how the weak and the wicked are initially contacted by God's grace. A person caught in a sinful habit of which he is unable to purge himself cannot expect God's pardon to help him, and the Church's rôle is merely to exhort him to further, seemingly futile, efforts. Such a person may receive Holy Communion only at the further peril of his soul. Taylor almost invariably insists upon the initiative of the sinner and not of God. The sinner must first endeavour, obey, believe, and love, then God will accept, forgive, pardon, love, and save.

However, this is by no means all that Taylor has to say about the application of the Gospel to sinners. We shall see in the next chapter that he elsewhere expounds a significantly different doctrine of God's dealings with man. This doctrine is set forth in his prayers and in his counselling of dying, desperate, or despairing people.

4

Contradictions in the Theology of Jeremy Taylor

In his public writings and in his sermons, Taylor argues that sins in the regenerate, if any, are minor. Romans 7.19-25, he says, is not a description of a regenerate man, nor should it be so construed. But in his prayers, obviously intended for use by Christians already in the covenant, Taylor maintains positions precisely contradictory to what is argued in his sermons and other public writings.

"A form of confession of sins and repentance, to be used upon fasting days; . . . especially in Lent, and before the holy sacrament"—Have mercy upon me, O God, after thy great goodness; according to the multitude of thy mercies do away mine offences: for I will confess my wickedness and be sorry for my sin . . . I am not worthy to be accounted amongst the meanest of thy servants; not worthy to be sustained by the least fragments of thy mercy, but to be shut out of thy presence for ever with dogs and unbelievers.—But for thy name's sake, O Lord, be merciful unto my sin, for it is great.

I am the vilest of sinners and the worst of men: proud and vainglorious, impatient of scorn or of just reproof; not enduring to be slighted, and yet extremely deserving it: I have been cozened by the colours of humility, and when I have truly called myself vicious, I could not endure any man else should say so or think so . . . But for thy name's sake, etc.

O Just and dear God, how can I expect pity or pardon, who am so angry and peevish, with and without cause, envious at good, rejoicing in the evil of my neighbours, negligent of my charge, idle and useless, timorous and base, jealous and impudent, ambitious and hard-hearted, soft, unmortified, and effeminate in my life . . . but passionate and curious in pleasing my appetite of meat and drink and pleasures, making matter both for sin and sickness; and I have reaped the cursed fruits of such improvidence, entertaining undecent and impure thoughts; and I have brought them forth in undecent and impure actions, and the spirit of uncleaness hath entered in, and unhallowed the temple which thou didst consecrate for the habitation of thy spirit of love and holiness.—But for thy name's sake, O Lord, be merciful unto my sin, for it is great.

Thou has given me a whole life to serve thee in, and to advance my hopes of heaven: and this precious time I have thrown away upon my sins and vanities, being improvident of my time and of my talent; and of thy grace and my own advantages, resisting thy Spirit and quenching Him . . . all my senses have been windows to let sin in, and death by sin. Mine eyes have been adulterous and covetous; mine ears open to slander and detraction; my tongue and palate loose and wanton, intemperate, and of foul language, talkative and lying, rash and malicious, false and flattering, irreligious and irreverent, detracting and censorious; my hands have been injurious and unclean, my passions violent and rebellious, my desires impatient and unreasonable, all my members and all my faculties have been servants of sin; and my very best actions have more matter of pity than of confidence, being imperfect in my best, and intolerable in most.—But for thy name's sake, etc. . .

Lord, I have abused thy mercy, despised thy judgments, turned grace into wantoness. I have been unthankful for thy infinite loving kindness. I have sinned and repented, and then sinned again, and resolved against it, and presently broke it; and then I tied myself up with vows, and then was tempted, and then I yielded by little and little, till I was willingly lost again, and my vows fell off like cords of vanity.

Miserable man that I am! who shall deliver me from this body of sin?

And yet, O Lord, I have another heap of sins to be unloaded. My secret sins, O Lord . . . and insufferable in their load.

And yet thou . . . hast not thrown me into hell, where I have deserved . . .

Miserable man that I am! who shall deliver me from this body of sin?

Thou shalt answer for me, O Lord, my God, Thou that prayest for me shalt be my judge.[1]

In this prayer Taylor plainly construes Romans 7.19-25 as the sentiments of a regenerate sinner to describe his condition in the season of Lent and in the preparation for receiving Holy Communion. Taylor was accused of Pelagianism on all sides because of his theological interpretation of repentance, but there is nothing in the prayer above which makes it Pelagian. In *Holy Living* Taylor makes it quite plain that he

> that resolves to live well . . . yet when the temptation comes again, sins again, and then is sorrowful, and resolves once more against it, and yet falls when the temptation returns, is a vain man . . . no true penitent, nor in the state of grace, and if he chance to die in one of these good moods, is very far from salvation: for if it be necessary, that we resolve to live well, it is necessary we should do so.[2]

This statement differs significantly, of course, from that in the above quoted litany, "I have sinned and repented and then sinned again, and resolved against it, and presently broke it; and then tied myself up with vows, and then was tempted, and then yielded . . ."

There is a clear understanding, in Taylor's prayers, of man's inability to please God except as God first accepts and pardons him. Not only does he stress the necessity that God act first, but he adds emphasis to the point by providing a vivid description of the evil and sin to be found in people who are already in the covenant. This description differs radically from what we find in the sermons and devotional writings.

> I am so evil and unworthy a person, that though I have great desires, yet I have no dispositions or worthiness toward receiving comfort. My sins have caused my sorrow and my sorrow does not cure my sins: and unless for Thy own sake, and merely because Thou art good, Thou shalt pity me and relieve me, I am as much without remedy as I now am without comfort . . . for Thou art good and gracious and I throw myself upon Thy mercy.[3]

This is obviously in marked contrast with what Taylor elsewhere describes as a regenerate state. In another litany he stresses the unequivocable necessity that God accept and act first, before we are enabled to do the least bit towards obedience and a holy life.

> I have broken Thy righteous laws and commandments, run passionately after vanities, and was in love with death, and was dead in sin, and was exposed to thousands of temptations, and fell foully, and continued in it, and loved to have it so, and hated to be reformed; yet Thou didst call me . . . with daily sermons . . . Thy gracious calling, and hast put me into a state of repentance and possibilities of pardon, being infinitely desirous I should live . . .[4]

Similarly, Taylor beseeches in another prayer the grace of humility:

> . . . and for what is my own, teach me to be ashamed and humbled, it being nothing but sin and misery, weakness and uncleaness . . . that despising myself, I may be accepted by Thee in the honours with which Thou shalt crown Thy humble and despised servants for Jesus' sake, in the kingdom of eternal glory. Amen.[5]

These prayers clearly commend to us a chronology of pardon and repentance opposite to that commended in the sermons and devotional works. The prayers invariably solicit God's pardon prior to any repentance or obedience.

> O Thou gracious Father of mercy, Father of our Lord Jesus Christ, have mercy upon Thy servants, who bow our heads, and our knees, and our hearts to Thee; pardon and forgive us all our sins; give us the grace of holy repentance, and a strict obedience to Thy holy word . . .[6]

This declaration and exposition of God's initial and unmerited action of forgiveness is missing in the sermons, but it abounds in Taylor's prayers.

> When David said he would confess, then thou forgavest him. When the prodigal was yet afar off, thou didst run out to meet him, and didst receive him. When he was naked, thou didst reinvest him with a precious robe; and what, O God, can demonstrate the greatest of thy mercy, but such a misery as mine, so great a shame, so great a sinfulness?[7]

> Lord, I put my trust in thee; and thou art ever gracious to them that put their trust in thee. I call upon my God for mercy; and thou art always more ready to hear, than we to pray. But all that I can do, and all that I am, and all that I know of myself, is nothing but sin, and infirmity, and misery; therefore I go forth of myself, and throw myself wholly into the arms of thy mercy through Jesus Christ, and beg of thee for his death and passion's sake, by his resurrection and ascension, by all the parts of our redemption, and thy infinite mercy, in which thou pleasest thyself above all the works of the creation, to be pitiful and compassionate to thy servant in the abolition of all my sins: so shall I praise thy glories with a tongue not defiled with evil language, and a heart purged by thy grace, quitted by thy mercy, and absolved by thy sentence, from generation to generation. Amen.[8]

There is no slightest appeal in the prayers to man's own righteousness, or holy life, or works of repentance as a basis for hope that God might forgive and receive. Acknowledgement of the mercies of God through Christ is the only hope and the only basis for prayer itself. It is almost as though someone other than Jeremy Taylor had written, "Charity with its twin daughters, alms and forgiveness, is especially effectual for procuring God's mercies in the day and the manner of our death."[9] The prayers stem from no private modesty in Taylor himself, for we find him praying for other sinners, too, on the basis of the mercy found in Christ for all our sins.

> Almighty God, Father of mercies, the God of peace and comfort, of rest and pardon, we, thy servants, though unworthy to pray to thee, yet, in duty to thee and charity to our brother, humbly beg mercy of thee for him to descend upon his body and his soul; one sinner, O Lord, for another, the miserable for the afflicted, the poor for him that is in need: but thou givest thy graces and thy favours by the measures of thy own mercies, and in proportion to our necessities. We humbly come to thee in the name of Jesus, for the merit of our Saviour, and the mercies of our God, praying thee to pardon the sins of this thy servant, and to put them all upon the accounts of the cross, and to bury them in the grave of Jesus; that they may never rise up in judgment against thy servant, nor bring him to shame and confusion of face in the day of final inquiry and sentence. Amen.[10]

In his sermons and works of devotion Taylor allows that a regenerate person may sin by omission and in thoughtless ways, but he insists the regenerate cannot hope for pardon of gross, wilful, and deliberate sins. In the prayers, however, it is for deliverance from precisely such sins that he most often petitions.

> I knew my sin, and I saw my danger, and I was not ignorant, and I was not surprised; but wilfully, knowingly, basely, and sensually, I gave thee away for the pleasure of a minute, for the purchase of vanity . . .[11]

> Bemired with sins and naked of good deeds, I, that am the meat of worms, cry vehemently in spirit; cast not me a wretch away from thy face; place me not on the left hand, who with thy hands didst fashion me; but give rest unto my soul, for thy great mercy's sake, O Lord.[12]

Elsewhere Taylor argues that hearty and thorough repentance alone make one worthy to receive Holy Communion, but in the prayers he conceives the Eucharist as that which will wash away the sin and nurture strength for proper repentance and a holy life.

> I know that a thousand years of tears and sorrow, the purity of angels, the love of saints, and the humiliation of the greatest penitent, is not sufficient to make me worthy to dwell with thee, to be united to thy infinity, to be fed with thy body and refreshed with thy purest blood, to become bone of thy bone, and flesh of thy flesh, and spirit of thy spirit . . . But what I cannot be of myself, let me be made by thee.[13]

Elsewhere Taylor insists that we may desire no sinful thing and must be pure ourselves through repentance before approaching Holy Communion, but in the prayers the Communion is food precisely for people who are beset with sins. He prays that God may

> . . . take away the partition wall, the hinderance, the sin that so easily besets me; and bring me unto Jesus . . . unite me unto him; and then, although in myself I am nothing, yet in him I shall be what I ought to be, and what thou canst not choose but love. Amen, Amen.[14]

> . . . my soul is dry, but not thirsty; it hath no water, nor desires none; I have been like a dead man to all desires of heaven . . . for the desire and the meat, the necessity and the relief, are all from thee.[15]

These prayers are intended for those preparing for Communion, but if one accepts what he elsewhere says about the qualifications necessary to be a worthy communicant, the penitents described in the prayers come to Holy Communion only to be damned.

We get another example of "the second Jeremy Taylor" from a work entitled *Christian Consolations*.[16] Bishop Heber says that *Consolations* was written *in private* to a "noble and religious lady" who was obsessed with feelings of guilt and unworthiness. Taylor tells the lady that we "are conceived in sin and it is so intimate unto us that we have no promise to be so spiritualized in this life that we shall not often trespass".[17] He also asserts explicitly that

> The scope of the seventh chapter to the Romans, as I apprehend the mind of the apostle, is, to refresh our guilty consciences, that a

regenerate man is not obnoxious to condemnation, though his flesh, upon some temptations, make him the servant of sin, because still in his mind he serves the law of God. And I am confirmed in that sense, because without all contradiction he teacheth the like doctrine: "The flesh and the spirit are contrary one to another, so that we cannot do the thing that we would."[18]

The Consolations are presented under five heads: Faith, Hope, The Holy Spirit, Prayer, and The Sacraments. Taylor's understanding of faith is limited, for the most part, to belief in doctrine except wherein faith is associated with justification, and there faith must include keeping the commandments.[19] Hence, in the "Consolations of Faith" there are a scant four pages. However, in the "Consolations of Hope" there are over seventeen pages and hope is used in a sense that embraces much that is usually associated with faith. Here, for example, he disparages the Novatians for blotting out the first part of the eighth chapter of the Gospel of St John because they objected to Christ's forgiving a woman taken in adultery. As Christ forgave the woman so shall he forgive us, according to Taylor, because our hope is in him. We are consoled by hope because we are forgiven by Christ through our hope in him. It might be said that here Taylor's doctrine is stated in terms of justification by grace through hope. Considering what he means by hope, his doctrine of justification scarcely differs in the *Consolations* from the doctrine expressed by Davenant and Hall which he severely criticizes in his public works.

We have, then, a description of the Gospel in Taylor's prayers and consolations which differs significantly from the description found in his other writings on four major points: 1. In his public works, man's works of repentance are the basis of God's initial acceptance. In the prayers there is clearly no other basis than the mercies of Christ. 2. Whereas Taylor publicly asserts that there is little or no sin in the regenerate, and that Romans 7.19-25 is not and could not be a description of a regenerate person, he presents the same passage in prayers as just such a description and as an indication of consolation to a Christian troubled with guilt. 3. In his public works, Taylor's doctrine of justification is by obedience in the covenant of repentance. In his prayers and consolations, justification is by grace through hope in the mercies of Christ. 4. In the public works, forgiveness and pardon are granted only after the obedience of repentance and the production of virtues contrary to the sins committed. In the prayers and consolations forgiveness and pardon are granted before any necessity for obedience and despite disobedience or lack of virtue.

What explanation can be offered for this double standard, this almost schizoid discrepancy? An obvious possibility might be that Taylor changed his mind at some time during the many years covered by his writings. However, this explanation is ruled out because many of the prayers were written at the same time and even bound up with the devotional works *Holy Living* and *Holy Dying*. Also, *Christian Consolations* and the contrasting three sermons on justification were all products of Taylor's last years.

It seems likely that the explanation for his contrasting doctrines of justification rests in Taylor's ineluctable and overruling concern for obedience and holy living. The understanding of the Gospel proclaimed in the prayers, and used to console the lady of deep guilt, is regarded by Taylor as too dangerous a doctrine to preach and teach openly. Thus, he says, there can be no hope for deathbed penitents "upon the stock of God's usual dealing and *open* revelation."[20] The fact that God justifies the wicked and helps the helpless might give some people the dangerous idea that it is unnecessary to behave. It is significant in this connection that the *Consolations* is a private document, never published by Taylor, and only made known after his death. It is also significant that in the introduction to it Taylor says that

> . . . The work of the ministry consists in two things, in threatenings or comforts. The first is useful for the greatest part of Christians who are led by the spirit of bondage, and fear to do evil, because of wrath to come; which grows out of love to themselves. The second is fit for the best Christians, that are led by the spirit of love; who endeavour to do righteousness . . .[21]

Taylor's reliance upon threatenings for "the greatest part of Christians" contrasts with Hooker's contention that "fear worketh no man's inclination to repentance, till somewhat else have wrought in us love also".[22]

Taylor could risk disclosing in private the consoling and comforting news of God's free forgiveness of sinners to a lady whom he considers one of the "best Christians" and with regard to whom he finds evidence that she is one "who endeavour[s] to do righteousness". Taylor's contrasting constructions of the Christian Gospel are occasioned, then, by his fear that gratuitous grace might be used as an excuse for moral chaos and antinomianism.

On the basis of such an understanding many of Taylor's idiosyncracies and peculiarities fall into an intelligible perspective. His objections to death-bed confession are an obvious result of his fear that if its validity is admitted, it will infringe upon the necessity for holy living. Death-bed confessions are "dangerous to the very being and constitution of piety, and scandalous to the honour, and reputation, and sanctity of the Christian religion."[23] After denying the efficacy of such a repentance in more than a score of places, Taylor makes the following qualification: "There must be some extraordinary way found out" that can be offered to one who has lived a vicious and habitually sinful life and has deferred repentance until death-bed. He offers the consolation that, "God hath an almighty power and his mercy is as great as his power. He can do miracles of mercy as well as miracles of mightiness."[24] Although God has revealed that one is forgiven only upon the fulfilment of certain conditions and that these conditions are impossible, yet one in such a hopeless state can hope in the same way that, "he that hath a deadly wound, whom the chirurgeons affirm to be hopeless, yet is willing to receive cordials, and to be dressed".[25] Taylor consistently argues that one who has led an impenitent life may on his death-bed rest his hope on nothing revealed by God. Yet when it comes to the immediacy of praying for such a sinner, he does not seem to believe what he has written, and he offers a prayer to be used "by the dying or sick penitents after a wicked life".

> Thou, O God, gavest mercy to the thief upon the cross, and from pain thou didst bring him to paradise, from sin to repentance, from shame to glory. Thou wert the Lamb slain from the beginning of the world, and art still slain in all the periods of it. O be thou pleased to

adorn thy passion still with such miracles of mercy: and now in this sad conjunction of affairs, let me be made the instance.[26]

Taylor's difficulties with respect to the doctrine of original sin, which caused accusations of Pelagianism not only by contemporary Presbyterians but by Bishops Warner,[27] Barlow,[28] and Sanderson,[29] and by Herbert Thorndike,[30] seem to be a direct consequence of his paramount anxiety for obedient behaviour and holy living. He is fearful that a more orthodox description of original sin, in which man's immediate responsibility for it seemed qualified, might also be an occasion for indolence in holy living. There can, however, be no question whatever of Pelagianism in the vivid descriptions of sin found in the prayers.

Taylor was frequently criticized because of his conditional qualifications as to the efficacy of baptism. This again is probably a consequence of his concern that a person encouraged to think of regeneration as accomplished in baptism might thereby be discouraged from the use of volition in subsequent holy life. For this reason, Taylor is inclined to the position that baptism is not efficacious until one's free consent is joined to it later in adult life.

Even the doctrine of Holy Communion is subjected to Taylor's overruling concern for holy living. He suggests, for example, that the holy sacrament should not be administered to dying persons when their condition is such as to limit "the concurrent actions and moral influences of the suscipient".[31] Concern for holy living is also the ground of his objection to the Roman Catholic distinction of mortal and venial sins.[32] In fact, Taylor's very doctrine of the Church seems to be qualified and inhibited by an assumption that the Church cannot actually do things that are of eternal significance except as it encourages amendment of life.

And even the judgment of the church, who hath authority to judge and sentence, yet it is only for amendment; it is universal, it is declarative, it is conditional: not personal, final, decretory, and eternal. For otherwise does man judge, otherwise does God.[33]

Whoever are reconciled to God, may be reconciled to the church, whose office it is only to declare the divine sentence, and to administer it, and to help towards the verification of it.[34]

For the church ought not to give pardon, or to promise the peace of God upon easier terms than God himself requires . . .[35]

Taylor frequently speaks of the relationship of God to the Church in a way that seems to imply that it is not through the Church that God's actions and will are made manifest. The Church

can, by sermons, declare all the necessary parts of repentance and the conditions of pardon, and can pronounce limited and hypothetical or conditional pardons; concerning which, the penitent must take care that they do belong to him.[36]

Concern for holy living at all costs seems to be the reason why Taylor includes several illustrations in his devotional works, which, to say the least, are less than Christian, but are included in the hope they will incline his readers towards good behaviour. Amongst his remedies against fear of death, for example, he offers us:

When St Hilary . . . went into the East to reprove the Arian heresy, he heard that a young noble gentleman treated with his daughter Abra for marriage. The bishop wrote to his daughter that she should not engage her promise nor do countenance to that request, because he had provided for her a husband fair, rich, wise, and noble, far beyond her present offer. The event of which was this: she obeyed; and when her father returned from his eastern triumph to his western charge, he prayed to God that his daughter might die quickly: and God heard his prayers and Christ took her unto his bosom, entertaining her with antepasts and caresses of holy love till the day of the marriage-supper of the Lamb shall come. But when the bishop's wife observed this event . . . she never let him alone till he obtained the same favour for her; and she also, at the prayers of St Hilary, went into a more early grave and a bed of joys.[37]

Also:

Cleombratus was so taken with this speculation, that having learned from Plato's *Phaedo* the soul's abode, he had not patience to stay nature's dull leisure, but leaped from a wall to his portion of immortality.[38]

To encourage chastity Taylor relates the following story:

I have read of a young hermit, who, being passionately in love with a young lady, could not by all the arts of religion and mortification, suppress the trouble of that fancy, till at last being told that she was dead, and had been buried about fourteen days, he went secretly to her vault, and with the skirt of his mantle wiped the moisture from the carcass, and still at the return of his temptation laid it before him, saying, Behold this is the beauty of the woman thou didst so much desire; and so the man found his cure.[39]

Taylor will accept and encourage almost any motive so long as the end he desires is produced. Thus, he encourages faith on the grounds that if there be no such thing as immortality and resurrection, we shall lose nothing for believing that there is; but if Christianity is true we are lost for not believing it.

Jeremy Taylor's unmistakable and unchallenged literary gifts have, perhaps, given his theology a prestige in the minds of subsequent generations that it does not in itself merit. The choice of words, the ringing phrases, and the aptness in the use of vivid examples make him always a pleasure to read. It is not surprising that his works have enjoyed such popularity. Samuel Taylor Coleridge warns us not to be misled by a writer whom he does not hesitate to rank with Shakespeare and Milton as a man of letters. "Let not the surpassing eloquence of Taylor dazzle you, nor his scholastic retiary versatility of logic illaqueate your good sense."[40]

It is unfortunate, however, that his theology has led to charges of Pelagianism based upon his doctrinal works. In his prayers, devotions, and sermons, Taylor displays a remarkable and extraordinary understanding of the subtlety, profundity, and power of sin. His sermon, "The Deceitfulness of the Heart", is comparable with the keenest insights of St Augustine (or of modern depth-psychologists) into the deep and complex infection which afflicts the heart of man. It would be preposterous to accuse Taylor of Pelagianism on the basis of this great sermon.

Although his "gospel" has serious shortcomings, and although he fails to emphasize the gratuitous nature of grace, Taylor has nevertheless made a significant contribution to theology by his exhortations to a holy life. Despite the ultimate helplessness of man and the gratuitous nature of grace, Christian salvation cannot be divorced completely from man's will or his freedom. Taylor gives full and eloquent testimony that the will of man is essential to a holy life. By exhortation, threatenings of future judgement, profound explication of the practical temptations of life, and all other means short of the kerygmatic good news of a gracious God, Taylor pleads the case for holy living and obedience.

This is all to the good, perhaps, but it should not be confused with the Christian Gospel. The only responsible critic of Taylor since the seventeenth century was a layman, Samuel Taylor Coleridge, who discerns not only Taylor's serious theological errors, but also the acute cruelty, from a pastoral point of view, of his teaching.

> If ever book was calculated to drive men to despair, it is Bishop Jeremy Taylor's on *Repentance*. It first opened my eyes to Arminianism, and that Calvinism is *practically* a far, far more soothing and consoling system.[41]

> Now the necessary consequences of Taylor's scheme is a conscience-worrying, casuistical monkish work-holiness.[42]

> In short, Socinianism is as inevitable a deduction from Taylor's scheme as Deism or Atheism is from Socinianism.[43]

Coleridge affords us some keen insights and suggestions as to what is awry in Taylor's theology.

> And yet Jeremy Taylor will not be called a Pelagian. Why? Because without grace superadded by Christ no man could be saved: that is, all men must go to hell, and this not for any sin, but from a calamity, the consequences of another man's sin, of which they were even ignorant. God would not condemn them the sons of Adam for sin, but only inflicted on them an evil, the necessary effect of which was that they should all troop to the devil! And this is Jeremy Taylor's defence of God's justice! The truth is, Taylor was a Pelagian, believed that without Christ thousands, Jews and heathens, lived wisely and holily, and went to heaven; but this he did not dare say out, probably not even to himself: and hence it is that he flounders backward and forward, now upping now downing.[44]

> The whole of Taylor's confusion originated in this;—first, that he and his adversaries confound original with hereditary sin; but chiefly that neither he nor his adversaries had considered that guilt must be a *noumena*; but that our images, remembrances, and consciousnesses of our actions are *phenomena*.[45]

[Taylor] constantly refers us to the deeds or *phenomena* in time, the effluents from the source, or like the *species* of Epicurus; while the corrupt nature is declared guiltless and irresponsible; . . .[46]

Taylor's exhortations to repentance, in other words, are directed at our conscious and deliberate transgressions without, however, first establishing the foundation of gratuitous and prior love and forgiveness required of a sound Christian soteriology of justification by faith, ontological incorporation into Christ at baptism, and nurture in a Church that joins our very being to God. His explication of the *phenomena* of sin fails to mediate the Word to man's *noumenous* guilt. The influence of orthodoxy in his immediate predecessors, and possibly the lesser danger of antinomian inferences, may account for the more acceptable theology of Taylor's prayers.

Coleridge seems not to have observed—at least, he does not mention—how different Taylor's theology is in his prayers. Quite justly, he docs point out that Taylor's adversaries also share in the fundamental error of confounding "original with hereditary sin". For example, Bishop Nicholson, a contemporary critic of Taylor's interpretation of original sin, may be found defending the charge of guilt against infants on the grounds of their *prior transgressions*!![47]

5

The Theology of
Henry Hammond and
Herbert Thorndike

Henry Hammond (1605-60) and Herbert Thorndike (1598-1672) were contemporaries of Jeremy Taylor. Their influential writings reflect the understanding of the Gospel found in Taylor's sermons, devotional writings, and theological works.

HENRY HAMMOND
1605-60

Hammond is principally noted for the *Practical Catechism*, his first work, published about 1644. The soteriology developed in this work immediately attracted considerable criticism from contemporary non-episcopal divines, but he did not, on this account, appreciably alter his views in subsequent writings. The *Catechism* is in the typical form of questions and answers by S. (Scholar) and C. (Catechist). Justification

> . . . is God's accepting our persons, and not imputing our sins, his covering or pardoning our iniquities, His being so reconciled unto us sinners that He determines not to punish us eternally.[1]

Such phrases are, of course, reminiscent of Hooker, Andrewes, and Davenant—"accepting our persons", "not imputing our sins", "covering . . . our iniquities", and "being so reconciled unto us sinners". Despite the similar language, however, Hammond's doctrine differs significantly from that of the earlier divines.

As for those that make justification to be before sanctification, I hope and conceive they mean by sanctification the sanctioned state, the actual performance and practice of our vows of new life, and our growth in grace; and by our justification that first act of pardon or reconciliation in God, and then they say true: but if they mean . . . that the first grace enabling to do these is a consequent of God's having pardoned our sins; this is a mistake . . .[2]

The classical Anglicans held, as we have seen, that the grace enabling man to lead a new life is a consequence of God's having pardoned his sins. Hammond, however, does not quite say to *lead* a new life but rather to *resolve* new life. He is ambiguous on this point in some places, but in others he clearly requires a new life as the condition without which the sinner may not be justified.

It is true indeed, those necessary qualifications which the gospel requires in us, are conditions or moral instruments without which we shall not be justified; but those are not properly called instruments or causes. *Scholar:* What are those qualifications? *Catechist:* Faith, repentance, firm purpose of a new life, and the rest of those graces upon which, in the gospel, pardon is promised the Christian; all comprisable in the new creature, conversion, regeneration, . . .[3]

Among the qualifications required for justification, then, Hammond includes not only faith, repentance, and firm purpose of a new life, but also the "rest of those graces . . . comprisable in the new creature . . . ". Whereas Hooker, Davenant, Andrewes, Hall, and Ussher had all held justification to be the forgiveness and acceptance that enabled the sinner to be sanctified, Hammond holds "that God justifies none who are unsanctified . . .".[4] Hammond's schema of salvation for man is as follows:

1. God gives His Son to die for him, and satisfy for his sins; so that though he be a sinner, yet on condition of a new life he may be saved. Then 2. in that death of Christ He strikes with him a new covenant, a covenant of mercy and grace. Then 3. according to that covenant He sends His Spirit, and by the word, and that Spirit annexed to it, He calls the sinner powerfully to repentance: if he answers to that call, and awake, and arise, and make his sincere faithful resolutions of a new life; God then 4. justifies, accepts his person, and pardons his sins past: then 5. gives him more grace, assists him to do, as before He enabled him to will, i.e. to perform his good resolutions: then 6. upon continuance in that state, in those performances,

till the hour of death, He gives to him, as to a faithful servant, a crown of life.[5]

Hammond, then, considers that justification comes *after* resolutions of new life and *before* the performance of such resolutions. The sinner, indeed, is enabled to execute his resolutions only with the grace he is given in his justification. However, the "Scholar" had previously asked: "But is not God first reconciled unto us before He gives us any graces to sanctify us?" To which the "Catechist" replies: "So far reconciled He is as to give us grace, and so far as to make conditional promises of salvation; but not so as to give pardon or justify actually . . .".[6] This would seem to mean that the justification referred to in Hammond's schema of salvation is not "actually" pardon or justification. On the other hand, he elsewhere states that "it is his free grace to pardon and accept us on such poor conditions . . .".[7]

Hammond's definition of sanctification is equally ambiguous. The word itself, he says,

. . . may note either a gift of God's, His giving of grace to prevent and sanctify us; or a duty of ours, our having, i.e. making use of that grace: and both these considered together, either as an act, or as a state. S.: What is it as it signifies an act? C.: The infusion of holiness in our hearts, or of some degrees of holiness, and parallel to that, the receiving and obeying the good motions of God's sanctifying Spirit, and laying them up to fructify in an honest heart; the turning of the soul to God, or the first beginning of new life. S.: What is it as it signifies a state? C.: The living a new, a holy, a gracious life, in obedience to the good grace of God, and daily improving and growing, and at last persevering and dying in it . . . the first part of sanctification, the beginning of a new life, must be first had before God pardons or justifies any: then when God is thus reconciled to the new convert upon his vow of new life, He gives him more grace, enables and assists him for that state of sanctification, wherein if he makes good use of that grace, he then continues to enjoy this favour and justification; . . .[8]

The classical Anglicans had held that the faith by which justification is received is a result of God's grace before justification. If this be interpreted as meaning what Hammond calls the "first part of sanctification", are they not all essentially in agreement? Hammond is, to be sure, careful to make clear that all that is required before justification, whether in resolutions and/or performance, is accomplished only by God's grace. Here, however, the similarity ends. For Hooker and Davenant God's initial grace provides the faith which receives the gift of justification, and this, in turn, enables the justified to perform the obedience of the new creature. According to Hammond, God's initial grace enables the sinner not only to *believe* but to *resolve* a new life (and in some places to *perform* this resolution) *before* any pardon as well as before justification—"Till that grace be received and treasured up in an honest heart, He will never be thoroughly reconciled to him, i.e. justify or save him."[9] In a sermon on 2 Corinthians 7.1 ("Having therefore these promises, dearly beloved, let us cleanse ourselves", Hammond exhorts his congregation to cleanse themselves as a prior condition of receiving the promises. "It is the property of conditional promises never to belong to any but those that perform the condition."[10] He goes on to say that

> God will not receive any uncleansed polluted sinner, will not be a father to any, be he never so importunate or confident in his Κράζειν Ἀββᾶ, will not own him to any degree of son-ship, that doth not bodily set a purifying.[11]

The classical Anglicans had considered justification as precisely such a cleansing, and, while Hammond accepts that cleansing is possible only by grace,[12] he also holds that it is a previous condition of forgiveness.

The most important difference, however, between Hammond and the classical Anglicans occurs on the subject of the new covenant. Hammond insists that the new covenant is free and that

> those necessary qualifications which the gospel requires in us are conditions or moral instruments without which we shall not be justified; but those are not properly called instruments of causes.[13]

But his conception of the relationship between the two covenants— between the righteousness of perfect, unsinning obedience and evangelical righteousness—differs considerably from that of his

Anglican predecessors. As with Taylor, Hammond's view is that the strictness of the law is now modified by Christ and the new covenant is more lenient than the old.

> The mercy and the pardon and the huge moderation of that court (of the new covenant), though it hath mollified the strict law into never so much chancery, will not proceed further, and mollify obedience into libertinism; it hath treasures of mercy for those who have not obeyed the law in the strictness of perfect unsinning obedience; the evangelical righteousness shall serve turn where the legal is not to be had; . . . Our Saviour hath brought down the market, provided as easy bargains of bliss for us as could be imagined; but this being granted, you must not now fancy another further second Saviour, that must rid you of these easy gainful tasks, which the first in mere kindness of benignity to you hath required of you.[14]

Nowhere in the writings of Hooker and the other classical Anglicans do we find any such description of the Gospel as that Christ has "brought down the market" to permit our imperfect righteousness to be that which renders us acceptable. God will not justify any who are not in part sanctified, Hammond asserts, and "it is His free grace to pardon and accept us on such poor conditions".[15]

Although Hammond employs in his discussion of the new covenant phrases similar to those used by the classical Anglicans, his doctrine of the lowered market is much more similar to the "more lenient covenant" of his contemporary, Jeremy Taylor. Hammond parallels Taylor's concern about the dangers of antinomianism. When, for example, he calls it mistaken to hold that the grace enabling a sinner to perform the vows of the new life is a consequence of God's pardon, he adds significantly,

> . . . besides, this is apt to have an ill influence on practice, and therefore I thought fit to prevent it. The issue of all is, that God will not pardon till we in heart reform and amend.[16]

Also, for another example, in criticizing the argument that faith is the only instrument of justification and a sure persuasion of election, Hammond is careful to say that a man "is fortified and secured by this one deceit from all obligation that Christian religion can lay upon him to superstruct Christian practice or holy living upon his faith."[17] He is thus echoing Taylor's concern for holy living and his fear that it may be threatened by prevalent assumptions about the Gospel. Hammond warns against

> . . . the persuasion of the Solifidians, that all religion consists in believing aright, that the being of orthodox, as that is opposed to erroneous opinions is all that is on our part required to render our condition safe, and our persons acceptable in the sight of God.[18]

On the contrary, Hammond says,

> . . . it is worth remembering, what Epiphanius observes of the primitive times, that wickedness was the only heresy, that . . . "impious" and "pious" living divided the whole Christian world into erroneous and orthodox, . . .[19]

This, too, is strikingly parallel with Jeremy Taylor's recurrent theme that correct living is more important than correct doctrine. Hammond's concern to avoid improper interpretations of soteriology even leads him to cite with approval that it

> . . . was a virulent objection and accusation of the heathen Celsus against Christ, that He called all sinners to come unto Him, publicans, harlots, all, and had an hospitable reception for such . . .[20]

He does quote Origen's reply to the effect that there is a distinction between thieves wanting company and a physician [Christ] who cures and heals. But this is nevertheless essentially an illustration of the conditional nature of God's promises ("His receiving us" and "His being our Father and we His sons"). Hammond clearly means to say that sinners must be cleansed before they can come unto Christ. This is, of course, similar to Taylor's point of view, particularly as set forth in the sermon called *Fides Formata*. Despite Hammond's use of phrases deriving from earlier divines, he belongs much more with Jeremy Taylor in his exegesis of the fundamental message of the Gospel. They share a profound ambition to avoid antinomianism; they are alike in placing emphasis upon holy living as against correct doctrine; Hammond's notion of "the lowered market" is strikingly parallel with Taylor's "more lenient covenant"; and, finally, both radically contradict their own public theology in composing their private devotions.

Hammond, as an example of this last point, argues that Romans 7.19-25 is misunderstood by those who consider that what St Paul says is "reconcilable with regeneration or repentance (for those two words certainly signify one and the same thing in Scripture)."[21] He maintains, in fact, that St Paul in this passage is figuratively assigning to himself what belongs to others. But in a prayer we find him saying:

> Nay, as if our old were too infirm, we have made new leagues with death, new agreements with hell, proceeding from evil to worse, and making every new calamity Thou sendest to reclaim us the occasion of some fresh impiety.

Also:

> O just and righteous Judge . . . we sinful creatures that are now under as great a degree both of guilt and punishment, do here cast ourselves down before Thee, acknowledging that we are not worthy any longer to receive the honour of Christian profession, that have . . . defamed it by enormous practices; and . . . who loved darkness more than light deserve to have our candlestick removed and to be given up to that inundation of atheism and profaneness which now invades this gasping church . . .[22]

HAMMOND'S CONTROVERSIES

Shortly after the second edition of the *Practical Catechism* appeared, three passages from it were listed "among current errors" in a work entitled *A Testimony to the Truth of Jesus Christ and to our Solemn League and Covenant as also Against the Errors, Heresies, and Blasphemies of these Times, and the Toleration of them,* "subscribed by the Ministers of Christ within the province of London". One of the three cited passages refers specifically to justification:

> That, neither Paul nor James excludes or separates faithful actions, or acts of Faith, from Faith, or the condition of Justification but absolutely requiring them as the only things by which the man is justified.

Hammond made reply to his critics in *A Brief Vindication of Three Passages in the Practical Catechism from the Censures affixt on them by the Ministers of London* (London 1648). (The very same reply in another edition is entitled, *A View of some Exceptions to the Practical Catechisme: from the Censures affixt on them by the Ministers of London*.) In this reply Hammond focuses his case upon St James, who holds, says Hammond, that works of faith are not separated from the office of justification as conditions. Hammond also asserts that St Paul, in his use of the witness of Abraham, intends to demonstrate that acts of faith are not separate from faith but are, in fact, required as conditions of justification. Hammond also contends that the faith described by St Paul is a faith, which

> . . . was not only a depending on God for the performance of his promise (which yet was a faithful action, or act of Faith), but also a resigning himself up wholly to him to obey his precepts; or more clearly, was a faith, which howsoever it was tried by promises or commands, did answer God in acts of faith, or faithful action; and so was accepted by God (without absolute unsinning obedience, much more without obedience to the Mosaicall law, i.e. without *works*) . . .[23]

Shortly after the second edition of the *Catechism* appeared, Mr Francis Cheynell of Merton College preached against Hammond's doctrine of justification at Carfax and St Mary's churches in Oxford. At Hammond's request Cheynell provided him with a copy of his objections to the *Catechism*. Subsequently, *A Copy of Some Papers Past at Oxford Betwixt the Author of the Practicall Catechisme and Mr Cheynell* was published. Cheynell's principal objection is, in substance, the same as that of the ministers of London:

> How doe you prove, that any soule whilst it remains unjustified doth cordially and wholly give up it selfe to bee ruled by Christ? I confesse it to bee a good evidence of justification, but not an antecedent to (much lesse a Condition to make us capable of) justification.[24]

Hammond's reply is as follows:

> For (1) I acknowledge not faith an instrument of that, any other then a morall instrument, by which I expresse my selfe to meane a condition accepted by God to justification: and a logicall or proper instrument of receiving Christ, (which Christ, not which Faith, justifies).

(2) Evangelical works, in the notion wherein I suppose you now take them, for fruits of faith, performances of obedience, I affirme not to bee either instrument or condition in the act of justification, or to that purpose; but I require them afterwards when occasions and opportunities of exercising that faith, of performing those resolutions, doe call for them. And therefore (3) I make no scruple to acknowledge that wee are not justified by any righteousnesse inherent in us, as I oft have said, but only by the righteousness of Christ imputed: Only that infusion of new righteousnesse (which when 'tis infus'd and rooted, is inherent in us) is the condition without which we shall not bee justified; not taking it againe for the actuall performances or acts of righteousnesse.[25]

Hammond contends, then, that "evangelical works" are necessary not as an instrument before justification but as a condition afterwards "when occasions and opportunities . . . of performing these resolutions do call for them". This contention is a significant modification of the position he argues in the *Catechism*, where the condition is not only "to resolve" but also "to amend". Nor is Hammond altogether consistent in his reply to Cheynell. Hammond insists, on the one hand, that the condition is not actual obedience but a vow of obedience and, yet again, that nothing less than faithful actions is that by which a man is justified. Cheynell presses this point in a rejoinder.

Pray Sir, shew mee what condition God requires unregenerate persons to perform, that they may attaine unto regeneration, which you take to be the condition of justification. I acknowledge that God doth never justifie an impenitent infidell *in sensu composito*, that is, the infidell doth not remain an impenitent infidell; but then you must grant on the other side, that God doth justifie the ungodly . . . Consider that you say in this last returne, p. 20 (The condition must bee undertaken before the Covenant belongs to me). This vow or resolution of obedience is, as I conceive, that which you call the undertaking of the condition; . . . Wee doe not receive a pardon by an act of charity, or bv a vow of obedience, or receiving of Christ as King, and giving up the obedience of the heart to him; I believe you have not forgotten these expressions which are scattered up and downe in your Catechisme and Papers. If faithful actions bee the onely thing whereby a man is justified, as you affirme page 28 then are wee not justified onely by a vow of obedience. If faith bee unsufficient to our justification, unlesse it bee consummate by love, that is, by acts of Christian charity, or keeping the Commandments of God, as you expound that phrase, page 35 then sure you cannot say you plead onely for justification by a vow of obedience. Unless you will make a first and second justification, I doe not see how you can come off. On the other side, if wee are justified by a vow of personall obedience, then wee are not justified by the obedience of Christ alone, or by faith onely; I meane, by the obedience of Christ, as that obedience whereby we are constituted righteous; nor by faith onely, as that whereby we receive pardon . . . and therefore truly Sir, I doe not yet see how you can agree with mee in my conclusion; namely that we are justified by the obedience of Christ alone, freely imputed by God, applyed and rested on by faith onely unlesse you will retract those passages in your Book, which were justly complained of, for the good of you and this whole University. I speak plainely and freely, as it becometh

Your friend to serve you

Octob. 30, 1646   Fr. Cheynell.[26]

In reply to this Hammond finds fault with Cheynell's spelling of Greek words and makes several slighting remarks on the latter's scholarship. He answers Cheynell's questions concerning the meaning of "conditions" of justification: "Yet for the condition prerequisite to regeneration also, I have given you my sense formerly and need not so soon repeat it to you."[27] He denies he ever held that any pardon is received by an act of charity. What he did say, he now says, is "that charity is a part of the condition, without which that pardon shall not belong to me"—not as a cause of efficiency but as a "meere condition".[28] He denies any first and second justification and insists that all he requires,

> . . . by way of condition is that sincere receiving of Christ in heart and resolution; which if it bee sincere will fructifie in its due season; and if it be not such as will doe so, 'tis not fit to bee accepted by God to our justification . . . And so once more I will agree with you . . . whether you will permit mee, or no; and doe it now againe without any need of the least syllable of retraction.[29]

Cheynell having asked whether he required a vow of obedience or actual obedience as a condition of pardon and justification, Hammond answers that when such occasions are not present, the faith . . . will serve the turne, without any actions; yet when the occasion is present, the action must be ready, or else the faith will not justifie.[30]

Hammond fails to answer directly whether the "due season" in which justifying faith must fructify is before justification or subsequent to, and by the grace of, justification. However, he clearly, if inconsistently, holds the former and Cheynell, consistently, the latter. They certainly do not agree. Much more important than the mere fact that Hammond requires obedience before justification (if the occasion permits), is that Cheynell claims that no such obedience is possible prior to the grace of justification. Hammond obviously maintains that it is not only possible but is generally required as a condition which must be fulfilled prior to justification.

HERBERT THORNDIKE
1598-1672

Herbert Thorndike, writing some years after Hammond's controversy with Cheynell, aligns himself with views similar to those held by Taylor and Hammond. Thorndike's understanding of justification and sanctification is, for the most part, developed in two of his works: *The Covenant of Grace*, published in 1659, and *Just Weights and Measures*, published in 1662. In Thorndike's opinion there are two gross errors—antinomianism and Socinianism; and two others which, while not actually heretical, are conducive to serious distortion and error—The Council of Trent and "those that labour most to interpret the Reformation".[31]

Thorndike maintains that in his efforts to avoid the errors of antinomianism Socinus went too far, denying any Godhead or being of Christ before his birth of the Virgin. It is, in fact, the antinomian misunderstanding of imputation that is the key, in Thorndike's opinion, to all the subsequent heretical tenets of Socinianism. He asserts that Socinus rejected imputation in the sense of "our fanatics",

that men are reconciled to God by the death of Christ (their sins being pardoned before they be done, and they adopted to the glory they shall one day have) without consideration of any condition qualifying for

it: which no man of common reason will take to be the sense of
St Bernard, or other learned divines of the Church of Rome, that have
allowed imputation to righteousness.[32]

Imputation, Thorndike says, is the true faith of God's Church, in
the sense that, because Christ's sufferings are immediately imputed
to mankind, God declares himself ready to be reconciled with "all
that turn good Christians; and accordingly makes good the promises
of his Gospel to them, performing their Christianity".[33] He suggests
that Socinus' rejection of the indispensability of baptism is an
excessive reaction to the view that the faith which *alone* justifies is

. . . believing that a man is predestinated by God to life everlasting,
as being of the number of them whom Christ was sent to redeem,
exclusively to the rest of mankind; and that therefore the whole consideration for which this faith justifieth, is the obedience of Christ,
imputed unto them which are of this number, upon no other account
than the eternal purpose of God to give Him for them alone; whereby
His sufferings are theirs in law, as much as if they had been performed by themselves; . . .[34]

Thorndike does not, however, explain how Socinianism is a reaction
to antinomianism, nor does he cite any examples that would confirm
such a relationship. He is not, it seems, so much interested to refute
Socinianism (which he feels represents no great danger to England—
". . . this heresy seems to be too learned to become popular among
us . . .")[35] as he is to refute the antinomianism from which he
believes it developed.

The antinomian doctrine of justification is rejected by Thorndike
as embracing a twofold error. First,

. . . that the promises of the Gospel, and our right in them, depends
not upon the truth of men's Christianity [thus] . . . there is no
mortal sin but repentance; because that must suppose, that a man
thought himself out of the state of grace by the sin whereof he
repents.[36]

Secondly, ". . . that justifying faith consisteth in believing, that a
man is one of them that are predestinate, whom God sent our Lord
Christ to redeem, and none else".[37] He goes on to say that the idea
of absolute predestination to glory is a heresy and must be disclaimed

in order to recover the unity of the visible church. He is careful to say that he does not accuse the Presbyterians of expressly professing such positions,

> . . . for they have an express confession of their faith, which expresseth them not . . . [but] particular divines and preachers of that party . . . maintain justifying faith and the knowledge and assurance of a man's salvation without and before repentance.[38]

Besides rejecting Socinianism and antinomianism, Thorndike also takes exception to the views of justification pronounced by the Council of Trent and, as well, the views prevalent among his contemporary Protestants.

> Now within these two extreme opinions of justifying faith, that of the School, which the council of Trent canonizeth, making it to consist in believing the truth of Christianity, and that of the Protestants, in trust and confidence of God's mercy to the faithful in and through Christ, . . . though both be clear of those heresies which the extreme opinions of the Socinians and the Fanatics run into, yet neither is able to shew them the sources of their errors . . .[39]

He asserts that the Reformation doctrine of justification consists

> . . . in the remission of sins, tendered and embraced by that faith, which consisteth in a resolution of trusting and reposing confidence in God for the obtaining of His promises tendered us in Christ Jesus; but supposing always and premising repentance, as a condition requisite to make this confidence lively and Christian, not sensual, carnal, and presumptive; and supposing always, and inferring upon it, the promise of God's Spirit, sanctifying, and enabling to perform that new obedience, which qualifieth for the world to come.[40]

While he argues that this doctrine is untrue, he does not consider that it is destructive to the faith.[41] He acknowledges, in fact, that it was his own view of justification while he was at the University of Cambridge. It is not destructive of faith, he says, because it does have the merit of urging repentance and it places appropriate emphasis upon new obedience. Repentance, in this sense, must, however, include a turning from all sin and a "resolution to all that goodness which Christianity prescribeth".[42] None the less, Thorndike continues,

I must say that this opinion is not true . . . I do conclude the sense of them, which this opinion inferreth, though it be not destructive to Christianity, yet is not deducible from the principles of it by good divinity. And, truly, to require repentance to the truth of that faith which only justifieth and not to make it part of that quality, in consideration whereof God for Christ's sake allows remission of sins; is to say things utterly inconsequent . . .[43]

The actual objection Thorndike has to such a doctrine seems to be that it is not sufficiently safe from antinomian misunderstandings.[44] He acknowledges that the position set forth in the Thirty-nine Articles (and the Homily to which they refer) is not coincident with his own judgement.

I will not say, that my position is laid down in that homily. For there are many passages of it, which shew them that penned it, no way clear in that point . . . But in the church catechism, and in the office of baptism, it is so clearly laid down, as will serve for ever to silence any other sense. And though that which the clergy subscribeth be, as it ought to be, a "wholesome doctrine", to wit, if soundly understood: yet that, by which Christian people are saved, ought to be that, which the offices of the church and the instruction which it proposeth contain.[45]

In another passage on the same subject he observes,

If it be said, that those homilies, which the article of the Church of England refers us to for the right understanding of justification and justifying faith, seem to express this opinion, which I esteem neither true nor yet destructive to the faith: I answer ingenuously, that they seem to me so to do; but that, so doing, the sense of it is utterly unreconcilable with those things which I have quoted out of the office of baptism, and the beginning of the catechism.[46]

Thorndike's "ingenuously" argued position concerning the Articles does not, however, mean that he subscribes to the doctrine of the Council of Trent. The latter

. . . is liable to a twofold challenge: first, for excluding the positive act of God's law, which the Gospel enacteth, by accepting the righteousness of a Christian as a condition sufficiently qualifying for the promises of the Gospel by God's original justice; secondly, for excluding the imputation of Christ's obedience from the consideration, in which a Christian is justified and saved, and, in a word entitled to the promises of the Gospel. A thing which that council need not have done. For it is manifest, that Pighius, Gropper, Cardinal Contarino, Cassander, and many others, the best studied in Luther's controversies of all that communion, had owned and embraced it for the doctrine of St Bernard, and divers other highly approved authors.[47]

Thorndike considers, in fact, that the Council of Trent is as out of harmony with the Gospel on the subject of justification as are the Protestants.[48] He finds in the Tridentine position two other serious errors: that faith is no more "than believing the Gospel to be true",[49] and that it inclines towards "making justification to consist, not in God's allowance, but in His act of infusing righteousness . . . ".[50]

Justification, according to Thorndike, is granted by God only under the conditions of the new covenant. Broadly speaking, those conditions are no less than "professing"[51] or "undertaking"[52] Christianity. We are justified by a faith which leads us to undertake and perform Christianity, and our justification ceases if we do not contrive to fulfil the conditions. Thorndike is a vehement critic of the doctrine of indefectible grace, and of any other position which does not admit that by gross sin we can lose the favour of God's justification. In commenting, for example, on John 4.14 ("whosoever drinketh of the water which He shall give, shall never thirst any more"), Thorndike observes that, "He supposeth that the water which He giveth is not vomited up again . . ."[53]

He is opposed to "infusion of inherent righteousness" as the formal cause of justification; he is opposed to justification by faith alone;[54] he is in favour of the doctrine of "imputation of Christ's righteousness",[55] but he considers this to be the *meritorious* and not the *formal* cause of justification; and he is particularly careful to assert that the grace of God precedes any work in Christian soteriology and is the initial cause and very foundation of justification.

However, as we have seen, he altered his views from those expressed in the Articles and Homily because he found that they did not sufficiently articulate the conditions upon which justification is granted. He objects to the doctrine of justification by faith alone because

... if a man be saved by living and dying a good Christian indeed, not by *finding himself* obliged so to do; then is he justified by undertaking to profess Christianity, and not by believing it: though by believing it he is obliged so to do.[56]

Thorndike is clearly more concerned to assert the importance, necessity, and value of performing Christianity than he is to proclaim the free gift of God's grace. Does he, however, understand justification to be growth in grace *after* God's initial acceptance? Is his position consistent with Hooker, Davenant, Hall, and Downame, or is there a different use of the same terms? Is Thorndike, in fact, describing as justification what the others describe as sanctification?

Such a conclusion might be drawn from the following passage:

... how those helps of grace, which the Gospel tendereth for the undertaking and performing of that Christianity which it requireth, are also granted in consideration of Christ's merits and sufferings put to our account; that is the helps of preventing grace, or the actual motions of God's Spirit (without which the Gospel were a mere abuse, supposing original sin) . . .[57]

If Thorndike means to describe justification as "those helps of grace, which the Gospel tendereth *for* the undertaking and performing" of Christianity, and sanctification to describe subsequent obedience in Christian life, he is then in close agreement with Andrewes and Davenant. He states, for example:

And thus it remaineth evident, that it is a covenant of unspeakable grace on God's part which His Gospel bringeth; notwithstanding that it requireth upon the condition of our salvation, that we live and die Christians. First, as tendering the assistance of God's Spirit, as well to undertake as to perform; and then, having performed, as tendering a reward which our performance cannot challenge: and both in consideration of Christ, whose merits and sufferings are free, pure, mere grace, before all helps of grace which they have purchased for us.[58]

If Thorndike here means that a sinner is freely accepted in the "covenant of unspeakable grace", and "that we live and die Christians" is the condition of final salvation and not a condition of being accepted into the covenant, then he is manifestly in accord with Hooker, Andrewes, Downame, Ussher, Hall, Donne, and Davenant.

This is not, however, the case. The two quotations cited above are exceptional statements in Thorndike's general discussion of Christian soteriology. The dominant argument of his soteriology cannot be reconciled with that of the earlier Carolines. Thorndike makes it abundantly clear that he considers that no one is admitted to the new covenant, forgiven of his sins, or accepted by God *until* and *after* he has fulfilled the conditions of the covenant. He declares, for example,

> . . . that neither remission of sins, nor right to the Kingdom, can be understood to be assigned under the title of justification in consideration of Christ, without consideration of that consideration which the Gospel of Christ requireth . . .[59] all that will undergo the condition are admitted to remission of sins and everlasting life.[60]

Thorndike's crucial and essential condition of the covenant is that we must undertake Christianity and faithfully live by it—but he is often ambiguous about whether we must *undertake* Christianity, *perform* Christianity, or *both*. As has been said, he denies that either infusion or imputation of righteousness may be the formal cause of justification. The formal cause of justification is, indeed, the very "condition of the covenant" about which he is so often ambiguous. Thorndike reports that he himself has abandoned the idea that justifying faith might be simply the trust and confidence of God's mercy through Christ, because this idea expresses only an inward act of faith which is an insufficient condition to qualify a Christian for the promises of the Gospel. Such an inward act of faith fails to do justice to the condition of the covenant of grace.[61] This condition of grace varies as Thorndike discusses it in different places. There are, in fact, three differing descriptions of the condition:

> (1) When therefore, the belief of Christ's Gospel causes a man to take up Christ's cross in baptism, then hath he that faith which justifieth; . . .[62] (2) Otherwise Socinius is free enough; in ascribing the effect of justifying, not to the worth of that faith which believeth, or of the Christianity to which it resolveth, but to the mere grace of God, of His own free goodness sending by Christ salvation to man-

kind overtaken in sin, *upon the condition of their Christianity for the future*;[63] (3) This is everywhere to be showed, in all writings any way allowed by the Church: that the justification of a Christian dependeth upon the *performance* of that which he professeth; . . .[64]

Thus the formal cause of justification is variously: (1) faith and baptism; (2) undertaking Christianity for the future; and (3) the actual performing of Christianity. It is not wholly clear what Thorndike means by "taking up Christ's cross in Baptism": it could be understood as consistent with either the mere undertaking to perform Christianity or the actual performing of Christianity. There is, however, significant distinction between (2) and (3) as the formal cause of justification (the condition without which the covenant relationship is not granted). It might be argued that in (3) his statement that justification "dependeth upon the performance" is meant by Thorndike not as a prior condition to the state of justification but rather that the state of justification depends upon performance in the sense that otherwise it might be lost. However, he frequently describes performance as a condition to be fulfilled *before* entering the covenant of grace. The very reason, indeed, for discarding his earlier view of justification was that it did not explicitly include profession of the outward man, and did not therefore sufficiently express the condition of the covenant of grace. Also, the condition is sometimes described as the "Word", and therefore to be fulfilled only by sincerely undertaking it and faithfully living by it.

Thorndike does consistently stress the necessity of grace for all the works of the "condition" upon which the covenant relationship and forgiveness is granted. But he is obviously opposed to earlier views which had insisted that such works were possible only by the grace of justification within the covenant relationship. The classical position, of course, had been that justification is free acceptance into the covenant relationship, and this, in turn, is the source of that grace which enables a sinner to live as a Christian. Thorndike, on the other hand, is adamant that Christian obedience is a necessary condition of the covenant relationship.

This "condition" upon which the grace of justification depends is, in effect, Thorndike's formal cause of justification. We have seen that he firmly rejects infusion of inherent righteousness as the formal cause, and insists instead upon the imputation of Christ's righteousness—"For the value of our Lord's obedience is necessarily extrinsic to us; to whose account it redoundeth only by imputation of grace."[65] But he also makes it clear that, for him, the imputation of Christ's righteousness is the *meritorious* cause and not the *formal* cause. The formal cause is the very condition itself upon which the covenant, merited and procured by Christ, is applicable,

> . . . for no man's debt is immediately paid by the pain which Christ suffered, but, in consideration of His obedience to God in undergoing such trials, all that will undergo the condition are admitted to remission of sins and everlasting life.[66]

The imputation of Christ's righteousness "is, immediately, to no further effect than of procuring the Gospel, to the effect of salvation, by the means of that Christianity which it requireth".[67] The obedience of Christ is imputed to men only "as they are qualified for it by being good Christians".[68]

The formal cause is, then, the condition upon which Christ's righteousness is imputed and one is justified. This is not, however, the principal thrust of Thorndike's discussion of the doctrine, nor does he actually consider the subject within the context of scholastic terminology. His exegesis of the Christian Gospel is for the most part a contrasting of the two covenants: the original law and evangelical law. Thorndike explicitly asserts that to call the Gospel a law "is no more than to make the covenant of grace a covenant, and not a mere promise: which is, to be no Fanatics".[69] Christ's death purchased a new evangelical law which admits "all to remission of sins and right to life everlasting, that will undertake to live true Christians".[70] One striking contrast Thorndike discerns between the two covenants is that the new "evangelical" law is more lenient than the old law.

> The positive will of God has tied the promise of salvation for the future, and justification (the title of salvation) for the present, to the positive act of professing Christianity; not to the perpetual obligation of all righteousness.[71]

The old law is set aside "as to the purpose of giving sentence by it".[72] Since "this law being under the state of original sin and the bondage of concupiscence, the condition of it cannot be to live without sin, but faithfully to fight against sin."[73] The new covenant is not infringed by "those sins which the present weakness of our mortal nature cannot easily avoid...".[74] Our Lord Christ will not judge the works of Christians according to what they might have done if Adam had not fallen "but according to that which everyone in his estate may attain to in the performance of his Christianity".[75] Thus, Christ's righteousness is imputed to us only in the nature of a *meritorious* cause, on account of which God grants easier terms of reconciliation within the Gospel covenant.[76]

DIFFICULTIES
IN THORNDIKE'S DOCTRINE

Such new, more lenient terms of reconciliation are characteristic of Thorndike's description of the new covenant, but they introduce significant difficulties. Not only does the new law exact a lesser measure of righteousness than the old, but it apparently requires less by way of conditions than is required initially to obtain justification:

> For, this law being settled for the condition of our reconcilement with God, the moral law comes in force as the matter of it: though neither according to the measure of original righteousness in paradise, nor that which was the condition of justifying faith before and under the Law . . .[77]

The prerequisites of justification are, then, represented as more arduous than the demands of obedience which are found within the new covenant.

This position leads Thorndike into a difficult quandary with respect to works of supererogation. He denies the possibility of such works because, he says, one

> . . . that cannot do what God's original law requires, cannot do more. *But* it is as easy to see, that some circumstances may conduce to the performance of our Christianity, that are not a part of it; and therefore

the vow of baptism binds not to them. If marriage stand with Christianity, what Christian is forbidden marriage? Yet single life is the safer way to perfection in Christianity. So is the profession of the clergy, and all the means of further retirement from the world than the taking up of Christ's cross signifies.[78]

His view that the demands of the new covenant are more lenient, and that there is an obedience short of perfection which is sufficient for salvation (is, in fact, the "title to salvation" (justification)) causes Thorndike to be less than successful in his denial that works of supererogation are possible. The "vow of baptism" and the "cross of Christ" apparently do not, for Thorndike, impose a demand for perfection. His concern that none be justified except those performing Christianity leads him to accept a minimum degree of righteousness as acceptable to God on the part of those who are in the new covenant. If one does *more* than is required one clearly goes beyond the "vow of baptism", and it is difficult to see how such unrequired works escape the title of supererogation. The "original law" does require perfection, and thus rules out works of supererogation, but the new "evangelical law", since it does not require perfection, would seem to permit supererogatory works.

Herbert Thorndike is as concerned to deny the Tridentine doctrine of infusion of inherent righteousness as any of the earlier (Caroline) Anglicans, but he differs significantly from them in many ways. He belongs with Jeremy Taylor and Henry Hammond in his discussion of soteriology. All three share an intense concern for "holy living", and a fear that the Gospel is frequently presented in such a way as to be conducive to antinomianism. Thorndike, specifically, abandoned his earlier view of justification because it did not sufficiently and explicitly express in repentance the conditions he subsequently thought necessary for forgiveness and acceptance. Taylor, Hammond, and Thorndike held similar views concerning sin in the regenerate, and though Thorndike did admit them, he admitted only those arising out of incurable ignorance or out of mere surprises of concupiscence.[79] All three describe Christianity in terms of a more lenient covenant, they tend to assign more arduous requirements to become justified than to remain so, and they all encounter logical difficulties in attempting to deny works of supererogation. Although Thorndike seems to have escaped the accusation of Pelagianism by contemporaries (and even joined in the chorus against Taylor on the matter),[80] he did so at the expense of inconsistency. When he defends himself from any possible charge of Pelagianism, he describes justification in a way that is contrary to the whole thrust of his other works:

> I do not grant any man to be justified by any thing that supposes not the Gospel of Christ, . . . that is, not by works as can be done by him, that hath not yet admitted and embraced the Gospel of Christ, and that by virtue of that grace of God which sets on foot the covenant of grace.[81]

He here conveniently forgets all he has elsewhere said about the "conditions" of the Gospel and of the covenant which must be fulfilled as conditions of justification: the "turning from all sin", the "undertaking" and "performing" of Christianity, "being good Christians", and "faithfully to fight against sin".

Thorndike, Hammond, and Taylor together represent a most important development in the Christian soteriology of the seventeenth century. There were, to be sure, other divines who departed somewhat from the classical position set forth by Hooker and his colleagues, but the departure of the "holy living" divines was far more significant. These latter three were contemporaries, and their doctrine was developed after the opening of the Long Parliament. Their major concern was for holy living, and they believed that the doctrine as held by the earlier divines did not sufficiently avoid antinomian interpretations of the Gospel. Although none of them dwelt at length on the question of causes, they all denied that we are justified by an infusion of inherent righteousness. The imputation of Christ's righteousness, however, was not, for them, the formal cause of justification but only the meritorious cause. That which makes our justification to be what it is, is God's acceptance of our faith, repentance, and sincere endeavours as righteous under the more lenient terms of the new covenant on account of the righteousness of Christ. Here we see the beginnings of a new moralism which is to have sinister consequences for Christian orthodoxy.

6

The Theology of George Bull

One of few works written by Anglicans after the Restoration devoted specifically to soteriology was published in 1670 by George Bull, later Bishop of St David's: *Harmonia Apostolica* or "Two Dissertations: in the Former of Which The Doctrine of St James on Justification by Works is Explained and Defended: In the Latter, The Agreement of St Paul with St James is clearly Shewn." As the title suggests, Bull seeks to reconcile any apparent contradiction between the two Apostles by approaching the doctrine fundamentally from the position of St James. Bull offers, first of all, a series of arguments in defence of the thesis that justification is by works, and he then attempts to reconcile St Paul's explication of the doctrine with that of St James.

His preliminary argument consists of citations from Scripture from two classes of texts: first, texts that speak of righteousness and good works as conditions that tend to make us acceptable to God; second, texts which apparently require some specific work, or works, for salvation or justification—particularly those which stress repentance without which none can obtain forgiveness.

Repentance, in other words, such as is necessary for remission of sins (and therefore for justification) is not any single work by itself but a collection of works. These include:

1. sorrow for sin; 2. humiliation under the hand of God, by which a man humbly acknowledges himself to have deserved His anger; 3. hatred and detestation of sin; 4. confession of sin; 5. an earnest and suppliant begging for divine mercy; 6. love of God; 7. a ceasing from sin; 8. a firm determination of new obedience; 9. a restitution of every thing acquired by sin; 10. forgiveness of all injuries done to us . . . ; 11. works of mercy or alms . . .[1]

Bull also contends, similarly, that faith which justifies includes "all the works of Christian piety".[2] Thus, it follows that because we are justified by our faith and repentance, and because both faith and repentance include works, we are, in fact, justified by works. Faith has two meanings for Bull. In its larger sense, as set forth in the New Testament, it includes the whole body and collection of divine virtues and graces, and is, indeed, a life lived according to the Gospel. However, when faith is taken in a more limited sense it connotes knowledge, assent, and reliance. Taken only in this latter limited sense, faith is neither the instrumental cause of justification nor an important condition for acceptance by God.

Bull's secondary argument is grounded in the familiar forensic analogy of the law court. The judge is God, the prisoner is man, and the rule by which judgement is passed is either the law of Moses or the law of Christ. No man may be judicially pronounced just except he be duly acquitted according to the rule of the law according to which he is tried. The law of Christ is interpreted by Bull as constituting the moral law of God as expounded, perfected, and illustrated by Christ in the Sermon on the Mount, and as expressly ratified by his own divine sanction (Matt. 7.24).

Bull concludes, in a tertiary argument, that no man can be justified in the sight of God by faith alone. Such a man must have those other virtues which Christ requires besides faith, because it is possible to have faith in the limited sense and yet rest in a doubtful and precarious condition. The wicked may have *knowledge* of the Gospel, even devils may *assent* to its truth, and many in bad estate do *rely* on the promise of it.

A fourth argument is developed from the assumption that everyone is justified in this world in exactly the same way that he will be judged by God in the world to come. Hence, because everyone will be judged in the last day by works (Matt. 25.21), and not by faith alone without works, therefore one is so justified in this life —not by faith alone but also by works. Bull denies that faith is as great as charity, or that charity is but the sign of faith. Justification is no less than the right to eternal life conferred principally for acts of charity. Charity is not, then, the meritorious cause, but is, in fact, the *sine qua non* of justification and salvation.

In a final argument, derived from what he calls the "implicit consent of all, and therefore of our adversaries themselves",[3] Bull endeavours to demonstrate that those who hold that a man is justified by faith alone do not thereby exclude works. His argument is that many understand faith to include the grace which answers it, and thus their formula implies that a man is justified by grace alone, and not by the *merit* of works. They do not, then, actually deny that justification is by works.

Having defended his thesis by an examination of St James' doctrine, Bull proceeds to relate it to the teaching of St Paul. This makes up Dissertation Two. He states quite frankly at the outset that

> . . . however incredible it may appear, . . . from what St Paul hath said concerning works, I will bring additional proofs for the doctrine of St James of justification by works.[4]

Bull at once refutes three other attempts to reconcile the two apostles. He rejects the suggestion that St James and St Paul are not speaking of justification in the same sense. St Paul, according to this argument, is speaking of justification before God which is a free gift and consequently not by works but by faith; St James, on the other hand, is speaking of justification before men in which works declare and manifest justification. Bull also rejects the opinion that St Paul speaks of a true and lively faith which justifies alone, but is followed inevitably by good works, whereas St James speaks of a false faith which neither produces good works nor justifies. The third opinion Bull rejects is that which seeks to reconcile St Paul and St James on the grounds that St Paul is speaking of a first justification which brings us to God and requires only faith without works, whereas St James is speaking of the second or continuing justification which requires works that proceed from the first or justifying faith. Though "many", both Roman Catholic and Reformed, accept this last solution, with adaptations to fit their respective systems, Bull holds it to be contrary to the statements of both Apostles.

The sensible way to overcome any apparent discrepancies, according to Bull, is to "explain St Paul by St James".[5] St James' doctrine is clear and simple, whereas any "obscurity and difficulty there is, must be attributed to the Epistles of St Paul".[6] The difficulty rests, Bull surmises, in St Paul's use of three terms: justification, faith, and works. He concludes, first, that the two apostles mean the same thing by the term justification. (He explicitly disagrees with Grotius and Bellarmine, however, that either apostle uses the terms to mean "to make righteous".) The difficulty is not with justification, then, but lies in the use of the terms faith and works. When St Paul uses the term faith, Bull asserts, he means "all the obedience required by the Gospel".[7] When St Paul denies that justification is by works he refers only to ritual works of the Mosaic law and/or works done in our own strength without benefit of grace. St Paul, thus understood, agrees with St James that justification *is* by works.

Bull uses this consensus as a spring-board for a general discussion of the relation of the law to the Gospel. He argues that St Paul speaks of the Mosaic law in two senses: one, as the whole law, and the other, as the ritual by itself. For the most part, according to Bull, St Paul has reference to the latter when he talks of "works of the law". When St Paul denies the power of the whole law to justify, he does so because he considers that it lacks pardoning grace and the promise of eternal life. Bull does not agree, however, that St Paul held the whole law to be inadequate, because, in fact, he deemed it to be a law of perfect obedience impossible to fulfil. To hold otherwise, Bull proclaims, is tantamount to describing God as one who cut off a man's legs and punished him for not walking.

Bull proceeds to contrast the Mosaic covenant with the new covenant. The law, he notes, lacks the gift of the Holy Spirit. Bull argues that, although St Paul certainly does not exclude true righteousness of the law as a condition of justification, he does nevertheless make it plain that the Gospel covenant is the source of the righteousness demanded by justification. The entire seventh chapter of Romans, says Bull, is a description of the unregenerate under the law *before* the grace of the Gospel, and can in no way be thought of as a description either of St Paul himself or of any other regenerate person. St Paul, Bull is asserting, rejects only the external and ritual observances of the law as being necessary to justification.

The final chapters of Bull's *Harmonia* describe certain Jewish errors with respect to the possibility of obtaining justification and salvation through the law. St Paul's purpose, Bull says, was to indicate the error in these positions. His last chapter contains a summary of Bull's doctrine with a specific admonition to avoid the following four errors concerning justification: 1. belief in works of condignity and pride, overlooking that the right to eternal life which good works purchase is available only within the Gospel covenant and promise; 2. the Solifidian and antinomian misunderstanding of "justification by faith only"; 3. The Pelagian heresy which neglects the necessity of a predisposing and all-powerful grace for works truly good; and 4. the Manichaean heresy which takes away free will and the co-operation of human industry. Bull summarizes his argument as follows:

> St Paul rejects from justification the following descriptions of works: first, ritual works prescribed by the ceremonial law; secondly, moral works performed by the natural powers of man, in a state either of the law, or mere nature, before and without the grace of the Gospel; thirdly, Jewish works, or that trifling righteousness inculcated by the Jewish masters; and lastly, all works separate from Christ the Mediator, which would obtain eternal salvation by their own power, or without reference to the covenant of grace established by the blood of Christ. St James, also, on his part, recommends none of these works, as appears from the whole tenor of his Epistle. On the other hand, that moral works arising from the grace of the Gospel do, by the power of the Gospel covenant, efficaciously conduce to the justification of man and his eternal salvation, and so are absolutely necessary, St Paul not only does not deny but is employed almost entirely in establishing. And this is the very point for which St James contends.[8]

Bishop Morley of Winchester issued a pastoral charge against the *Harmonia*, Thomas Barlow, later Bishop of Lincoln, lectured against it at Oxford, and two nonconformists, John Tombes and Joseph Truman,[9] objected in whole or in part to Bull's doctrine. In 1675 Bull published *Examen Censurae* in answer to some unpublished criticism by Charles Gataker, son of Thomas Gataker, which had been forwarded to him by Bishop William Nicholson. In the same year, 1675, Bull also published *Apologia pro Harmonia* which was an answer to *Justificatio Paulina* by Thomas Tully, the Principal of St Edmund Hall. Bull's two defences are almost twice the length of his original treatise, but they provide almost no substantive addition or alteration. He consistently holds in all three works that whoever is acquitted by the law of Christ must necessarily fulfil that law, and no one fulfils the law without works. Therefore, by faith alone without works no one is acquitted by the law of Christ. "Whosoever denies this is not fit to be argued with and is a subject rather for the physician than the divine."[10]

The argument of the seventh and eighth chapters of the Epistle to the Romans, according to Bull, is that the bond of Mosaic law is broken, and no one henceforth shall be condemned for not performing its ceremonies, "provided he seeks for salvation according to the Gospel".[11] To justify, for Bull, means to acquit or pronounce guiltless, and he contradicts Grotius' claim that it means to make righteous.[12] Justification is sometimes equated with salvation. He claims, for example, that there is no condition in the Gospel covenant which is not also a condition of gospel justification.[13] He also asserts that the Strasburg Confession "plainly teaches . . . that the idea of righteousness or justification and of salvation is the same . . .".[14] He implies the same point when he states, "first, observance of the law is necessary for anyone to acquire a right to salvation by grace of God in Christ, i.e., be justified".[15] Finally, he in one place says directly anything required of salvation the same is required of justification.[16] Justification, for Bull, seems to be indistinguishable from remission of sins, and the former without doubt includes the latter. In a reference to the Homily on Salvation he states that remission of sins is "equivalent to justification".[17] In yet another place he implies that remission of our sins is a part of justification— ". . . remission of our sins (which is not the least part of our justification)".[18]

Thus, whatever is required for justification is also required for remission of sins. Consequently the sinner must produce good works of repentance before he is forgiven. Bull insists that repentance is as necessary as faith to justification. Describing what repentance includes he makes this point:

> . . . and hence rose that custom in the ancient church, by which they demanded of those who had fallen, for any of the heavier offences, under censure of the church, not only confession of sins, and a more regular conduct in future but also works of mercy, called good works, before absolution was granted to them.[19]

He relates favourably Clement of Rome's claim that "true love and its works are necessary to the remission of sins, that is, to justification . . .".[20] Forgiveness is granted for all sins committed after baptism and regeneration, Bull asserts, upon condition that repentance be "exact, and perfectly worked out".[21] What he means "by perfectly worked out" he explains specifically for the benefit of those who trust in a death-bed repentance. Saving repentance is much more than merely asking God to have mercy but must include the putting off of the old man, mortified, and the flesh be crucified with its affections.[22]

Bull's discussion of good works is strangely ambiguous. He asserts that there is nothing wrong in good works except trust in their merit, but on page 31 of the *Harmonia* he denies that good works of themselves deserve eternal life, and on page 39 he explicitly declares that they obtain a right to eternal life. He does deny absolutely works of condignity,[23] not even allowing condignity to works proceeding from grace. Works of supererogation are similarly ruled out by Bull,[24] and he is adamant about the necessity of grace as the source of all good works if they be truly good. Thus, there is no place for boasting, and no possibility of merit or credit accruing to any but God.

Bull uses the term sanctification in only one paragraph of the entire *Harmonia*, "Justification is certainly subsequent to sanctification, at least the first and yet imperfect sanctification."[25] He nowhere defines what distinction, if any, there may be between first and second sanctification. He attempts to prove this distinction concerning the order of the two doctrines by reference to 1 Peter 1.2. He maintains that St Peter is here describing the order of human salvation as, first, sanctification to obedience, and then, "sprinkling of the Blood", i.e. justification". Charles Gataker condemns this interpretation, and says flatly that Bull is confusing justification with sanctification. Bull replies that justification must presuppose sanctification because

> . . . it is inconsistent with the righteousness of God (as we have said elsewhere) to forgive any man his sins, and withal to give him a right to a heavenly life, who is not cleansed from his sins, nay, who is not also in a manner made a partaker of "the Divine nature"![26]

Bull also asserts that the author of the Epistle to the Hebrews limits the

> . . . expiation or freedom from sin, obtained by the blood of Christ to those who are sanctified in heart and deed, strongly hinting that none are justified by the merits of Christ who are not first sanctified by the Spirit of Christ. Justification is certainly subsequent to sanctification.[27]

There is not only first and second sanctification but also first and second justification, according to Bull, but these latter are no more fully explained than the former, being mentioned, in fact, in but five places in all three works.[28] A right to the Kingdom (revocable) is granted in first justification, but Bull makes it clear that "inward works", at the least, are necessary to any first justification. Second justification is the final fruit of perfect righteousness produced by grace. Hence, the plan of salvation for Bull seems to be: (1) prevenient grace; (2) first sanctification; (3) first justification; (4) second sanctification; and (5) second justification. He is not, however, consistent in his use of this schema. He elsewhere asserts, for example, that Romans 8.1 indicates "that those who believe in the Gospel are fully and perfectly justified".[29]

Bull explains Ephesians 2.8-10 ("For by grace you have been saved through faith; and not of yourselves, it is the gift of God, not of works, lest any man should boast") in the following passage:

> By faith here, I understand obedience to the Gospel, of which faith especially so called, is not only the beginning, but the root also and foundation [and] . . . "of works" has the same force as "of yourselves".[30]

Despite his preliminary definition of faith as knowledge, assent, and trust, Bull continually speaks of faith as that obedience which is the root of charity and all other virtues.

> You will see (unless you shut your eyes) that the faith to which . . . according to the Gospel covenant . . . justification and salvation is granted, is by no means a single virtue but . . . is effectual in the will through the true love of God and our neighbour; or that sort of assent to the Gospel which is accompanied by a reformation of the whole man, his heart and actions; or a sincere observance of what is taught in the Gospel.[31]

One passage in the *Harmonia*, in particular, signifies Bull's conception of faith in relation to justification. Paraeus, it seems, had claimed that works truly good are not required for justification and can be produced only by the justified, and he had quoted St Augustine to the effect that good works do not precede but follow justification. Bull objects to this argument on the grounds that faith itself is a good work. If good works can only follow justification, then we cannot be justified even by faith, because faith itself must then follow justification. Paraeus had contended that faith is not a work, but merely the instrument of apprehending Christ. Bull dismisses this contention with a rhetorical assertion that "all in their senses allow" faith to be a work.[32] Bull also differs from Paraeus by interpreting St Augustine's statement, cited above, as meaning that *most* good works follow but *some* precede justification.

Bull manifests typical Caroline respect for the early Church Fathers (with the possible exception of St Augustine) quoting some seventeen of them in the *Harmonia*. He depends less upon the English divines, but in reply to Charles Gataker he warns, "How many names [of our English Divines] can I recount . . . take heed you drive me not to recount them."[33] He does, in fact, in the course of his subsequent controversy with Tully, refer to a goodly number of English divines including Hammond, Hall, Taylor, Jackson, Montague, Jewel, Hooker, and Davenant. With the exception of the latter two, however, these references have no connection with the issue of justification. He appeals to these divines on such other matters as: the importance of Scripture, of the first four councils, and of the creeds; the fatalism of the Pharisees; the last judgement as being contingent upon both faith and works; and the interpretation of Romans 7 (Jackson, Taylor, and Hammond).[34] He acknowledges divergencies from Richard Hooker who had held that actual righteousness may only follow justification, whereas Bull, as we have seen, contends that it must precede justification.[35] Thus no English divine is quoted in support of his essential position.

His references to Davenant are numerous, but puzzling and ambiguous. He quotes or refers to Davenant some six times, but the following is perhaps his most significant reference:

> I will finish this discussion with the words of a most learned and excellent Prelate of our Church, who both well knew and firmly retained the orthodox doctrine on this point and hath successfully defended it against the sophistry of Bellarmine and other Roman Catholics. I mean Davenant, Bishop of Salisbury, who in his very learned Disputations concerning habitual and actual righteousness, thus explains and confirms in two brief but clear theses, whatever we have advanced here and elsewhere in these Dissertations concerning the necessity of good works.[36]

This statement is, at the least, surprising in light of obvious contradictions between the writings of the two theologians. Davenant clearly holds that justification precedes sanctification, and Bull equally clearly holds the opposite. For Davenant justification is the beginning of salvation, and for Bull it is the end (at least in the case of "final justification"), and is, indeed, almost *synonymous with* salvation. The whole thrust of Davenant is that works have their principal place in relation to sanctification. Bull contends with comparable force that they have their principal place in relation to justification.

It may appear that we could reconcile the two divines by clarifying semantic rather than doctrinal discrepancies. For instance, if Bull is using the term justification to describe God's action in granting that grace without which no good work is possible, would he not then be in accord with Davenant? Bull is certainly consistent in arguing for the *initial* necessity of grace in the schema of salvation, and he seems also to be as concerned to disclaim any merit of works as is Davenant. Both agree as well in differing from Bellarmine, and in condemning works of condignity and supererogation. There is, indeed, some basis in Bull's brief remarks about first and second justification and first and second sanctification to suggest the possibility at least of some underlying agreement on the two doctrines.

There are, however, several other considerations that tend to negate any hope of actual agreement. Bull evidences a thorough familiarity with Davenant's work, which had, after all, been in circulation some thirty years before Bull began to write. (Davenant is even quoted by Bull, for example, in an obscure discussion of the proper use of the Greek preposition ἀντί.[37]) Yet there are numerous direct contradictions, of which Bull could scarcely have been unaware, inasmuch as he frequently quotes from the very passages in Davenant's works which are explicitly contradictory to Bull's own argument.

Bull disagrees with Davenant, for example, concerning the relationship of works to eternal rewards, specified in reference to Matthew 25.21-5.[38] Bull also denies that the imputation of Christ's righteousness is the formal cause of justification,[39] which position Davenant is occupied in defending at considerable length. Bull asserts, in fact, that "the righteousness of Christ is . . . that on account of which our faith is imputed for righteousness".[40] Even more contrary to Davenant's doctrine is Bull's statement that our works "are the very things on account of which (by the merciful covenant of God through Christ) eternal life is given us".[41] The *Harmonia* includes the following statements which are directly contradicted by a passage Bull later quotes from Davenant. Anything that is said to be a condition of receiving a reward is part of a covenant and promise or agreement upon performance of which, one, thereby, obtains a right to a reward.[42] He proceeds to disagree with those, among them, surely, Davenant, who deny that by work a right is obtained to salvation.

> . . . a promise, agreement, or covenant confers a right to the benefit contained in it only on the performance of the condition, and, therefore, a condition always refers to some right to be obtained.[43]

Having said all this, Bull thereupon blandly cites Davenant, presumably to support his argument. He first quotes the illustration (given above) of a person to be knighted for whom it is a condition that he go to court and kneel before the king. It would be, as Davenant put it, "absurd for anyone thence to conclude" that the fulfilling of these conditions granted one a right to knighthood. In this long quotation from Davenant, however, he omits two illustrations without indication that anything has been omitted. One is of the patient who must admit his infirmity, desire health, and apply to the physician, but the fulfilment of these conditions does not, in itself, confer a right to the benefits thereby gained. The other is that of the beggar who must admit his need, go to the place where alms are distributed, and hold out his hand, but by the fulfilment of these conditions alone he gains no right to the alms. Bull continues to quote Davenant on page 215 of the *Harmonia* as to the necessity of good works for preserving a state of justification, but stops the quotation with "etc." when Davenant qualifies what he is saying with the words, "Let us then not think that the act itself of believing, repenting, and mortifying the flesh effects or merits the preservation of justifying grace."[44] Or, again, he quotes Davenant out of context on page 354 of the *Apologia* on the necessity of good works for justification, failing to mention, however, the cautious and qualified context in which the Bishop of Salisbury made such a statement.[45]

Such radical differences between Davenant and Bull render the possibility of some underlying agreement remote. On yet another point agreement is altogether excluded—that is, their quite opposite views of chapter 7 of the Epistle to the Romans. Bull argues that the phrases in chapter 7 "to be carnal", "unable to do that which is good", etc. cannot be understood to describe one of the regenerate. "If ye walk in the Spirit [which Bull claims "all regenerate persons do"] ye shall not fulfil the lusts of the flesh" (Rom. 8.1), because, Bull holds,

. . . by the grace of the Holy Spirit alone, freely obtained of God for us by Christ, we are enabled to perform those things which by the Gospel covenant lead to justification and eternal sanctification.

Bull strongly maintains that the latter part of chapter 7 cannot be understood to describe the state of a regenerate person, one blessed with the grace of the Gospel.

> That opinion certainly besides being contrary to all antiquity before Augustine, and which Augustine himself at one time rejected, is clogged with insuperable difficulties and most evident absurdities.[46]

The crux of Davenant's argument is that sin does remain in the regenerate, and Romans 7 is specific evidence that it does. Bull agrees with Davenant only as to the importance of the issue, but he holds precisely the opposite view: "and thus . . . concerning the sense of the seventh chapter of Romans, . . . if the contrary interpretation be admitted, the cause we are upholding plainly falls to the ground . . .".[47] The two divines, then, agree that they disagree, and each grounds his argument in an opposite interpretation of Romans 7.

Does Bull's denial that the latter part of Romans 7 is a description of a regenerate person mean that he holds a regenerate person to be sinless? Apparently not, since he acknowledges some unavoidable faults and defects even in the regenerate which he describes as "that solicitation of concupiscence",[48] though he holds that, "it extort no assent of the will whatever".[49] Such small taints of sin remain as a reminder, according to Bull, of that state of perfection from which we fell and our continued need, therefore, to rely upon grace. This statement is made within the context of a discussion in which Bull argues the possibility of perfect obedience, not only as demanded by God, but factually as performed by man. He agrees with St Augustine that perfect obedience is possible, but he denies the latter's contention that none actually has been perfectly obedient.

Bull states his position thus: that there is a

> . . . lowest degree of righteousness, which is absolutely required for us in the Gospel . . . before we depart this life; we rid ourselves of all sin on which eternal death is denounced by the Gospel . . .[50]

Similarly,

> For not on account of every the least failing, even such as through grace we might have avoided, does the law of the Gospel denounce on

man exclusion from the kingdom of heaven, much less inflict the pains of hell; but on account of certain sins only, which are inconsistent with the end of the law, charity, or the love of God above all things, and consequently with the friendship of God.[51]

In still another passage Bull argues that in the Gospel covenant one may commit venial sins without being deprived of eternal reward, but he carefully qualifies the distinction between venial and mortal sins by asserting that all sin is mortal to him who does not earnestly labour to escape such sins.

Another peculiar discrepancy arises in Bull's discussion of the law of Christ. He at one time states that "the Gospel, or law of Christ, although it teaches a high religion . . . yet enjoins nothing on fallen man which cannot be fulfilled through the grace which it promises".[52] In the *Harmonia*, however, he identifies the law of Christ with the Sermon on the Mount and says, the observance of this law tempered by the grace of the Gospel is demanded by Christ of all Christians, as an absolutely necessary condition of his covenant.[53] Such descriptions of the arduous conditions of the covenant are exemplified also by other statements to the effect that "no one, therefore, is a friend of Christ except upon this condition, that he observe all His commands".[54] "Here it is perfectly clear that to enjoy the love of God, i.e., to be justified, a man must have such love as will ensure obedience to the commands of Christ."[55]

Bull's essential argument is most clearly stated in his description of the atonement through which runs the proposition that the conditions of the Gospel covenant *must be fulfilled*. These conditions include:

> . . . not only faith, but repentance and the study of good works. Here the merit of Christ does not perform that office which many so dangerously and absurdly dream. For Christ hath not merited, nor is His righteousness imputed to us for this purpose, that we should be freed from the conditions of the Gospel . . . but by His merit He hath obtained, that upon a most just condition we might become partakers of salvation, and He also purchased grace, by which we are enabled to perform that very condition.[56]

This latter grace is obtained not by justification but is, in fact, required for it. Davenant, on the other hand, maintains that Christ's righteousness is imputed not to free us from the conditions of the covenant but rather to enable us to fulfil those conditions. Forgiveness and the grace that enables us to do good works is, according to Davenant, freely given in justification. Not so, says Bull, it is rather that good works are our part of the covenant which must be performed before God will justify us.

Although his doctrine of justification differs radically from that of Davenant, Bull is nevertheless critical of Bellarmine's view that justification means to be made righteous by the attainment of inherent righteousness.[57] Bull contends, indeed, that the formal cause of justification is the remission of sins granted upon fulfilment of the covenant conditions.[58] On account of Christ's righteousness our works, faith, and repentance are accepted as righteous, our sins forgiven, and thereby are we justified.

George Bull belongs, then, to the "holy living" school, and his doctrine of justification is closer to that of Taylor, Thorndike, and Hammond than it is to Bellarmine or to Davenant and Hooker. Like Taylor, Thorndike, and Hammond, Bull considers that Christ's righteousness is not the formal but the meritorious cause of justification. He argues that works not only follow from but also must precede justification. Unlike Davenant, he concurs with the "holy living" divines on the question of sin in the regenerate. Romans 7 is not to be understood as a description of the regenerate person. God will, nevertheless, forgive any who earnestly labour to escape all sins, and he will damn no one for an occasional lapse owing to the "solicitation of Concupiscence" (provided there is no act of the will). As for Taylor, Hammond, and Thorndike so also for Bull there is a minimum degree of righteousness required in the new covenant, and this causes him a similar difficulty when he atempts to deny works of supererogation. (How are we to regard works over and above the minimum required for salvation?) Bull, too, tends to prescribe more arduous conditions of righteousness before justification (outside the covenant) than he does after justification (within the covenant of mercy). Finally, Bull shares with the "holy living" divines a fear of the danger of antinomianism when discussing justification. Thus, he laments to Gataker:

Read the writings of those who in the late anarchy of our church (never to be thought of without tears) openly defended Antinomianism: specially the sermons of Tobias Crisp, styled a D.D. to the disgrace of that sacred title. It shames me to tell my foreign readers how many deductions, loathsome to Christian ears, this Crisp draws from your assertion, and that with so plain an inference, that I confess I cannot refute his writings on your hypothesis; what you may be able to do, I know not.[59]

The radical ambiguity in Bull's plan of salvation is that nowhere does he actually allow that it is possible for the unjustifiable to be justified, the unforgivable to be forgiven, and the unlovable to be loved by Christ. No one, he insists, will be accepted and forgiven until he has performed works of love. In effect, Christ, who first loved us, according to Bull, demands none the less that we love him in order to be loved by him.

For God, though He justify the ungodly through Christ (Rom. 4.5) i.e. him, who *having been such*, nevertheless will not justify the ungodly (Ex. 34.7), i.e. him who still remains in his wickedness;[60] a wicked man is [not] justified in the concurrent sense, i.e. while he is still wicked;[61] [one must] approach to God, seek His favour in prayer, serve Him with the whole heart, and keep all His commandments. But *when* we in this manner approach to God, God on His part approaches to us, that is, closely embraces us with the arms of His love, most perfectly forgiving all our sins . . .[62]

It is true that he qualifies this emphasis upon works by acknowledging that they are possible only by grace. However, according to such statements as above, neither Christ nor God can be approached by one who is defiled by sin. Bull argues, in other words, that the righteousness required for justification is possible only *by* the Gospel covenant, but, at the same time, he also claims that this righteousness is required *for* the Gospel covenant. He never explains how God can give grace to a man defiled by sin and outside the covenant if that man must first be righteous to obtain the grace. That God loves, forgives, and justifies sinners, and the sinners are then bound to obedience through gratitude, is termed, by Bull, an antinomian heresy.

> Pray tell me, tell me plainly are we bound to obey the moral law, as confirmed by Christ, at the hazard of our soul, or only by the bond of gratitude? If you affirm the latter you embrace the pestilent heresy of the Antinomians . . .[63]

Perhaps the most curious passage in the *Examen Censurae* has to do with justification considered as a reward. Bull argues in the *Harmonia* that "to impute anything to a man for righteousness, and to impute a reward to a man for anything, is the same, or at least are both contained in the same idea of justification".[64] Gataker objects to this statement on the grounds that it makes justification itself into a reward. He points out that St Paul's whole concern is to demonstrate that justification is a gift and to deny that it is a reward for performance of works.[65] Bull's reply to this objection significantly includes the observation that

> . . . what you mean in the first part of your remark, I do not exactly understand nor does it matter whether I understand it or not; for whatever it is that you there say, you express your agreement with and approval of what I have asserted.[66]

It is not surprising that Bull elicits such criticism, however, since, for example, he writes,

> It is moreover evident that the same faith, which if it could be separated from love, would profit nothing, when united with love, has no weight by its own influence, neither any power or virtue of justification, which it does not owe to love.[67]

It may well be that Bull does "not exactly understand" what St Paul means by justification. There is, at any rate, a startling contrast between his early exposition of St Paul in the *Harmonia* and that with which he concludes the *Examen Censurae*. He begins by proclaiming that

> I will, moreover, venture to promise, however incredible it may appear, that from what St Paul hath said concerning works, I will bring additional proofs for the doctrine of St James of justification by works.[68]

This confident assertion is in bold contrast to a passage found at the conclusion of his defence against Charles Gataker. There, he candidly acknowledges that he *may* have erred in expounding some

of the more difficult arguments of St Paul (though he denies that
Gataker has pointed out such errors). He closes with this quotation
from "a holy and learned man".

> In St Paul's Epistles there is room for an elephant to sink; how much
> more a flea such as myself? Whence, in passages like this, I will eat as
> much as I can: What remains, I will burn with fire, following the
> exposition of the holy Catholic doctors, and [be?] contented with it.
> For no mortal man can penetrate the depth of the Epistles of St Paul
> the Apostle.[69]

It is quite likely that the Reverend George Bull, writing in the
turbulent Restoration period, conceived the Epistle of St James as
a basis for countering the immorality of the times, and as a corrective to certain weaknesses in the position of the Church with
respect to justification. His concern about the behaviour of the
common people is evident when, for example, he writes that,

> . . . whoever of the common people shall receive this doctrine un-
> disguisedly delivered, namely, that faith is the only instrument of
> justification and that good works have no weight, are of no impor-
> tance . . . you will never persuade him to perform any good
> works . . .[70]

The phrase "undisguisedly delivered" is an odd but apt expression.
It seems to suggest that the doctrine of justification by faith must be
disguised from the "common people" not because it is wrong, but
rather because it tends to dissuade such people from the performance
of good works. Another similar parenthetical remark is made in the
Harmonia, ". . . to her modesty . . . fidelity also, an uncommon
virtue among women, is added".[71]

Bull seems to have begun his work with such concerns as these
paramount in his mind, and he found St James an easy and con-
venient vehicle to convey his assumptions. But when he comes to St
Paul he is forced to stretch his interpretations of the text ("Faith",
for St Paul, "comprehends in one word all the works of Christian
piety" and "denotes the whole condition of the Gospel covenant").[72]
Later, attempting to defend himself against the criticism of Gataker
and Tully, he is driven to confusing qualifications (first and second
justification and first and second sanctification, for example).

Bull acknowledges in a preface that he began his work in the expectation that it would be "the brief employment of an hour", but "as the abundance" and "tide of matter" (profundity of St Paul?) flowed in upon him, it developed into a much greater length. Had he begun with St Paul, could he have expected that his work would be the "brief employment of an hour"? It is significant that he complains because Gataker's criticisms on the first Dissertation (St James) were more lengthy than those on the second Dissertation (St Paul). This seems to indicate that Bull's original position, as expressed in his discussion of St James, is much more vulnerable to criticism. It is also significant, in the same way, that he discusses St James in a mere forty pages as compared with the 179 pages devoted to St Paul in the *Harmonia*. Less than one fourth of his work, then, drew more than half the criticism.

Bull's explication of the doctrine of justification is highly puzzling, especially his attitude towards Davenant. Despite the fact that the two differ greatly about justification, Bull nevertheless seems to believe that he and Davenant hold the same doctrine. It is not credible that Bull was unaware of the vast discrepancies in view of his obvious familiarity with the work of the Bishop of Salisbury. He not only cites Davenant's use of Greek prepositions, but quotes from him in contexts where it would have required singular obtuseness to avoid noticing the differences.

It is also difficult to explain Bull's inconsistent discussion of sin in the regenerate. Tully's principal objection to the *Harmonia* is that Bull denies that Romans 7 is a description of the condition of a justified person. Tully directly asks Bull if he would deny that he himself is a wretched sinner, who, in his present estate, deserves death.[73] Bull answers:

> I willingly confess before God and men, that I was once a most grievous sinner, and therefore most miserable: and I acknowledge, that even now, I offend in many things: but I trust that by the grace of God without arrogance, I can deny that I am a sinner in the sense that the word is used in the Scripture, or that I am under the body of death, of which the Apostle speaks, and therefore miserable . . . the whole scripture . . . declares . . . [a regenerate person] to be blessed and happy.[74]

This extraordinary disclaimer is in striking contrast to Bull's more modest remarks in his preface to the *Harmonia*:

> . . . then entreat the Lord by your fervent prayers for the author who, though disputing about Gospel righteousness, confesses himself to be (and he says it from his heart) the chiefest of sinners, and in the same Lord Farewell.[75]

Either Bull changed his mind radically in the five intervening years, or he did not really believe what he wrote in one or other of these passages. His ambiguous discussion of Davenant, his failure to grasp Gataker's objection that justification is not a reward, and his contradictory statements with respect to his own condition, are, perhaps, most plausibly explained if we assume that Bull deliberately "disguised" his views about justification on account of his fear of the dangers of antinomianism. He must have understood that Davenant's doctrine differed profoundly from his own, but he refrained from saying so because he feared that the Gospel of forgiveness would not persuade the "common people" to obedience and "holy living". He must have understood Gataker's contention that justification is not a reward, but this doctrine, he seems to have felt, must not be "undisguisedly delivered". He must have known in "his heart" that he was a sinner, but the logic of his stated doctrine drove him to deny that there could be sin in the regenerate.

Bull, then, departs radically from the classical (Caroline) Anglicans, and he emphatically differs from the doctrine of the Council of Trent and Cardinal Bellarmine. He must be placed with Taylor, Thorndike, and Hammond in the vanguard of what was to become the predominant school of Anglican moralism.

7

Exegesis of the
Gospel after the Restoration
1660

The "holy living" doctrine did not completely displace the classical Caroline understanding of soteriology. Contemporaries of Taylor, Thorndike, and Hammond did adhere to and sustain the basic argument of the earlier divines. Robert Sanderson (1587-1663), John Bramhall (1594-1663), and William Nicholson (1591-1672) were three influential Carolines who lived into Restoration times, and yet maintained the classical doctrine that the formal cause of justification is the imputation of Christ's righteousness. None of the three wrote any work devoted exclusively or specifically to soteriology, but their teaching on other matters reflects the Caroline position on justification. Like the earlier Carolines they argue that righteousness is infused into the sinner at justification, but that this righteousness is not in itself sufficient to be the formal cause of justification (nor does it exclude the possibility of sin in the regenerate). Bramhall, for example, writes that all true Christians have

> . . . true inherent justice, though not perfect . . . as gold is true gold though it be mixed with some dross. [But] . . . it is not our inherent righteousness that justifieth us . . . but the free grace of God for the merits of Jesus Christ.[1]

By way of contrast to the more lenient requirements of the new covenant as described by the "holy living" divines, Bramhall argues that

> The gospel, . . . bindeth us yet to our good behaviour in every respect as deep as ever the law did, if not in some respects deeper,

allowing no liberty to the flesh for the fulfilling of the lusts thereof in any thing, but exacting entire sanctity, and purity both in inward affection and outward conversation, in all those that embrace it.[2]

The most notable difference in doctrine between the "holy living" divines and the classical Anglicans is the contention of the latter that justification is the means whereby the sinner, as a sinner, is reconciled to God and begun to be made righteous. Nicholson, however, after making clear that it *is* sinners who are justified, significantly adds that faith and repentance are required of such sinners for their justification. Faith and repentance are, in fact, the instruments by which sinners receive that which justifies them— the righteousness of Christ. This argument differs importantly from that of the "holy living" divines who held essentially that faith and repentance are that very righteousness *by which* sinners are justified through the more lenient covenant *on account* of the righteousness of Christ. Nicholson rejects this understanding of faith because, he says, faith may be said to justify only as it apprehends Christ.

> For take it [faith] as a quality, a virtue, a habit infused into the heart by the holy Spirit, and so it justifies not; for that were to make our Faith our Christ. But reflect upon faith in another notion, as it hath for its object Christ Jesus, and layes hold on his whole ransome, and applies it; and so faith may be very properly said to justifie, because the object which it apprehends doth justifie.[3]

Nicholson does declare that the righteousness of Christ "is of no more power than physick, though never so precious, not applied";[4] but he makes it plain that the faith and repentance which apply this righteousness are no more than instruments. That which actually justifies is the righteousness of Christ imputed to the sinner.

> Now upon this imputation of Christ's righteousness, there follow three admirable benefits to a Christian soul; redemption from sin, remission from punishment, Reconciliation to God.[5]

All three of the late Caroline divines agree with their classical predecessors as to the relationship of justification to sanctification. We are, as Sanderson puts it, delivered first "from the guilt of sin in our justification . . . [and then] from the dominion of sin in our sanctification".[6] Good works and holy life are enabled by the grace *received in* justification and are *not* conditions *required for* justification. Nicholson, for example, asserts that, God,

> . . . imputing to them the obedience of His own Son, and His righteousness accounts them just in His sight . . . [those] who are justified, and thus acquitted, have holiness in some degree, according to the condition of this life, inherent in them: which, though it cannot wholly discharge from sin, yet it frees from the dominion of sin so that no justified person yields himself a slave and a vassal to sin, but resists its commands, mortifies, crucifies it, and makes it die daily.[7]

There was considerable reluctance, it should be said, on the part of Anglicans to criticize fellow-Anglicans on controversial doctrines such as justification. Isaak Walton, in his *Life of Sanderson*, notes that Sanderson differed from Henry Hammond on several subjects, and then he adds that when fifty-two ministers of London objected to Hammond's *Practical Catechism*,[8]

> Dr Sanderson was with much unwillingness drawn into this Debate . . . who in his judgment of God's decrees differ'd with Dr Hammond (whom he reverenced and loved dearly) and would not therefore ingage him into a Controversie . . .[9]

Similarly, Charles Gataker, at the conclusion of his work reconciling St Paul and St James, writes

> . . . that this brief discourse was prepared for the publick, and indeed submitted unto Censure some months before that book called *Harmonia Evangelica* [*Apostolica*], was exposed to the World . . . I think it not fit at present to enlarge my discourse with any reflection upon those dissertations in particular, because I am unwilling to stir, or to increase the waters of strife . . .[10]

Gataker's explicit criticism of Bull was not printed, but rather sent privately to Bull's bishop, William Nicholson. This reluctance to "increase the waters of strife" in the discussion of justification may have prompted Tully's complaint (in a preface) that his contemporary divines were sluggish in defending the doctrine of the Church of England.[11]

THOMAS BARLOW
1607-91

Reluctance to generate controversy may also explain why Thomas Barlow, Bishop of Lincoln, did not see fit to publish two letters he wrote to a priest in his diocese. These letters, printed posthumously in 1701 with a preface by "Ri Mayo", strongly condemn the spread of the doctrine of justification by works. The priest addressed in the letters is identified only as "J.W.". "Ri Mayo" tells us that his "character is already published to the world, in his funeral sermon: But I being to publish (mostly) his blemishes, may be allow'd to conceal his Name."[12] The occasion of the letters was a protest by "J.W." against Barlow's admonition that no one in his diocese was to preach the doctrine of justification by works. "J.W." argues that he should be allowed to preach the doctrine provided only that the works are not assigned as *meritorious* causes of justification "J.W.'s" argument is that, since faith is a work itself, justification is necessarily by works. He rejects the doctrine of the imputation of Christ's righteousness, and suggests that Barlow's admonition would apply to Hammond, Bull, and Baxter (among others) if they were in the Bishop of Lincoln's diocese, Barlow, in reply, asserts that all Anglicans who have written on justification

> . . . before the late unhappy Rebellion (at least all I have yet met with) such as Bishop Jewel, Hooker, Reynolds, Whittaker, Davenant, Field, Downham, John White, etc. do constantly prove, and vindicate the imputation of our blessed Saviour's Righteousness against the contrary Doctrine of Racovia and Rome, Papists and Socinians. So that in Truth, it is only you, and some Neotericks, who (since the year 1640) deny such imputation . . . to the prejudice of Truth, and the scandal of our Church and Religion.[13]

Barlow accepts his correspondent's contention that their age is cold in charity and void of good works, and that good works should, accordingly, be diligently preached to the people. But "this is not enough".

> See then, as for your purpose to Preach up good works, I do highly approve it; there is a necessity that you and every Faithful Minister,

should do so. But you must take heed, that you Preach them up, to those ends and purpose to which they are appointed; otherwise it may be (as in Socinians and Papists it is) a bad work in you to Preach up good ones.[14]

Barlow adheres, then, to the doctrine of the classical Carolines. His argument in the two letters is that the theologians of the Church of England fully agreed on justification until 1640. Whereupon, especially with the publication of Baxter's *Aphorisms*, some younger divines arose in the Church of England who follow Socinus in attributing justification to our own works of faith and repentance. Barlow asserts that this doctrine is, in some ways, more dangerous than that of the Council of Trent. He notes that Roman Catholics and Protestants alike agree that justification is given by God and they deny that it is "acquired by our acts and industry", as the followers of Socinus maintain.[15] According to Barlow, the doctrine that our faith and repentance is accepted as the righteousness by which we are justified is expressly gainsaid by Ephesians 2.8: "By grace you are Saved through Faith, and that not of your selves, it is the gift of God; not of works, lest any man should boast." Good works are necessary to salvation because they are the way, but they cannot be considered the *cause* of salvation.[16]

Barlow reiterates the classical argument that righteousness is infused into the justified but it is *not* that *by which* we are justified. Our righteousness is imperfect and marred by many sins. It is only the righteousness of Christ imputed to us (covering us) that makes us acceptable unto God. "J.W." attempts to argue that St Paul could not have been speaking of his own evangelical obedience in Romans 7, and that when St Paul denies that we are justified by works he means to disclaim only works of the Mosaical law and works performed by our own strength. Barlow answers that, on the contrary, St Paul *is* speaking of his own inherent righteousness which, in comparison with the spiritual law of God, is "loss and dung".[17] Such inherent righteousness is a fruit of faith and is the righteousness of sanctification. It is a real but imperfect righteousness *even* in St Paul. Barlow asserts that Socinus and his followers are wrong when they say that St Paul in Romans 7 is speaking of some other person. He flatly declares that

> St Augustine and the Fathers before him, the Church of England, Hooker, and (till of late) all her Learned Sons; many Learned Papists say, and firmly prove, that St Paul in that place speaks of himself.[18]

Inherent righteousness is the righteousness of sanctification and it cannot, because of its imperfection, be the righteousness of justification. Barlow argues that St Paul is speaking of justification *coram Deo* and St James *coram hominibus*. We "are justified before God by the merits of Christ only, supplied by Faith only",[19] and it is the meaning that St Paul attaches to justification. St James, far from contradicting St Paul, attributes justification to works only in the sense that works are evidences before men "of our antecedent Justification, and declares a person already just before God".[20]

"J.W." says, in his first letter to Barlow, that St Paul frequently asserts the proposition that justification by faith means no more than justification by *continued acts* of faith. Barlow replies that, "this proposition is so far from being frequently asserted by St Paul, that it never occurs, not once, in any of his 14 Epistles".[21] In a second letter to Barlow, "J.W." reiterates his previous argument, apparently not dissuaded by Barlow's reply and admonitions. He also tries to argue that, since we are justified by faith and faith is subjective and inherent in us, we are, therefore, justified by inherent righteousness. Barlow replies that this is false because faith is said to justify only as it receives, relies upon, and applies the righteousness of Christ. "J.W." repeats his statement that works not only declare justification but constitute it. He interprets the doctrine of the imputation of Christ's righteousness to mean only "that for the sake of Christ's Righteousness we are reputed Righteous".[22] Barlow answers that only perfect righteousness can satisfy God's justice, only Christ's righteousness is perfect, and hence we are justified only by Christ's righteousness imputed to us.

Barlow (as does Lancelot Andrewes) suggests that the simplest way to determine the whole issue is to ask on what righteousness we shall rely when we are judged in the last day, our own inherent righteousness or the righteousness of Christ imputed to us.

I say, when you shall come before that Great and Just Judge, you will reject your own works, and inherent Righteousness, and rely upon the sufferings and satisfaction of our blessed Saviour, and say, as a late Learned and Pious Prelate [Sanderson] did (in his Last Will and Testament), "I commend my Soul to God, beseeching him, not to look upon it as it is in it self, infinitely polluted with Sin (no mention of good works, or performance of the condition of the Covenant by them, though had there been any such thing, he might justly have pleaded and depended upon it); but as it is Redeemed, and Purged with the Precious Blood of Christ. In confidence of whose merits alone (not of his performance of the Condition of the Covenant by his own works) it is, that I cast my self upon his mercy for the Pardon of my Sins." So that Pious and very Learned and Judicious Person.[23]

EDWARD FOWLER

1632-1714

JOHN BUNYAN

1628-88

Another Anglican of the Restoration period who discusses the doctrine of justification was Edward Fowler. His doctrine is contrary to that of Barlow, and he is, in fact, another representative of the "holy living" school in his exegesis of the Gospel. *The Design of Christianity*[24] elicited as much criticism as had Bull's *Harmonia*. The principal argument of Fowler's work, as indicated by the title, is that righteousness is the true end and purpose of the Gospel. When Fowler discusses justification he sees it as a doctrine "designed for a Motive to quicken and excite Men in their Endeavours after . . . Righteousness . . .".[25]

On the surface, Fowler may seem to agree with the "imputation" rather than the "holy living" divines since he does say that the imputation of Christ's righteousness is the true explanation of justification. However, he defines the doctrine in such a way that he clearly belongs with the "holy living" school. Imputation, he writes, is true in the sense that

. . . it consists in dealing with *sincerely* righteous Persons, as if they were perfectly so, for the Sake of Christ's Righteousness . . . it is not possible that any other Notion of this Doctrine should have any truth in it.[26]

He denies that faith justifies only as it apprehends the righteousness of Christ, or that faith is merely the instrument of justification. Faith is actually that righteousness which is accepted by God for justification on account of Christ's righteousness. This understanding of justification leads Fowler, as it did the other "holy living" divines, to describe the demands for righteousness in the new covenant as simpler and more lenient than those of the old covenant.[27] He quotes favourably Jeremy Taylor's statement that "if ye walk in the Light and live in the Spirit, your Doctrine will be true . . . ".[28] The "Design of Christianity", the business of Christianity, is to make us righteous. According to Fowler whatever does not encourage this end cannot be Christian.

Fowler's work was attacked the same year it appeared by John Bunyan, writing from Bedford prison in a work entitled:

> A Defence of the Doctrine of Justification by Faith In Jesus Christ shewing True Gospel-Holiness flows from Thence, or "Mr Fowler's Pretended Design of Christianity, proved to be nothing more than to trample under Foot the Blood of the Son of God; and the Idolizing of Man's own Righteousness. As also, How while he pretends to be a minister of the Church of England, he overthroweth the wholesome Doctrine contain'd in the 10th 11th, and 13th of the 39 Articles of the same, and that he falleth in with the Quaker, and Romanist against them." By John Bunyan, Disalowed indeed of men, but chosen of God, and precious, 1 Pet. 2.4.

Bunyan's essential point is that Fowler exhorts a sinlessness and cleanliness on the part of the unregenerate that is possible only in the regenerate. Fowler requires as a condition of justification a quality of righteousness impossible to achieve because of original sin. Bunyan contends that only by the free gift of justification are sinners enabled to be truly righteous. He tells Fowler, you

> . . . suppose that it is within the power of a man's own Soul, always to keep sin out of it self, and so guilt out of the conscience; albeit the Scripture saith, that both the mind and it are defiled with the filth of

sin, in all whosoever do not believe the Gospel, with which belief this description medleth not.[29]

A reply to Bunyan was published the next year, unsigned, but probably by Fowler, entitled

> Dirt Wipt off: or "A manifest Discovery of the Gross Ignorance, Erroneousness and most un-Christian and Wicked Spirit of one John Bunyan, Lay-Preacher in Bedford which he hath shewed in a vile Pamphlet . . . written for the disabusing of those poor deluded people that are followers of him . . ."

Here it is alleged that Bunyan, to his perpetual infamy, has shown "most woful ignorance, and notorious dishonesty, and ill nature, besides the foulest erroniousness" in his book against Fowler.[30] Bunyan is not, as a matter of fact, altogether accurate in his objections to Fowler. In Dirt Wipt Off it is complained that Bunyan put "hearty" where Fowler had "barely" in a significant context quoted in The Defence. Fowler had actually written, "Let us declare that we are not barely relyers on Christ's Righteousness by being immitators of it."[31] It must have been dark in Bedford gaol because another inaccuracy occurs in Bunyan's list of forty doctrines destructive to Christianity. Fowler actually had stated that Christ came "to fulfil, or perfect them, that is, by giving more and higher instances of Moral Duties than were before expressly given . . .".[32] Bunyan's quotation reads "lighter" instead of "higher".

However, it is, in general, true that Fowler describes "lighter" conditions within the new covenant, and Bunyan's criticism, despite this inaccuracy, is not irrelevant. This latter inaccuracy, perhaps for this reason, goes unmentioned in Dirt Wipt Off.

Fowler claims that his teaching is supported by the major Reformation theologians, but this seems not to have impressed Bunyan, who replies:

> As for your saying, That Calvin, Peter Martyr, Musculus, Zanchy, and others, did not question, but that God could have Pardoned sin without any other Satisfaction, then the Repentance of the sinner. page 84, It matters nothing to me, I have neither made my creed out of them, nor other, then the Holy Scriptures of God.[33]

EDWARD STILLINGFLEET
1635-99

This question of satisfaction had an important bearing on disputes about the doctrine of justification. The "holy living" divines were accused of Socinianism, of falsely arguing that Christ's satisfaction is not necessary in the atonement, and of wrongly suggesting that God forgives us our sins for no more satisfaction than our own sincere repentance. Edward Stillingfleet published *A Discourse Concerning the True Reason of the Sufferings of Christ* which discusses satisfaction and grace in relation to the atonement. Although there is little in Stillingfleet's work about justification as such, his discussion of satisfaction has a direct bearing upon the Gospel. To the objection, for example, that free grace is inconsistent with the doctrine of Christ's satisfaction, Stillingfleet answers:

> Either God's Grace is so free as to exclude all conditions, or not: If it be so free, as to exclude all conditions, then the highest Antinomianism is the truest Doctrine; for that is the highest degree of the Freeness of Grace, which admits of no conditions at all.[34]

Thus, the nature of God's grace consists in free satisfaction freely given, but the effects of this satisfaction are given conditionally. God, though justly provoked by the sins of mankind, has accepted the sacrifice of Christ as a sufficient satisfaction for the sins of the world. In consideration of this satisfaction God has offered

> . . . those terms of pardon, which upon man's performance of the conditions required on their part, shall be sufficient to discharge them from that obligation to punishment which they were under by their sins.[35]

This resembles the conditions of the covenant described by Taylor, Thorndike, and Hammond, but Stillingfleet differs from the "holy living" divines in one important respect. Faith, he says, is indeed the condition of the new covenant, but it does not include within itself obedience and good works. The latter are, according to Stillingfleet, the fruits of faith.[36]

WILLIAM BEVERIDGE
1637-1708

Another late Caroline who considers that good works are not included in faith but are rather its fruit, was William Beveridge. Like the classical Anglicans of the first half of the century, Beveridge argues that the formal cause of justification is the imputation of Christ's righteousness because our own is insufficient and God's demand is absolute. Hence, no righteousness can serve for our justification but the righteousness of Christ imputed to us. Beveridge maintains that it is faith only that justifies, and he reconciles this position with St James' doctrine by contending that the Apostle is speaking only of works which follow justification. Like Thomas Barlow, Beveridge suggests that St Paul is speaking of justification before God, which is by faith only, whereas St James is speaking of justification before men, which is declared and manifested by works.[87]

ISAAC BARROW
1630-77

A contemporary of William Beveridge with a similar understanding of the Gospel was Isaac Barrow. Barrow's soteriology is found, for the most part, in his sermons. Although he manifests many of the same concerns as did the "holy living" divines, he clearly belongs fundamentally to the classical school. Barrow declares that justifying faith does not consist in being persuaded of one's own election and pardon, but rather it connotes a firm resolution to live by and perform all the conditions of the Gospel. Justification can be lost by disobedience, and may be regained only by repentance. He stresses the conditions of the new covenant but, unlike the "holy living" divines, these conditions, for Barrow, refer to *obligations within* the covenant and not to *prerequisites for* the covenant. He nowhere mentions any righteousness or obedience required as conditions *before* justification. The new covenant, he says, is granted to us on "gentle terms" and easy conditions, but these refer to terms and conditions of faith before justification and not to demands made within the covenant.[38] When Barrow speaks of conditions of obedience and righteousness he refers to conditions for remaining in the covenant, whereas the condition of initially entering the covenant is

> . . . sincerely believing, and seriously repenting; returning to God with hearty desires and earnest resolutions to serve him; God is ready to dispense mercy and pardon, and immediately receiveth the person into grace and favour with him . . .[39]

Barrow shares the view of classical Anglicans that justification is by the imputation of Christ's righteousness.[40] He denies the contention of Grotius and Bellarmine that to justify means to make righteous. Like the earlier divines he says that, while God does infuse righteousness into the justified, this righteousness is not that by which they are justified. Barrow even asserts that if the Council of Trent is right in proclaiming that infused righteousness is the formal cause of justification then Christianity itself is insufficient.[41] According to the Tridentine doctrine, he remarks, no one is justified because no one is without sin and consequently there are no Christians. Barrow insists that justification may be apprehended by faith alone because if it were attained by works men might boast. We are justified freely by God's grace without regard to our former actions, and therefore *"Where is boasting? it is excluded."*[42]

> From the justification St Paul speaketh of, all respect to any works, and to any qualifications in men, (such as might beget in them any . . . boasting) is excluded; it cannot therefore well be understood for a constituting man intrinsically righteous, or infusing worthy qualities into him; but rather for an act of God terminated upon a man as altogether unworthy of God's love as impious, as an enemy, as a pure object of mercy; so it is most natural to understand those expressions, importing the same thing; God justifieth the ungodly; We being sinners, Christ died for us . . .[43]

Barrow concedes that the terms of soteriology in Scripture are not used with undeviating consistency. He asserts that justification connotes chiefly God's initial forgiveness and acceptance, especially in Baptism, but that any subsequent pardon may also be termed justification. However, he candidly adds, "But whether St Paul ever meaneth the word to signify thus, I cannot affirm."[44] Barrow acknowledges that in some passages of Scripture justification seems to mean the same thing as sanctification, but he adds that, for the most part,

> God's justifying soley, or chiefly, doth import his acquitting us from guilt, condemnation, and punishment, by free pardon and remission of our sins, accounting us and dealing with us as just persons, upright and innocent in his sight and esteem...[45]

Edward Fowler, "J.W.", and George Bull represent an extension under Charles II of the "holy living" understanding of the Gospel that first arose during the Commonwealth in the works of Taylor, Hammond, and Thorndike. The characteristic and distinctive argument of these divines consists in the assumption that faith and repentance is accepted by God as the righteousness of justification on account of the righteousness of Christ. On the other hand, Sanderson, Bramhall, Nicholson, Gataker, Tully, Barlow, Beveridge, and Barrow argue that we are justified by the righteousness of Christ imputed to us and received by faith only. This is the doctrine also, as we have seen, of Hooker, Andrewes, Davenant, Downame, Hall, Ussher, and Donne.

"THE WHOLE DUTY OF MAN"

More influential perhaps than any other single work, with respect to the subsequent understanding of the Christian Gospel among Anglicans, was an anonymous devotional work, *The Whole Duty of Man*, which appeared with a preface by Henry Hammond dated 7 March 1657. This work was to become a standard devotional guide over the next two centuries, and was to be far more widely read than almost any other contemporaneous theological work.

It has been suggested that it may have been written by John Fell, or by Richard Allstree, or by Hammond himself. It could have been written by any of the "holy living" divines in that it is a typical example of their understanding of the Gospel. Faith itself is regarded as a duty, and is defined as belief in the literal validity

of every word in Holy Scripture, together with certain other affir-
mations concerning the Godhead, and the commands and threatenings of the new covenant. All the threats of wrath, punishment,
miseries both temporal and spiritual, and everlasting destruction
in the life to come "we are most steadfastly to believe, that these
are God's threats."[46]

This same teaching concerning repentance and the conditions of
the new covenant are featured also in Jeremy Taylor's works. Baptism confers upon us a claim upon all the benefits that flow from
Christ "on condition we perform our part of the covenant".[47] This
condition is clearly defined. "Obedience to all God's commands is
the condition required of us."[48] There is "no promise of forgiveness of any sin but only to him that confesseth and forsaketh it".[49]
Anything short of complete repentance "will never avail him toward
his pardon; nothing but an entire forsaking of every evil way being
sufficient for that".[50]

> This repentance is, in short, nothing but a turning from sin to God,
> the casting off all our former evils, and, instead thereof, constantly
> practising all those Christian duties, which God requires of us. And
> this is so necessary a Duty, that without it we certainly perish.[51]

The prerequisites for Holy Communion are also the same as for
Jeremy Taylor. Before receiving Holy Communion

> . . . you must cast off every Sin, not bring any one unmortified lust
> with you to that table; for it is not enough to purpose to cast them off
> afterwards, but you must then actually do it, by withdrawing all
> degrees of love and affection from them; you must then give a Bill of
> Divorcement to all your old beloved sins, or else you are no way fit to
> be married to Christ. The reason of this is clear; for this sacrament is
> our spiritual nourishment, we must have spiritual life (for no man
> gives food to a dead person). But whosoever continues not only in the
> act but in the love of any one known sin, hath no spiritual life, but is
> in God's account no better than a dead carcass, and therefore cannot
> receive that spiritual food. It is true, he may eat the Bread and drink
> the Wine, but he receives not Christ, but instead of him, that which is
> most dreadful; the Apostle will tell you that *I Cor. xi. 29* He eats
> and drinks his own Damnation. Therefore you see how great a
> necessity lies on you thus actually to put off every Sin before you
> come to this table.[52]

This qualification of "any one *known* [italics supplied] sin" is also reminiscent of Taylor's allowance for inadvertent and non-wilful sins. One can be a friend of God and a worthy communicant so long as one's sins, if any, are unconscious or are not deliberate. (This notion has sinister pastoral implications that will be discussed in the final chapter.) But

> . . . if thou breakest this League (as thou certainly dost, if thou yieldest to any wilful sin), then God and thou art enemies; and if all the world then were for thee, it could not avail thee.[53]

Little in *The Whole Duty of Man* would lead one to suppose that there is any good news in the Gospel. The purpose of preaching is seen as merely to remind us of our duties.[54] The Gospel is described as though it were made up predominantly of threatenings. The way to overcome sin is to consider first the heinous guilt of it, and then the danger in which it puts one of damnation. "And sure, if this were but thoroughly laid to heart, it would restrain this sin."[55] (How different this is from Hooker's understanding of the limitations of fear in redemption!) The problem as set forth in this devotional work is that "men do either not heartily believe that this sin will damn them, or if they do, they look on it as a thing way off, and so are not much moved with it".[56] The solution, therefore, is to help sinners to apprehend their damnation and to grasp its nearness.

Like Taylor (and unlike Hooker, Andrewes, and Donne) this work finds a special meaning for the "wedding garment" in Scripture. The classical Anglicans had interpreted it to mean that we, in Christ, are clothed with his righteousness and only thus are acceptable to God. For the "holy living" divines and for *The Whole Duty of Man* it is our charity and devotion which are the "spiritual graces our souls must be cloathed with, when we come to this Feast, for this is that Wedding Garment . . .".[57]

Yet another similarity of this work to the works of Hammond and Taylor is the inclusion in it of contradictions which are made in its prayers. In the prayers it is plainly assumed that God, when he forgives sinners, does give them also the grace to achieve subsequent repentance. "O fit me for that mercy, by giving me a deep and hearty Repentance . . ."[58] Instead of assuming that our pardon and forgiveness depend wholly upon our own acts of repentance and charity, the prayers, more modestly, ask of God only that he "Look upon me in thy Son . . ."[59]

8

The Theology of
Richard Baxter and controversies
it provoked

Seventeenth-century soteriology cannot, of course, be fully understood apart from the teaching of non-Anglican divines of the same
period. Following the Long Parliament there was a flood of material
published by such divines which had a profound effect upon the
course of English doctrine. Richard Baxter (1615-91) published his
first work, *Aphorisms of Justification*, in 1649. It immediately
elicited a storm of protest, and Baxter found himself involved for
the rest of his life in controversies about justification. Among those
who objected to the *Aphorisms* were Anthony Burgess, John Wallis,
Christopher Cartwright, George Lawson, John Crandon, John
Warner (not the Bishop of Gloucester), Thomas Tully, John
Tombes, and William Eyre. Baxter replied to the objections of the
latter four in his *Four Disputations of Justification*, published in
1658. In 1676 he published *A Treatise of Justifying Righteousness,*
containing two volumes: "An Answer to Dr Tullies Angry Letter"
and "An Account of my Considerations of the Friendly, Modest,
Learned, Animadversions of Mr Christopher Cartwright of Yourk
on my Aphorisms". Among other works in which he discusses
justification were *Richard Baxter's Admonition to William Eyre,
The Christian Directory, The Life of Faith, An End of Doctrinal
Controversies,* and *Richard Baxter—A Confession of His Faith,
especially concerning the interest of repentance and sincere obedience to Christ, in our justification and salvation.*

In a sermon he preached in Pinner's Hall Baxter was accused
of rejecting the imputation of Christ's righteousness and of

supporting justification by one's own righteousness. He replied in *An Appeal to the Light: or Richard Baxter's Account of Four Passages of a Sermon on Ephesians 1.3*, "Published in hope either to procure the convincing instructions of the wise, or to humble and stop the erroneous Registers of the Truth". He failed, however, to convince at least one "of the wise" who replied anonymously in *Animadversions on a sheet of Mr Baxter's, "entitled 'An Appeal to the Light', for the further Caution of his Credulous Readers"*. This critic alleged that Baxter has unjustly charged others with antinomianism, and he objects specifically to Baxter's interpretation of imputation. In 1671, Baxter wrote *How far Holiness is the Design of Christianity*, a defence of Edward Fowler[1] against an attack by John Bunyan. A year before his death, in 1691, he published *The Scripture Gospel defended and Christ, Grace, and Free Justification Vindicated Against the Libertines*. This work was in two volumes: "A Breviate the Doctrine of Justification Delivered in many Books", and "A Defence of Christ and Free Grace against the Subverters commonly called Antinomians or Libertines". The first was directed against a Mr Troughton who had denied that there were any conditions for justification. The second was provoked by a re-publication of the works of Dr Tobias Crisp with the implicit approbation of several eminent nonconformist divines. Baxter considered that Dr Crisp was an antinomian, and he regarded the re-publication of Crisp's work as a renewal of the doctrine against which he had laboured all his productive life.

Refutation of antinomianism was the motive of his first as well as of his last work. As a young chaplain he warns that the army is

. . . falling in with Saltmarsh, that Christ hath repented and believed for us, and that we must no more question our faith and Repentance, than Christ. This awakened me better to study these points and being young, and not furnished with sufficient reading of the Controversie, and also being where were no libraries, I was put to study only the naked matter in itself. Whereupon I shortly wrote a small book called Aphorisms of Justification . . .[2]

Baxter complains in his reply to Tully's letter that the latter attacked the *Aphorisms* twenty years after they were printed when he,

Baxter, had publicly amended his views. His complaint, however, is not altogether justified, since Baxter never in fact, changed his basic argument.

Though he modified some other views, William Orme's claim can be accepted that "he adhered to the substance of its (the *Aphorisms*) sentiments to the last".[3] Justifying faith, for Baxter, is that which is imputed and reckoned for righteousness as a condition of the new covenant. Such faith is

> . . . no less than our unfeigned taking Christ for our Saviour, and becoming true Christians, according to the tenour of the baptismal covenant. As to the acts, it is formally trust—one in three; the understanding's assenting trust, the will's consenting trust, and the executive power's practical, venturing obeying trust.[4]

It was the latter "obeying trust" which provoked so much of the criticism of his contemporaries. In the *Aphorisms* Baxter argues that no one is justified except he produce "evangelical" works which render him worthy of justification. He explicitly declares that it is not God's will, "that any man should be justified . . . who hath not some ground in himself of personall and particular right and claim thereto . . .".[5] When queried on this point by Tully he explains further that we are not justified by "any Evangelical Works of Love, Gratitude, or Obedience, to Christ as Works are distinguished from our first faith and Repentance".[6] He implies that such works are included in faith and repentance:

> Faith is imputed for Righteousness . . . because it is an Act of Obedience to God . . . Faith is so reputed, or imputed as it is the performance of the Condition of the Justifying Covenant or Donation.[7]

These remarks differ somewhat from those in the *Aphorisms*, but Baxter's original views on justification were never substantially altered as is clear from an examination of his teaching on justification taken as a whole.

Fundamentally, Baxter takes the position that Christ himself fulfilled the conditions of the old covenant, and thereby purchased for us easier terms within the new covenant. On account of Christ's righteousness, our own righteousness (faith and repentance) is accounted, or imputed, as acceptable righteousness. We are, in other words, justified by our own righteousness *on account of* the righteousness of Christ. Baxter distinguishes two kinds of righteousness: legal (old covenant), and evangelical (new, or Gospel), covenant. When we fulfil the conditions of the new covenant by "our own actions of Faith and Gospel Obedience", legal righteousness is automatically ours because "Christ has fulfilled the first covenant"[8] for us. Asked whether Christ's righteousness or our faith is imputed to us for righteousness, Baxter answers that

> Christ's Righteousness is reputed the meritorious Cause . . . And our Faith is reputed the Condition . . . and all that is required in us to our Justification . . . Are we any way Justified by our own performed Righteousness? Answer: yes; Against the charge of non-performance (as Infidels, Impenitent, Unholy), and so as being uncapable of the free-gift of Pardon and Life in Christ.[9]

He is careful to specify that righteousness, which he includes in the term faith, is given to us by God. It is by this righteousness that we are justified, and it is this righteousness which obtains our justification under the conditions of the new covenant. Thus, according to Baxter, the imputation of our *own* faith is the formal cause of justification.

> He giveth us both the Renovation of his Spirit (to Evangelical Obedience), and a Right by free gift to Pardon and Glory for the Righteousness of Christ that merited [it]; And this thus given us, he reputeth to be an acceptable Righteousness in us.[10]

Baxter, then, differs from the classical Anglicans who held that the imputation of *Christ's* righteousness is the formal cause of justification. His views on justification are, in fact, remarkably like those of Taylor, Thorndike, and Hammond.

His interpretation of the doctrine of the new covenant, for example, is not dissimilar from that of Taylor and Thorndike, and his view that Christ, in fulfilling the old covenant law of innocency, gained for us easier terms in the new covenant, is suggestive of Hammond's remark that "Christ has brought down the market". Baxter says flatly that though

. . . without Grace we can no more beleeve, then perfectly obey, . . . yet the conditions of the Gospel . . . are far more facile then the old conditions.[11]

And thus God Reputeth Faith, and Imputeth it to us, requiring but this Condition of us (which also he worketh in us) by the Covenant of Grace, whereas perfect Obedience was required of us by the Law of Innocency.[12]

Thorndike's understanding of the doctrine of the covenant of grace finds an echo in Baxter's observation that "we are now under a covenant that doth not so charge all culpability on mankind, as the Law of Innocency did alone".[13] The concept of a more lenient covenant even leads Baxter to speak of the *covenant* itself as that which justifies us. When the conditions of the new covenant are fulfilled by penitent believers, "that covenant doth pardon all their sins (as God's instrument) and giveth them a right to Life eternal for Christ's merits".[14] Asked whether pardon or justification is perfect before death Baxter answers that, though no pardon extends to future sins, "the same Gospel-covenant, doth morally perform a new act of pardon, according to the Redeemer's mind and will".[15] Also, he asserts that the "covenant which first justified us, doth continue to justify us . . . ".[16] Christ has purchased the new covenant for us, but it is the covenant itself that justifies us in consequence of its more facile conditions.

Baxter is, then, in accord with the "holy living" Anglicans that faith includes obedience and charity, that the new covenant is more lenient than the old, that Christ's righteousness is the meritorious and not the formal cause of justification, and that antinomianism is to be shunned by an emphasis upon holy living. He agrees as well that justification is the imputing of our faith for righteousness on account of the obedience of Christ which has purchased for us the new covenant. Our own inadequate righteousness (repentance and faith) is made acceptable under the more lenient terms of the new covenant.

The following paragraph (from his reply to Tully's letter) stresses the cogent particulars of Baxter's doctrine of justification.

And that the Law of Grace being that which we are to be judged by, we shall at the last Judgement also be judged (and so justified) thus far by or according to our sincere Love, Obedience, or Evangelical Works, as the Conditions of the Law or Covenant of free Grace, which justifieth and glorifieth freely all that are thus Evangelically qualified, by and for the Merits, perfect Righteousness and Sacrifice of Christ, which procured the Covenant or free Gift of Universal Conditional Justification and Adoption, before and without any Works or Conditions done by Man Whatsoever . . . If this be Justification by Works, I am for it.[17]

First, then, the nature of free justification, for Baxter, consists *only* in the procurement of the new covenant by Christ's sacrifice "before and without any Works or Conditions done by Man Whatsoever". Second, Baxter plainly refuses, despite abundant criticism over a period of twenty-five years, to abandon his fundamental contention that our faith is "imputed" and accepted for righteousness under the more lenient terms of the new covenant on account of the merits of Christ's righteousness. Thirdly, he adheres to the last to an ambiguous (and confusing) use of the term justification which was characteristic of his teaching for some forty years.

Baxter's use of the term justification is, in fact, more perplexing than was that of Thomas Jackson. In the above cited passage Baxter identifies justification with final judgement, but elsewhere he gives it a variety of other meanings. He defines justification in one case as:

1. Sometimes signifieth to be made just and justifiable in judgement; and then it sometimes includeth both the gift of saving faith and repentance, and the gift of pardon, and of right to life everlasting; and sometimes it presupposeth faith and repentance given, and signifieth the annexed gift of pardon and life.

2. Sometimes it signifieth God's justifying us by his sentence in judgement, which containeth both the justifying of our right to impunity and salvation, and the justifying our faith and holiness as sincere, which are the conditions of our righteousness.

3. And sometimes to justify us, is to use us as just men, and as long as we understand the matter thus signified by pardoning and justifying, we must not strive about words so variously used.[18]

This definition is not too helpful because it is obviously in itself ambiguous. Baxter seldom gives any indication which of these definitions is intended in any particular context, and at times he slips almost imperceptibly from one meaning into another. To justify, for Baxter, can mean variously: to forgive initially, to judge in final judgement, to make righteous, to treat as righteous, to give faith and repentance, or any of a number of combinations of the same. He even proposes yet another definition of justification in his defence against objections to the sermon he preached at Pinner's Hall. He was accused of substituting our own righteousness (under a cloak of the "imputation of faith") for the righteousness of Christ as that by which we are justified. Baxter concedes that the righteousness of Christ is that which gave us the new covenant, but he insists, none the less, that we are justified by our faith.

> We must be justified by our faith against the charge of Infidelity, and by our Repentance against the charge of Impenitency, and by our Love, Holiness, Obedience and Sincerity against the charge of . . . being hypocrites . . .[19]

Here, while answering a claim that he makes the imputation of our faith and repentance the formal cause of justification instead of the imputation of Christ's righteousness, he drifts conveniently into quite another understanding of the phrase "to be justified".

Answering a similar complaint of Tully he asserts, "that what I usually call Evangelical Righteousness he [Tully] supposeth me to call Justification".[20] However, this does not really meet Tully's point. Tully's criticism is that Baxter requires good works before justification whereas St Augustine declares that they follow justification. Baxter goes on to say that

> . . . good Works follow the Justified, and go not before his initial Justification: as also in the sense that Austin spoke it, who took Justification for that which we call Sanctification or Conversion.[21]

Twelve pages previous, however, Baxter says that the "performance of the condition is strangely here [by Tully] supposed to follow the Right or Benefit of the Gift or Covenant". In yet another passage, noting that St Augustine does not argue that justification means "make righteous" and, consequently, that works follow justification, he remarks that, "no doubt but as to many texts of Scripture, Austin was mistaken . . .".[22]

After twenty-five years of controversy and some three works on the subject, it is odd that Baxter finds it surprising when Tully argues that the performance of Christianity must follow the gift of the covenant. Disagree though he may, he must have known that many of his critics, and even some whom he cites for support (Downame, Davenant, and Bradshaw) held the same opinion. In his *The Appeal to the Light*, Baxter claims that Mr William Bradshaw had expressed "in what sense Christ's righteousness is and is not imputed to us, just as I mean and to that I stand".[23] Now Bradshaw does deny that imputation means that God considers a sinner to have done and suffered the very acts that Christ did. Such an interpretation of imputation is one that Baxter also consistently denounces as pernicious. However, Bradshaw proceeds to describe the imputation of Christ's righteousness as the formal cause of justification; Baxter, on the other hand, plainly considers it the meritorious cause only, assigning imputation of faith as the formal cause. Bradshaw, furthermore, explicitly says that "Repentance and good works do necessarily follow justification".[24] Bradshaw, then, specifically joins in two of Tully's most telling criticisms. Baxter is less than accurate when he claims that Bradshaw describes the imputation of Christ's righteousness "just as I mean and to that I stand".

Thomas Edwards, among others, sought to demonstrate Baxter's affinity with the Roman Catholic doctrine of justification. Tully went so far as to suggest that Baxter, along with Bull and Bellarmine, were real threats to true Christianity. In reference to Baxter's distinction in the *Aphorisms* between first and second justification, Tully emphatically denies that even *evangelical* works justify for the first justification. Baxter replies, somewhat unjustly, that Bellarmine and other Papists "commonly say, that the first Justification is not of Works, or Works do not first justify us. Have I not now proved that he [Tully] erreth and complyeth with the Papist?"[25]

The "friendly, modest, learned" Christopher Cartwright's objections to Baxter's thesis are entirely divorced from those of Tully, and seem to have been less disturbing to Baxter. Cartwright takes exception to Baxter's description of the reign of law in the Old Testament, and to Baxter's pronouncement that God no longer judges but has given his judgement to Christ. Cartwright does not, however, disagree that the requirements of the new covenant are more lenient, and he is in accord that the imputation of our own faith is that by which we are justified.

Another critic of Baxter, George Lawson, stresses the distinction between the imputation of Christ's righteousness and the imputation of our own faith as being the formal cause of justification. Lawson argues that good works are the fruit of faith, and are not, therefore, included in faith. He alleges, indeed, that those who conceive good works as a *means* to the forgiveness and rewards of the Gospel

> . . . must contradict the Doctrine of St Paul, agree with the Papists in their Doctrine of Justification by Works, for the main, use the same arguments to maintain it, and give the same Answers to Objections against it, which they do; though, in some Terms and Circumstances, they may differ.[26]

Lawson concedes that Christ's righteousness is imputed only to penitent and believing sinners, but he nevertheless clearly denies that faith and repentance constitute the righteousness by which we are justified. Though he acclaims Lawson to be the ablest of his critics, Baxter nowhere disposes of this penetrating objection.

A TENTATIVE EXPLANATION OF
THE AMBIGUITY IN BAXTER'S POSITION

Baxter was criticized for his soteriology by at least sixteen other theologians and divines, and he produced six works devoted to the subject over a period of forty years. He never, however, really came to grips with the criticism of his interpretation of the formal cause of justification. He frequently cited for support Bradshaw, Davenant, Downame, and Ussher, who held, in fact, a view diametrically opposite to his. How did Richard Baxter manage to write so much about justification over such a long period of time and end up nevertheless with such an ambiguous doctrine? Baxter began his work on justification, as we have seen, to counteract antinomianism in the Army. The doctrine which most perniciously manifested such libertine tendencies to Baxter was the doctrine of the imputation of Christ's righteousness. Throughout his career he therefore sought to deny: that we are reputed personally to have suffered on the cross and to have satisfied God's justice for our own sins; that Christ had repented and believed for us; and that our faith and repentance are no more to be questioned than is Christ himself. Baxter understood such teachings to be the essence of the doctrine of the imputation of Christ's righteousness (as it was preached, for example, by such divines as Saltmarsh and Crisp). In his very first work (written without the benefit of libraries or other pertinent reading) Baxter affirms that justifying faith must include sincere Christian obedience. He was promptly accused of Pelagianism, and to defend himself against this grave charge he is subsequently diligent to make plain that the righteousness of faith, which is ours and which is "imputed for righteousness", is accomplished only by God's grace.

Taylor, Hammond, and Thorndike had said much the same thing, but Baxter comes perilously close to carrying the point into a further and dangerous area. He concedes that St Augustine had required righteousness only *after* justification, and in trying to reconcile this limitation with his own volition he suggests that St Augustine actually meant sanctification. This argument contains certain ominous implications. If we are justified only by a righteousness of our own (made acceptable on account of Christ's sacrifice), and if our own righteousness is in fact directly given to us by God, as Baxter seems to say, then it is difficult to distinguish Baxter's position from that of the Council of Trent.

Baxter was frequently accused of advocating a "Papal" doctrine of justification. And indeed, if he means to deny the imputation of Christ's righteousness as the formal cause of justification, and if he seeks to avoid Pelagianism by arguing that the righteousness by which we are justified is given or infused by grace, and if he then goes a step further and suggests that this given, or infused, grace is actually sanctification (in order to reconcile himself with Augustine): then it would create a situation in which there might be, under the circumstances, a premium upon confusion.

JOHN GOODWIN
1594?-1665

Baxter specifically commends for its discussion of justification a work of John Goodwin, entitled *Imputatio Fidei*.[27] Goodwin concurs with Baxter that our faith is that righteousness which is imputed for our justification, and he rejects the view that we are justified by Christ's righteousness imputed to us (on the grounds that, since Christ fulfilled the law, the imputation of his righteousness would make our justification to be by works of the law). He objects also that by such a doctrine "the Antinomian Sect among us, will be able to justify their non-necessitie of personall sanctification or inherent holynesse . . .".[28] He expressly challenges Bishops Davenant and Downame with respect to the imputation of Christ's righteousness. He assumes that formal righteousness and the formal cause of justification are one and the same.[29] Hence, he cannot accept that we are formally righteous by imputation of Christ's righteousness or by the infusion of inherent righteousness. His rebuke of Davenant, though amusing, is not wholly accurate. Goodwin asserts that

> . . . if the judgement of the late Bishop of Sarisburie (a learned man, doubtless, though a Bishop) be of any authoritie, he is absolutely declared against the imputation of Christ's righteousness and pleads for the righteousness itselfe imputed as the formal cause of Justification.[30]

Possibly he is referring here to Davenant's refusal to make the formal cause of justification be an effect of the imputation of Christ's righteousness. Davenant's essential position is unequivocally that which Goodwin is criticizing.

There is no necessity for the imputation of Christ's righteousness, according to Goodwin, because sinners are fully and absolutely made righteous before God by the act of having their sins pardoned. There can be no middle ground between perfect absolution and freedom from all sin because the only thing that can diminish or qualify perfect righteousness is sin. Thus, a man who "is perfectly freed from all sinne whatsoever, must of necessitie be compleately and perfectly righteous with all".[31] The effect of Christ's righteousness is that forgiveness will be granted upon the condition of faith. Justification cannot take place without perfect righteousness but this is achieved simply by the remission of sin. Goodwin does not agree that the only perfect righteousness is the righteousness of Christ.

> We have heretofore shewed that there is a righteousness in the Law, as absolute and complete, as the righteousness of Christ it selfe . . . that perfect righteousnesse wherein Justification consists, and wherewith men are made formally righteous when they are justified, is nothing else but the remission of sinnes . . .[32]

GEORGE WALKER
1581?-1651

Goodwin himself found a critic in George Walker, author of *A Defence of the True Sense and Meaning of the words of the holy Apostle: Rom. 4. ver. 3.5.9*. Walker asserts that it is the heresy of Socinus and the Arminians to corrupt the words of St Paul in the way that Goodwin has done. He accuses Goodwin of defining faith as assent to the proposition that Christ has so merited favour with God that God will now accept and account this faith to be the righteousness of justification. Walker's criticism is that to assign Christ's righteousness as *only* the meritorious cause excludes any provision for his righteousness to be communicated to us. Faith is imputed for righteousness only as it apprehends its object, Christ. Walker argues that

> . . . faith seeketh that righteousness which makes him righteous by the communion of it, when in himself by nature he is ungodly, his faith comprehending in it Christ, and his righteousness, is counted for righteousness because it settles him in the state of a righteous man; and God's setting on his skore Christ's satisfaction and righteousness, doth accept him for a man justified.[33]

Since Goodwin considers faith to be a part of our conformity and obedience to the law, Walker alleges that he is thereby teaching justification by works. He says flatly that Goodwin is heretical and his doctrine "more impious than the Pelagian and Popish Heresies concerning justification".[34] Walker also argues that to deny that God can justify us by the righteousness of Christ is to deny the union of the faithful in Christ, "for if he be one with us, and we with him, then are our sinnes made his, and in him satisfied, and his righteousness made ours and we are Justified by it, as it is ours . . .".[35] Goodwin and his followers have been, he says, less than Christian in their conduct of the controversy: "As for his rude, impudent, and unmannerly followers, their owne lying and slanderous tongues, proclaime their pedigree from the Father of liers."[36] He utterly rejects a rumour

> . . . that Mr Goodwin did confute and confound me of late . . . by the powers of his Arguments, that first he made me rage through anger and fury, and after made both my Brother and me, to yeeld, and to confesse our former *ignorance* and *errors*, and to embrace him as one sent from God to turne us from *darknesse* to *light* . . . From such Spirits, the God of Truth, defend his Church and People.[37]

WILLIAM EYRE

Another critic of Baxter was William Eyre, who preached against Baxter's doctrine of justification. Mr Benjamin Woodbridge (the first graduate of Harvard College) published a sermon attacking Eyre, which was, in turn, commended by Baxter. Eyre replied to Woodbridge's sermon in his *Vindiciae Justificationis Gratuitae*:

> Justification without conditions; or The Free Justification of a Sinner, Explained, Confirmed, and Vindicated, from the Exceptions, Objections, and seeming Absurdities, which are cast upon it by the Assertors of Conditional Justification: More especially from the Attempts of Mr B. Woodbridge in his sermon, Entitled Justification by Faith and of Mr Cranford in his Epistle to the Reader, and of Mr Baxter in some Passage, which relates to the same Matter. Wherein, also, the Absoluteness of the New Covenant is proved, and the Arguments of it are disproved.

Eyre's tract has a preface by John Owen in which he asserts that Baxter "makes Works, by virtue of God's Promise and Covenant, to be meritorious causes of Justification and Salvation, and in no other sense doe the Papists affirm it".[38] Owen says, however, that he consented to write the preface because of the importance of the issue, and not because he wholly approves Eyre's position. Eyre's approach derives basically from the doctrine of predestination. Since God determined to justify certain men before creation they have been, in fact, justified before they acquire Faith. Hence, it is impossible to be justified by the imputation of faith, as Baxter teaches, because justification was decided by God before we believed, before we even existed. He defends his argument analogically by observing that

> . . . as the Righteousness of Christ was actually imputed to the Patriarchs before it was wrought; and our sins were actually imputed to Christ before they were committed; so I see no inconvenience to say, That Christ's Righteousness is by God imputed to the Elect, before they have a Being.[39]

JOHN GRAILE
JOHN EEDES
1609?–1667?

Eyre's doctrine was criticized by John Graile in *A Modest Vindication of the Doctrine of Conditions in the Covenant of Grace and the defenders thereof, from the Aspersions of Arminianism and Popery, which Mr W. E. cast on them.* Graile insists that it is not any sinner but only a believing sinner who is the subject of justification. Another more extensive work directed against Eyre (and including objections to Baxter) is John Eedes' *The Orthodox Doctrine concerning Justification Asserted and Vindicated Wherein the book of Mr Wm. Eyre . . . is examined and also the Doctrine of Mr Baxter concerning Justification is discussed.* Eedes maintains in his preface that the

> . . . doctrine concerning the Justification hath been soundly taught by the Protestants; and the Papists, Arminians, and now those that cry up free Grace, have opposed that truth, and while Mr Baxter doth

oppose these Antinomians, as they are called, he falls himself into another error that may prove of dangerous consequence.

Protestants consistently have affirmed that faith justifies instrumentally and relatively, but, according to Eedes, Mr Eyre, Dr Hammond, and Mr Baxter have rejected that tradition. Eedes grants that before the world was made God intended to justify men, but he denies against Eyre that such intention is itself justification. We are not justified before or without faith. It is not bestowed on us until we believe. Faith and repentance are conditions of justification required by the Gospel, but they are not to be confused with our evangelical righteousness "nor are we justified by works that are from obedience of faith".[40] Eedes concedes that faith is a condition required on our part, but it does not, he says, justify "by its owne merit, worth or dignity, as a work, or quality in us, but in as much as it receives Christ . . .".[41]

Eedes rejects Baxter's doctrine on the grounds that it counts our repentance and faith as the righteousness by which we are justified. "It is . . . agreeable neither with truth nor with the humilitie required of us to call our faith and repentance, our righteousness, to be justified by it."[42] He accuses Baxter of evading the issue when he draws a distinction between co-ordinate and subordinate righteousness. Another evasion, Eedes says, is contained in Baxter's assertion that Paul does not exclude from justification works of faith which are from grace. Baxter's position is untenable in any event, Eedes concludes, because good works cannot be required as a condition of justification—"they are not required of us that we may be justified, but that being justified we may glorifie our heavenly Father . . .".[43]

THE ANTINOMIANS

Baxter undertook his work on justification primarily to refute the antinomians. Eedes complained that Baxter fell into other errors in his effort to avoid the antinomian errors. The "holy living" Caroline divines considered the antinomians to be a real and present danger to society and a threat to Christianity itself. Who were the antinomians, and what did they teach concerning justification? John Eaton was denominated "father of Antinomianism in this diocese" by Bishop Joseph Hall.[44] In his book, *The Honey-Combe of Free Justification,* Eaton sets it forth that the justified are perfect and sinless in God's sight. When a sinner is accepted by Christ, and covered by Christ's righteousness, God no longer sees him as he was (and as he still is, in part). He states that in Romans 7.24 St Paul is not describing the

> state he and the justified children of God doe stand in the sight of God, but what he and all the true children of God by the imperfection of their sanctification doe feele in themselves . . .[45]

Eaton is acutely conscious of the imperfection of man's righteousness, yet for him the new covenant is not a more lenient one, as it is for Baxter and so many others. Because of Eaton's emphasis upon the absolute nature of God's demand, and the imperfect nature of righteousness in the regenerate, he is particularly occupied to proclaim the free acceptance of sinners in justification. All men, even the justified, are assuredly in a state of wretchedness compared with that perfection demanded by the spiritual law of God. Thus, any man can live before the eyes of God only provided that through faith he is covered by the righteousness of Christ, a righteousness found only *in* Christ. Justification, he fancies, is like a beam of sunlight shining into dark hearts and reflecting there the image of God, mirroring, as it were, some light of sanctification.[46] Eaton argues that it is futile to exhort works of righteousness and obedience except they be first grounded in justification. Works of sanctification are the fruits of justification. Justification is like fire of which sanctification is the heat:

> So that take a kettle of cold water which we would have to be hot, it would be a foolish part to set it beside the fire and then charge it to be hot, and to threaten it that else it shall be spilt; but put fire under it, then will it begin to be warme; but if it grow not hot enough, put more fire under; and if there lie a green stick or block that keepeth away the heat, yet put more fire, and then it will burne up the block and make the water thoroughly hot. So our soul is this block, our affections are like to water, as cold to God as may be: but if we call

unto people for Sanctification, zeale and works, the fruits of the same, only with legal terrours, not putting under the fire of justification, we shall either but little move them, or else, with a constrained sanctity, make them worse hypocrites, twofold more the children of hell than they were before (Matt. 23.15).[47]

Another minister often accused of antinomianism was John Saltmarsh, author of *Free Grace or the Flowings of Christ's Blood Freely to Sinners*. "Being A Display of the Power of Jesus Christ on the Soul of one who had been in the Bondage of a troubled Conscience upwards of 12 years . . .". Saltmarsh differs from Baxter and the "holy living" Carolines on the nature of the new covenant. The distinction between the new and the old covenants, for Saltmarsh, is that man "was to have his life upon performing certain conditions"[48] in the old, but in the new he is perfectly free. In the new covenant "God is our God of Free Grace and righteousness on his part, not for any conditional righteousness on ours . . .".[49] The new covenant is properly not with us but with Christ. Christ stood for us and fulfilled all the necessary conditions, and it is only a covenant with us in the sense that we are with Christ. Those who presume that they can fulfil certain conditions for the covenant merely seek to bargain with God, falsely supposing that they can thereby satisfy the price required by God. They fail to give due glory to God because they are preoccupied with the notion that they must first perform some conditions within themselves. The law commands men "to obey, to love, to be holy, that God may be their God, and they his people; the gospel commands us to obey, and love, because we are the people of such a God".[50] The law continues to command these things of the justified in the new covenant, and it can still point out the sins of the justified, but it "cannot tax him with damnation".[51]

Saltmarsh acknowledges freely that a converted person may fall back into sin, but he denies that by such a fall the sinner may be excluded from the covenant. He also insists that the fact that the justified slip back into sin is no reason to question the validity of justification. Spiritual assurances of forgiveness, he asserts, and of God's love are acquired more by way of the Gospel news than by any works originating from justification. Thus, no one should despair of God's forgiveness and love because he has fallen back into sin. Saltmarsh is conscious that his doctrine of free forgiveness might lead others to sin more freely.

> If any man sin more freely because of forgiveness of sins, that man may suspect himself to be forgiven; for in all Scripture and Scripture-examples, the more forgiveness the more holiness. Mary loved much, because much was forgiven to her . . .[52]

Saltmarsh stoutly maintains that no sin by us can alter the love of God, but nevertheless urges that the faithful be penitent and aggrieved for any sin he may commit because it

> . . . grieves the Spirit of his God, and though he knows sin cannot alter the love of God, yet, because it hides it, he hates it; in this sense it separates not eternally but from the temporal communion with God, "grieving the Holy Spirit of God".[53]

Perhaps the most famous (or notorious) "antinomian" was Tobias Crisp. The publication, in 1690, of the second edition of Crisp's work, *Christ Alone Exalted*, stirred the aged Baxter to write his final diatribe against antinomianism. Crisp is in accord with Saltmarsh that to require conditions of justification is "but to receive Christ as upon bargain and sale".[54] Crisp denies utterly that our obedience and good works are the way to heaven. They are, he says, neither causes of salvation nor the way of salvation. Sanctification is indeed an inseparable companion of justification, but sanctification is not the way to salvation: Christ is the way. Sanctification, for Crisp, is the business we have to do on the way, *in* Christ.[55] Like Eyre, Crisp is persuaded that a person is justified before he has faith. Faith is not a condition of the covenant. No one, to be sure, will be saved without faith, but first comes justification, *then* faith in that justification.[56] Unlike Eyre, however, Crisp does not go so far as to assume that we are justified before we believe on account of the doctrine of predestination. Rather, Crisp is concerned to avoid any notion that faith as a condition of justification might somehow be construed as a work. The theme throughout Crisp's work is contained in its title, "Christ Alone Exalted". He avoids scrupulously any pretension that *our* faith might be a condition of

God's action. He is led to concur that we are justified before we believe, because he wishes to avoid any boasting on our part that we attained our justification by our own faith. It is understandable that some of the examples used in Crisp's sermons did arouse criticism. For example:

> But let me tell you, Christ is a free way for a drunkard, for a whoremaster, for a harlot, an enymy to Christ; I say, Christ is as free a way for such a person to enter into him, as for the most godly person in the world. But do not mistake me; I do not say, Christ is a free way to walk in him, and yet to continue in such a condition; for Christ will never leave a person in such a filthiness to whom he hath given to enter into himself: mark well what I say; but for entrance into him, Christ is as free a way for the vilest sort of sinners, as for any person under heaven.[57]

Crisp defends himself against charges of antinomianism by alleging that there is no effective way to get people to forsake their sins except to tell them that they are already forgiven and that forgiveness was bought at a terrible price. We must be holy and righteous in order to "glorify God in our bodies and in our spirits for they are God's".[58] He rejects works only as they are required *before* justification or *for* heaven. Christ *alone* must be exalted.

In theological content there is little of substance in the published works of Eaton, Saltmarsh, and Crisp that is not also found in the works of Davenant, in the sermons of Donne, and in the prayers of Taylor. There is a certain poor taste manifest in Crisp's examples, there may well have been even more rash statements from the pulpit which he eliminated or qualified when submitting to the printer. On the basis of theological content, however, such as was printed, the "antinomians" do not seem to have been especially shocking, and it is difficult to see why they aroused so much concern among so many divines during the century, and later.

THOMAS GATAKER
1574-1654

A principal critic of antinomianism, in general, and of Saltmarsh, in particular, was Thomas Gataker. In 1652 Gataker published

Antinomianism Discovered and Confuted and Free-Grace . . . shewed to be other then is by the Antinomian Party in these times maintained. He is most concerned to refute the contention "that God doth not, will not, cannot, in these times see any sin, in any of his justified children".[59] Saltmarsh specifies that the promises of the Gospel belong to sinners *as* sinners and not as repenting or humbled sinners. Gataker retorts that Christ came to call sinners to repentance and unless they do repent they shall perish. He suggests that "Mr Eaton's spirit seems to be in this man revived".[60] Gataker refers to a certain divine who told a woman to reason thus: God will save sinners, I am a sinner: therefore God will save me. Gataker suggests that the woman might equally well reason thus: God will damn sinners; I am a sinner: therefore God will damn me.

Another work by Gataker, discussing justification more fully, was published in 1670 by his son Charles, under the title *An Antidote Against Errour concerning the True Notion of Justification.* Here, Gataker's argument resembles that of the "imputation" Carolines. He considers that there is an actual change in justification, but he denies the Tridentine doctrine that such "infused" grace is the formal cause of justification. Nor does justification as defined by St Paul mean "to make righteous". We are never so inherently righteous in this life that "it can be more then du debt, we ow . . . to God".[61] However, Gataker condemns the Socinian error in regard to justification as being worse than that of Rome. The Socinians, he asserts, do not appreciate the actual satisfaction made by Christ, and therefore consider our imperfect endeavours to be an acceptable righteousness for justification.

Gataker is equally critical of those who conceive justification to be simply the remission of sins. He argues that, contrary to what many others have claimed, Calvin did not say that justification is merely the remission of sins. Even Bellarmine, he notes, acknowledged that Calvin found there was a real satisfaction by Christ's righteousness in the remission of sin different from the mere "condonation" that Socinus taught.[62] Gataker declares that

> . . . much time and pains ar spent and wasted on either part, by them on the one side, in contending against such an *imputation of*

Christ's righteousness, as none of ours ever dreamed of; and by manie of ours on the other side, in confuting what they deliver of *justification*, when as by that term they mean no justification, strictlie so termed, but *Sanctification* improperlie by them so stiled, and so the Air onelie is to no purpose between them both beaten, while the one either will not see or marks not what the other means.[63]

Gataker resolves the issues posed by Christian soteriology by arguing that every Christian has a twofold righteousness. There is, first of all, righteousness that cleanses from the *guilt* of sin. This is the righteousness of justification, which is perfect and equally shared by all Christians. The other righteousness cleanses from the *filth* of sin. This is the righteousness of sanctification, which is never perfect in this life and is unequally shared by Christians. Gataker (like Davenant) is not disposed to assign inherent righteousness as the formal cause of justification; he denies (like Downame) that justification is the mere remission of sins; he is (like Baxter) a vehement critic of the antinomians; and yet, despite all this, he strenuously takes exception to Baxter's doctrine that our own works of faith and repentance are acceptable as the righteousness of justification.

JOHN OWEN
1616-83

One of the more influential non-Anglican divines of the Caroline period was John Owen. In 1677 he published *The Doctrine of Justification by Faith*, "through the imputation of the righteousness of Christ, explained, confirmed, and vindicated". As was noted, Owen wrote the preface for Eyre's work attacking Baxter. He did not, however, hold the same understanding of election and predestination as did Eyre. Owen denies that justification precedes faith, or that our justification is simply the apprehension of the purpose or decree of our election.[64] We are justified only, he argues, *after* we receive Christ by faith. On the issue of justification Owen belongs to the same school as Hooker, Andrewes, and Davenant. Justification is the gracious and free act of God imputing the righteousness of Christ to a believing sinner. He considers, in other words, that the formal cause of justification is the imputation of Christ's righteousness.

> This position . . . is that [which] the learned Davenant laid down [and] . . . is the shield of truth in the whole cause of Justification, which whilst it is preserved safe, we need not trouble ourselves about differences that are among learned men . . .[65]

Following Davenant and his predecessors, Owen is severely critical of the Tridentine doctrine that the formal cause of justification is the infusion of inherent righteousness. This doctrine is a fiction, he says, because "then a man is judged righteous, who indeed is not so. For he who is not perfectly righteous, cannot be righteous in the sight of God unto justification."[66]

Owen is adamant that the imputation doctrine is no judging or accounting righteous of a man who is not, in fact, truly and really so. A sinner in justification becomes truly righteous as he becomes a member of Christ whose righteousness is thereupon imputed to him in such union. A justified person is truly righteous, then, because he is *in Christ*. Owen places more explicit emphasis on this union with Christ than even Downame does, and perhaps more than anyone of the period with the exception of John Donne.

> The foundation of the imputation . . . is union . . . This by the Holy Spirit inhabiting in him as the head of the church in all fullness and in all believers according to their measure, whereby they became members of his mystical body.[67]

Such a description of justification as a union with Christ implies a continuing imputation which is itself the basis of forgiveness of sins committed after the act of justification. Union with Christ is the basis of Owen's argument that by the imputation of Christ's righteousness a sinner is actually and truly righteous, not by any infusion of righteousness adequate to satisfy God's justice, but by very membership in Christ whose righteousness manifestly does satisfy God's justice.

Like the classical Anglicans, however, Owen does argue that there is an actual infusion of inherent righteousness in justification. Bellarmine is wrong, he states, to assert that no Protestant writers acknowledge an inherent righteousness except Bucer and Chemnitius. In fact "there is no one of them, by whom either the thing itself, or the necessity of it is denied".[68] Inherent righteousness, however, cannot be that by which we are justified. Nor can it be considered to precede justification.

Owen disagrees also with those who distinguish a first and second justification, attempting thereby to reconcile St James and St Paul. Owen reconciles the two Apostles by basing his exegesis on the teaching of St Paul. His rule, indeed, for interpreting Scripture where it appears to contradict itself is that

> . . . if some, or any of them do treat directly, designedly, and largely about the matter . . . and others . . . only . . . occasionally, transiently, in order unto other ends, the truth is to be learned, stated, and fixed from the former places.[69]

The doctrine of justification, then, must be approached from the views expressed by St Paul. According to Owen, the two Apostles do not have the same design or end. They mean the same thing by works but they do not speak of the same faith or of justification in the same sense. St James is speaking of a false faith; St Paul is speaking of a true (justifying) faith. St James discusses justification only as to evidence, signs, and manifestations of it; St Paul describes the very nature and causes of our justification before God. Hence, we are indeed justified by grace alone without works, but works are an inseparable manifestation of our justification. "For James only declares that by the works which he performed after he was justified, he was manifested and declared so to be".[70]

The non-episcopal divines discussed in this chapter are only a few among some thirty who wrote about justification and sanctification after the opening of the Long Parliament. The two doctrines became an issue which divided Puritans and Presbyterians, Anabaptists and Independents. It is upon the issue of formal cause that we discern most clearly the differing understandings of justification. Baxter, Goodwin, and Woodbridge argue that the formal cause of justification is the imputing of faith for righteousness (on account of the merits of Christ). This is also, in essence, the view of the "holy living" Carolines, whose doctrine significantly resembles that of

Baxter. On the other hand, Owen, Eedes, Gataker, and Walker concur with the classical (early Caroline) Anglicans that the very imputation of Christ's righteousness is the formal cause, and their doctrine of justification, accordingly, is remarkably reminiscent of Hooker, Andrewes, Downame, Davenant, Donne, Ussher, and Hall.

9

Summary

The seventeenth century began, as we have seen, with an understanding of the Gospel according to which Anglican divines (such as Hooker) discerned as the crucial problem of Christian soteriology the question: What is the formal cause of justification? These divines agreed that in justification a change is effected in the regenerate person and his inherent righteousness is established. They were, however, equally agreed that assigning inherent righteousness as the formal cause of justification was a profound error on the part of the Council of Trent which inevitably introduced other grave distortions of the Christian Gospel.

About the time of the Civil War, English Christianity was exposed to another doctrine of justification, equally incompatible with the doctrine of Trent, and also a radical departure from the earlier Anglican position.

The only theological unanimity detectable in this period (embracing Roman Catholics, Anglicans, and Protestants) is a universal assumption that the formal cause of justification is the key to the problem of soteriology. Disagreement about the nature of that formal cause abounded, but, with rare exceptions, all were agreed that therein lay the crucial issue. Whether it be "infusion of inherent righteousness", "imputation of Christ's righteousness", "imputation of faith", or some combination of the same, the formal cause invariably appears as the crux of each system, statement, or controversy concerned with soteriology. The very definition of formal cause—"that which makes a thing what it is"—assures, of course, that it will be (must be) the crux of the issue.

Is the formal cause, however, really in fact what is crucial in the development of soteriology? Anglicans did indeed differ among themselves as to precisely what is the formal cause, but it is significant that the groupings, or schools of thought, into which they divided themselves, were groupings most clearly distinguished by what each concluded the formal cause to be. Anglicans primarily concerned with the gratuitous nature of grace agreed that the formal cause of justification is the imputation of Christ's righteousness. Those whose primary emphasis is placed on holy living and a fear of antinomian inference from the Gospel proclaimed the imputation of faith to be the formal cause. The most coherent understanding of the doctrine as set forth by the "non-episcopal" divines was directly drawn from discussion of the nature of the formal cause. The two notable attempts at synthesis of conflicting doctrines were focused upon the problem of the formal cause: Jackson's solution was simply to deny its existence; Forbes attempted the other way out of the dilemma and postulated a twofold formal cause.

Jackson, as has been demonstrated, actually did assume a formal cause (the imputation of Christ's righteousness) and his soteriology does not, in point of fact, differ from that of the classical Anglicans. When he denied the existence of a formal cause, he was equating the term "to be righteous" with the term "to be justified". (In that sense, when he denied a formal cause of justification he was really denying the existence of justification itself.) Forbes' twofold formal cause is an attempt at a soteriology that would combine the doctrine of the Council of Trent with that of Taylor, Jackson, and Hammond. It is also intersting to note that John Owen's adherence to the imputation of Christ's righteousness as formal cause leads him to describe justification in a way that differs very little from the classical Anglican doctrines (which also assumed the same formal cause).

On the other hand, Richard Baxter was in accord with the "holy living" divines that the imputation of faith is the formal cause, and this accord finds a parallel in other points of agreement he had with Taylor, Hammond (in their public works), Thorndike, and Bull despite radical differences he had with them on many other issues of Christian doctrine and polity.

The doctrine of imputation of faith for righteousness as argued by the above-named four, and as enunciated by Baxter in his *Aphorisms*, generated a major controversy among non-episcopal divines of the Caroline period. Baxter's statement was challenged by at least eight ministers, and the consequent confusion found Independent and Presbyterian divines on both sides of the argument. Some thirty writers were eventually drawn into the dispute. Much of the argument was concerned with attempts to clarify the relationship of the doctrine of predestination to the doctrine of justification, but the major issue, once again, was over the formal cause of justification. Owen, Graile, Thomas Gataker, Jessop, Eedes, Lawson, and Walker insisted that the formal cause is the imputation of Christ's righteousness. Baxter, Cartwright, Goodwin, Wooton, and Woodbridge insisted just as firmly that it is rather the imputation of faith for righteousness. Thomas Tully, Principal of St Edmund Hall, also stressed the centrality of the issue of formal cause in his argument denouncing Bull, Baxter, and Bellarmine as the real enemies of Christianity. All three differed from Tully radically on the question of formal cause. Tully might have included Robert Barclay, the Quaker, who would have fitted in not only alliteratively, but was also yet another who denied Tully's doctrine of the formal cause of justification. Barclay, agreeing with Bellarmine, held the formal cause to be the infusion of inherent righteousness,[1] whereas Baxter and Bull considered it to be the imputation of our faith. It may be that this apparent relationship between the formal cause of justification and one or another particular school of soteriology was coincidental or causal, or it may be that the different understandings of soteriology were symptoms or results of the various doctrines of formal cause. In either case, it remains an historical fact that during the seventeenth century divines on all sides of theological controversies considered formal cause to be the crux of the soteriological problem. It is certainly significant that agreement on any one doctrine of the formal cause invariably was accompanied by agreement on many other issues of soteriology.

THE SUBSTANCE OF
ANGLICAN CRITICISM OF
THE COUNCIL OF TRENT

No matter what their internal differences the Caroline theologians were virtually unanimous in criticism of the Tridentine doctrine of infusion of inherent righteousness as the formal cause of justification. There were six basic objections to the doctrine of Trent.

First, the Anglicans argued that any inherent righteousness infused into the regenerate is less than the righteousness God demands of us or intends for us. Inherent righteousness, furthermore, is acceptable only on account of God's mercy in Christ and never on the basis of his justice alone. The forgiveness of justification is granted by, and on account of, Christ's atonement. The gratuitous nature of forgiveness precludes, for the Anglicans, any association of it with inherent righteousness, which they considered only begun in justification and to be continued in the process of sanctification.

Second, if the formal cause of justification were to be inherent righteousness infused into the regenerate at justification, then there would be no point in the regenerate praying "forgive us our trespasses . . .". Such a doctrine would also preclude the "eternal priesthood" of our Lord and the necessity of his continued mediation.

Third, such a doctrine would place the concept of a "state of grace" on the basis of the righteousness of the regenerate rather than on the righteousness of Christ where it belongs. If our inherent righteousness were to be considered the very *form* of justification, the resultant "state of grace" would be no more or other than what the Anglicans regarded as the grossly inadequate righteousness of the justified.

Fourth, the Anglicans complained that if inherent righteousness infused into the regenerate were to be considered perfect, or nearly perfect, this would breed presumption in the regenerate. If a regenerate person, in other words, were to consider himself acceptable and forgiven because of sufficient righteousness infused into him and by which God's demands have already been met, then he would no longer need humbly to beg mercy.

Fifth, if, on the other hand, inherent righteousness were considered to be only the minimum that God will accept, then any growth in righteousness, any righteousness over and above the righteousness infused in justification, would appear to be *more* than what God requires as acceptable righteousness. Thus, what Hooker, Donne, and Hall called the "pernicious" doctrine of works of supererogation becomes a logical and ineluctible consequence of the inherent righteousness doctrine.

Sixth and finally, although the "infusionists" firmly asserted that any description of the cause by which one is justified that does not provide for actual infusion of inherent righteousness is merely a "legal fiction", they did not themselves altogether escape the same problem. It was argued that for God to justify the ungodly, for him to pronounce as righteous those not actually righteous, was in fact, to base the doctrine of justification upon a lie. The Anglicans retorted that acknowledgment of flaws or imperfection (or even venial "concupiscence") in the regenerate necessarily includes even those who advocate the "infusion" doctrine; they, also, are embraced by the "lie" that God has justified anything less than what is righteous. To avoid such an absurdity the only alternative would seem to be either to adulterate the quality of God's righteousness or to be dishonest and hypocritical about sin in the regenerate. Thus argued the Anglicans. It was this very dilemma, of course, which led the Council of Trent to visit anathema upon any who profess that concupiscence in the regencrate has the formal nature of sin and to assert that God hates nothing in the regenerate.

This question—whether there be any sin in the regenerate—was so closely associated with justification and the issue of formal cause that it became an integral part of the controversy over Christian soteriology. For many Anglicans the question of sin in the regenerate was the test of the dispute. If there be no sin in the regenerate, then they were prepared to grant that infusion of inherent righteousness is the formal cause of justification. But they found it so evident that the regenerate indeed do sin that they felt compelled to conclude that inherent righteousness cannot be the formal cause of justification.

There was a vast disagreement about the proper exegesis of Romans 7.19-25. Most Anglicans considered it a description of St Paul *even* in his regenerate state, or, if not that, it was at the least theologically a description of a regenerate person *after* justification. Those others who conceived the infusion of inherent righteousness to be the formal cause of justification were compelled to deny that this passage from Romans could be a description of a justified person. The later "holy living" divines were similarly inclined, but they were less consistent about it than was the Council of Trent. It is significant that Bellarmine and Bull and Davenant, representatives of the three important doctrines of justification, were agreed on one thing, that the doctrine of justification depended upon how sin in the regenerate was understood. If Romans 7 is a description of the regenerate, Bull acknowledged that his doctrine was thereby false, and Bellarmine conceded, on the same basis, that his doctrine of inherent righteousness would be rendered untenable.[2] Davenant, on the other hand, allowed that if there is no sin in the regenerate, then the infusion of inherent righteousness must be the formal cause of justification. Thus, the question of sin in the regenerate was regarded on all sides as the supreme test of validity for the doctrine of justification, and the controversy over exegesis of Romans 7 is a notable indication of the central emphasis assigned by all to a satisfactory definition of the formal cause of justification.

The formal cause of justification was considered, by most of the Anglicans, to be the imputation of Christ's righteousness. Archbishop Ussher; Bishops Andrewes, Davenant, Downame, Hall, Sanderson, Barlow, Nicholson, Beveridge; Richard Hooker, John Donne, Isaac Barrow, and Thomas Tully—all rejected the Tridentine doctrine of inherent righteousness, and all embraced the imputation of Christ's righteousness as the formal cause of justification. Despite Jackson's explicit denial that there is such a formal cause, he actually entertained, as we have seen, the essential doctrine of the classical Anglicans.

THE DOCTRINE OF
"THE LOWERED MARKET"

Jeremy Taylor's doctrine must be described as exceptional. His theological works, sermons, and *public* devotional writings consistently reflect a doctrine of justification by imputation of faith, which Taylor defines in such a way as to include repentance, amendment of life, and sincere endeavours. We are justified, according to Taylor (in his public works), by God's acceptance of our inadequate strivings and sincere endeavours on account of the more lenient terms of the new covenant purchased for us by Christ. Taylor cautioned that much of what was said or written about justification included inferences that tended to discourage serious concern for Christian ethics and casuistry. It was this threat to "holy living" which motivated him to undertake his work on repentance. He sought, in other words, to rectify a doctrine which might undermine holy living, before he launched his major work on ethics.

Much of Taylor's public theology—especially that which focuses discussion on soteriology—is contradicted by the theology of his (private) prayers. In the prayers it is not our "sincere endeavours" that render us righteous; the grounds of petition are, on the contrary, Christ's righteousness *alone*. Sinlessness is the ground and prerequisite for forgiveness and justification in his public works, but in his prayers sinlessness is precisely what we are incapable of except by God's merciful forgiveness and justification through Christ. In the pulpit, justification is said to be by repentance and holy living; in the attitude of prayer, it is said that justification is by Christ's gratuitous and merciful forgiveness of sinners. In his public theology Romans 7.19-25 is not (cannot be) a description of a regenerate person; in a litany to be recited prior to Holy Communion the very words of Romans 7.19-25 are used as a description of the regenerate. In certain sermons Taylor contests the validity of death-bed confessions on the grounds that God does not forgive without repentance, which specifically includes turning from all unrighteousness and performing those acts of obedience which are necessary for forgiveness; there are, none the less, certain prayers of Taylor composed especially for such occasions, which invoke God's mercy, his gratuitous grace and forgiveness, and (significantly) the example of the thief on the cross. Taylor's theological description of the worthy communicant excludes all who are not confident of their own righteousness; his prayers for communicants explicitly proclaim deliberate and/or unconscious unworthiness. Taylor, in short, did not practise in prayer what he preached from the pulpit (or published for the edification of the public).

Apparently Taylor fundamentally believed what he said in his prayers, but his profound concern lest antinomianism be encouraged by preaching and teaching gratuitous forgiveness led him publicly to exhort holy living as the only hope for justification. His publicly stated conditions *for* justification become, in the prayers, consequences *of* the grace of justification. Taylor's teaching that sinlessness is a condition of entrance into the covenant of grace involved him in a doctrine which Bishops Warner, Sanderson, and Barlow (as well as Herbert Thorndike) condemned as Pelagian. There is, however, no suggestion whatever of Pelagianism in Taylor's prayers, which repeatedly make clear that no righteousness is possible for man without God's grace. If we assume that Taylor is fundamentally to be judged by his prayers, then we may place him within the classical Anglican tradition.

Dr Henry Hammond's soteriology was similar to that found in Taylor's sermons and theological works. We possess fewer of Hammond's prayers, but such as we have suggest a dichotomy like Taylor's in so far as the problem of sin in the regenerate is concerned. Herbert Thorndike's public theology was also in line with that of Taylor and Hammond, but he published no prayers, and further parallel is therefore not possible to make. We may speculate that Hammond's theology of justification was at least more ambiguous than what he wrote. This speculation is supported by his statement that he gave up the imputation doctrine because it did not seem sufficiently to guard against the pestilent heresy of the antinomians. Thorndike too, in other words, doctored the doctrine of justification largely out of fear of antinomianism and of the moral chaos that might be encouraged by improper inference. He escaped the charge of Pelagianism but the price he paid for his escape was inconsistency.

Bishop William Forbes of Edinburgh was moved particularly to settle the prolonged, confusing, and heated controversy over justification and only secondarily by any fear of antinomianism. His motive was more irenic, and less a concern for holy living such as was characteristic of Taylor, Hammond, and Thorndike. He failed in his primary objective. Combination of "infusion" with "remission of sin" as the formal cause of justification involved him in the difficulties of both but solved the problems of neither. He admitted (as had the classical Anglicans) that inherent righteousness is not adequate as a doctrine of justification, but refused to concede that his position was thereby overthrown. We are also, he noted, justified by remission of sin, "nay by it principally".[3]

THE CLASSICAL VIEW

The work on justification by Bishop Davenant of Salisbury was probably the most impressive produced in the Caroline period. He was certainly most frequently and favourably quoted by his contemporaries. He was also the most representative theologian of the dominant school of seventeeth-century Anglican theology. His work established the classical position with respect to formal cause, the relationship between works and salvation, the problem of sin in the regenerate, the gratuitous nature of justification, and, in general, the relationship between justification and sanctification.

On this last subject alone Davenant was not representative of the prevalent school of thought. While the major concern of this school was to safeguard the gratuitous nature of justification, they did not (Davenant excepted) minimize the importance of works. To resolve the dilemma they tended to argue that works are necessary for sanctification but not for justification. We are, the argument went, accepted and covered by the imputation of Christ's righteousness, and we are thereby established in a relationship to God which enables us to perform the works of sanctification. Justification was conceived as the beginning and ground of salvation, freely given, without works, and to be apprehended only by faith.

Sanctification is not an action but a state of being: a growth in grace little by little in the life of obedience and good works. That is to say, justification, while preceding sanctification, is concomitant also with it. Hooker, Andrewes, Jackson, Downame, and Ussher (classical Anglicans all) felt that, although sanctification is consequent to justification, the latter cannot be an act once and for all and "in a moment", as Davenant said, because justification is just as necessary to the process of sanctification and for the final judgement. Forgiveness of sins in the regenerate and our disposition at the last judgement cannot be made to depend upon our own imperfect sanctification, but must be assigned wholly to Christ's righteousness imputed to us. Thus, sanctification follows justification in the same sense that the righteousness and obedience of sanctification follow necessarily the grace of justification.

Justification is, nevertheless, a continuing relationship with God. We never cease to suffer the need of being freely justified and forgiven by an acceptance of our imputed righteousness, despite the unworthiness of our sanctification. Thus, instead of holding justification to be "in a moment" as Davenant did, Hooker, Andrewes, Ussher, Donne, and Downame affirmed the continual necessity of justification. Justification is concomitant with sanctification throughout the whole state of salvation. The dominant concern of Lancelot Andrewes, when he attempted to refute the doctrine of inherent righteousness as formal cause, was not so much to stress the gratuitous nature of initial forgiveness and adoption, but rather specifically to deny that at the final judgement we shall be able to plead anything other than Christ's free, unearned, unmerited love, mercifully forgiving us despite the utter inadequacy of any (inherent) righteousness of our own. Ussher and Downame emphatically concurred that justification is necessary for the process of sanctification. It was Jackson's conjecture that the continuing necessity of Christ's atoning work is the real meaning of his eternal priesthood (which, Jackson alleged, was contravened by the inherent righteousness doctrine of the Council of Trent).

John Donne adhered in substance to this same school of thought, but his method of discussion is very different, even idiosyncratic.

Other sermons of the period which discussed justification tended to be scrupulously worked out essays expounding a particular statement of formal cause, the relationship between justification and sanctification, imputation, infusion, and so on. This was true of Andrewes, Ussher, Barrow, Taylor, and, to a somewhat lesser extent, of Hooker. Contrasted with the other surviving sermons of the period the sermons of Donne are unique. Donne's discussions of the doctrine of justification eschew the technical theological language, the special vocabulary, and the abstraction of most seventeenth-century polemical theology. His sermons do manifest a clear soteriological doctrine, but we do not find in them much use of such terms as formal cause, imputation, infusion, and the like. Justification is described in particular situations and proclaimed in terms of specific actions. He preached justification; he did not preach *about* justification. He eloquently evoked the qualities and properties of sanctification, but he did not preach *about* sanctification. It might be contended that Donne preached of soteriology "existentially"— and that he was alone in his century in so doing.

The predominant view of the Gospel held in seventeenth-century England assumed justification to be a doctrinal description of the application to sinners of the atonement. Justification initially confers entrance into the new covenant, and it is subsequently the ground of all forgiveness and sanctification. All Anglicans rejected the Tridentine doctrine of justification and most considered the formal cause of justification to be the imputation of Christ's righteousness. Justifying faith was regarded not as "assent to doctrine" but as trust and affirmation in the atoning work of God in Christ. Faith was said to justify only as an instrument which apprehends grace, and not as a work imputed for righteousness. Justification, however, was regarded as only an aspect of salvation, inseparable from sanctification, the growth in grace through good works of obedience.

There were certain questions posed by the classical Anglican doctrine which did not receive altogether satisfactory answers. Few of the Anglican divines attempted to explain how the unrighteous are initially contacted and justified, and most contented themselves with the assertion that a sinner's transgressions are, in fact, freely forgiven, his sin is rooted up (though not totally extirpated) and covered, and himself, therefore, reckoned or imputed as righteous, pronounced so, and begun to be made so. This would seem to mean that, for example, if an unrighteous man were to die immediately after his justification, he would be granted entrance into heaven without that righteousness specifically required by Scripture—"unless your righteousness exceeds that of the scribes and Pharisees you will in no wise enter into the kingdom of heaven".

ORIGINS OF ANOTHER, NEW DOCTRINE

Solutions to such difficulties in the classical position were attempted by the school of Taylor, Thorndike, and Hammond. To guard against the possibility that an unrighteous sinner might get to heaven they postulated a minimum degree of righteousness under the term "faith", which would be acceptable to God as righteous on account of the righteousness of Christ which has purchased the new covenant. The Council of Trent had, on the other hand, attempted to circumvent the same difficulty by a declaration that in justification God actually infuses into the sinner a righteousness for which, since it *is* in him (inherent), God regards him as righteous. A justified person, therefore, who died at once would be already righteous, and there can be no question of his entrance into heaven.

Taylor, Thorndike, Hammond, and Bull agreed with the earlier Carolines that the regenerate had in them no such inherent righteousness infused at justification. They differed, however, from other Carolines and from Trent, in the way they attempted to meet the two difficulties. They approached the problem, in fact, by formulating a new doctrine of the covenant of grace. Sinners are justified when they turn from their wickedness and show a measure of true righteousness. Thus, if a person dies soon after justification, he may have at least some righteousness on entering heaven. Righteousness required as a condition of the covenant is not, however, considered acceptable for justification in the way that Trent's inherent righteousness is, but it is considered and accounted as *adequate* because of the *more lenient* conditions of the new covenant. Some measure of righteousness is required for justification, then, but such imperfect righteousness is acceptable for salvation because the conditions of the new covenant are more lenient. This doctrine disposed of the problem of an unrighteous justified person (who dies immediately afterwards) getting to heaven by requiring only that he be a little righteous. The problem of "legal fiction" was solved by asserting that God in justification reckons as just one who may, in fact, be only a little just.

Not only does this argument fail adequately to remove the difficulties it was meant to answer, but it also introduces two new problems which are even more vexatious. One problem concerned the possible Pelagianism involved in requiring righteousness as a prior condition of forgiveness and justification. This was the basis of much of the contemporary criticism of the new school. Another problem concerned the propagation of the strange doctrine of a "more lenient covenant" with its concept of a "lowered market". Having denied that the infusion of inherent righteousness or the imputation of Christ's righteousness may be taken as the cause by which one is justified, this doctrine forced a conclusion that, on account of Christ's atonement, God accepts and reckons as righteous our sincere but otherwise wholly inadequate righteousness. Taylor, Hammond, Thorndike, Bull, Baxter, Fowler, "J.W.", and the author of *The Whole Duty of Man* were so preoccupied with antinomian inferences in the more gratuitous descriptions of the Gospel, that they frequently prescribed for the unregenerate more severe and arduous conditions for justification than they required of the regenerate within the covenant.

The works of Hooker, Jackson, Andrewes, Davenant, Donne, Downame, and Ussher were produced before the shock of the Civil War (and the subsequent flood of published Puritan theology). The "second generation" of Carolines were removed by more than time from their predecessors, and it is perhaps not surprising that they introduced radically new and strange doctrines to Anglican theology.

Bishop Barlow's observation that their new "moralism" could be dated from 1640 is substantially correct.[4] The responsible Anglican figures, so far as the doctrine of justification is concerned, belonged to a previous generation. The two generations were separated not only by their respective doctrines but also by convulsive historical events. The effect of those events upon Anglican soteriology, and the subsequent significance for theology of the new teaching that came about, will be the subject of the concluding chapter.

10

Conclusions

A radically significant and often unnoticed turning point for English Christianity was the watershed in the middle of the seventeenth century which separated the view of the Gospel held in the first half of the century from the view of the second half with its trend toward moralism. The earlier view, though by no means perfect,[1] manifested a blend of doctrine and ethics, Christian dogma and morals, justification and sanctification, and produced a devotional literature that was profoundly and functionally pastoral. The later view rent the fabric of soteriology and split the elements of religion so radically that doctrine became almost irrelevant and ethics became so harsh as to be cruel. There was an ineluctable movement away from the Christian faith of the earlier divines towards a moralism masquerading as faith.

The divines who introduced this trend towards moralism postulated a freedom of will in sinners that was of Pelagian proportions. Their remedy for sin consisted largely of exhortations to lead a holy life. Moreover, the only vertible significance attached to the atonement was the *moral* example of Christ. (One of the titles of Jeremy Taylor's life of Christ was, appropriately, *The Great Exemplar*.) Starting from assumptions that can be characterized only as Pelagian, soteriological thought, by an implacable logic, moved inexorably through an exemplarist atonement, to an adoptionist christology, to a Socinian deity, and finally from deism to atheism. The tragedy is that many of the divines responsible saw what was happening but were unable to see how they themselves were contributing to it.

George Bull, for example, clearly discerned the threat to Christian faith inherent in Socinianism and tried desperately to forestall it with his *Defence of the Nicene Faith.* However, it is impossible to defend the Trinitarian position of Athanasius while in effect confuting his soteriology.[2] Trinitarian theology is unnecessary and irrelevant to such a doctrine of salvation as Bull unfolds in *Harmonia Apostolica.*[3] Coleridge's dictum, directed at Jeremy Taylor, is actually applicable to the whole situation—"Socinianism is as inevitable a deduction from Taylor's scheme as Deism or Atheism is from Socinianism."[4]

It is, therefore, certainly worthwhile to evaluate the meaning of this trend away from orthodoxy, to attempt to explain why it occurred, and to point out some of its unfortunate consequences, especially for devotional and pastoral theology.

The "holy living" school of thought was not merely a minority position expounded by a few Anglicans during the seventeenth century. On the contrary, Hammond, Taylor, and Thorndike belonged to the "second generation" Carolines, and their doctrine of justification, along with that of Richard Baxter, seems to have been proposed no earlier than 1640. Despite the many opposing views on the subject of justification among contemporary Carolines, there was relatively little criticism of the "holy living" school of thought. Though there was indeed abundant criticism of Bull's work, the mere fact that it was produced and twice defended by him in subsequent works is evidence of the strength of the newer doctrines, especially notable when contrast is made with the virtual unanimity that had prevailed among the Carolines before 1640.

It is, however, easier to demonstrate the existence of the trend towards moralism than to weigh its importance. It is true that Hammond, Taylor, Thorndike, and Bull are but a few by comparison with the far larger number of Anglicans who adhered to the "gratuitous justification" school, but the former were enormously more influential than their numbers might suggest. Few divines of the seventeenth century (and probably no Anglicans) had so vast an influence as Jeremy Taylor. *Holy Living* had reached its fourteenth edition in the year after the death of Charles II, and *Holy Dying* its twenty-first edition by 1710! Henry Hammond's *Practical Catechism* had had its twelfth edition by 1685. Nor may we ignore the widespread impact of *The Whole Duty of Man* upon such as William Law, John Wesley, Charles Simeon, and the Tractarians. If the influence of Thorndike was restricted on account of his preponderously awkward style, this was more than offset by the promulgation these views enjoyed in the more lucid works of Richard Baxter. It is indeed unlikely that we could overstate the influence of the latter great Independent divine. It is, for example, astonishing to contemplate the uncritical use made of Baxter's writings by John Wesley, who published without any criticism whatever Baxter's earliest and least defendable work, *Aphorisms on Justification*.

The prodigious influence of Taylor, Baxter, and *The Whole Duty of Man*, the relative absence of contemporary Anglican criticism of their new doctrine, the mere fact that Bull produced his works at all, and the absence of any respectable alternative discussion of soteriology, make it incontestably apparent that the trend during the seventeenth century away from the classical or orthodox Anglican position possessed a remarkable virulence and an implacable momentum.

SOME HISTORICAL OBSERVATIONS

The trends in doctrine during the seventeenth century can be understood only in the light of other transitions occurring at the same time. The shaking of the very foundations of established society in the mid-seventeenth century had a profound effect upon the theology produced in the midst of it. The concern about immorality and lawlessness, occasionally expressed under Charles I, grew into a spectre of antinomianism which cast a darker and darker shadow over nearly all the theology written well into Restoration times. Seventeenth-century teaching concerning the Gospel cannot be separated from antinomianism and the fear of it.

Until 1640 English theologians were in substantial agreement in their understanding of the Gospel, but following the upheavals in society which began with the Long Parliament a new soteriology began to emerge. Richard Baxter, as a young chaplain in the army, became alarmed by what he considered to be a lawless and libertine gospel being preached to the soldiers. To counteract such libertarian practices he produced his first work, *Aphorisms on Justification*. Although he belatedly excused himself by noting that this work was written without benefit of libraries, he nevertheless spent much of his career defending it without ever appreciably modifying his position. Thorndike acknowledged that it was fear of antinomianism which moved him to alter his position on the doctrine of justification from that which he had been taught at Cambridge. Bull, like Baxter, began his work with similar motives (to correct the immorality of Restoration behaviour). Again, like Baxter, he defined his position in his first work and spent much of the balance of his career defending it. It would seem that the most plausible explanation of the dichotomy within the works of Taylor and Hammond is that they believed that they could not preach or teach during such chaotic times what they really believed to be true concerning the Gospel because of the antinomian inferences which might be drawn from such a candid exposition.

Some historians of the period reckon the doctrine of "free justification" or "justification by grace" as a Puritan concept unleashed during the Long Parliament.[5] Quite the contrary is the fact. Nearly every theologian, prior to 1640, whether Anglican, Roman Catholic, or Protestant, accepted "free justification" and "justification by grace". It was only during and after the events of "the troubles" that a new doctrine, that of Baxter, Taylor, Thorndike, Hammond, and Bull arose—a doctrine also propounded by numerous non-episcopal divines and by the Quaker Barclay.

There were, to be sure, a few exceptions to the unanimity that prevailed before 1640. While Bishop William Forbes' work, written in 1634 (but not published until 1658), was not in detail parallel to the position of the later "holy living" divines, it did afford a foretaste of that doctrine, by requiring, for example, obedience as a prior condition of justification. But Forbes basically considered justification to be both free and by grace (the formal cause, he held, is infusion of inherent righteousness together with remission of sins). Forbes was, however, in at least some of his teachings an exception to the Caroline theology of justification prior to the Civil War. His departures from orthodoxy may be explained by the special historical and geographical context in which he lived and worked. He was, after all, a bishop in Scotland in the 1630s, and the disruption of religious order had reached Scotland well before it overtook England. Forbes was the first major Caroline divine to demur importantly from classical Anglicanism. When events led to upheaval in England, many more would demur, Anglicans and non-episcopal divines alike. Bishop Forbes was, in fact, their precursor.

Antinomianism (coupled with the fear it engendered) must be accounted a very significant contributor to the growth of the new moralism. It is evident, from any point of view, that antinomian inferences could more easily be drawn from the soteriology typical of Anglicanism at the beginning of the seventeenth century than from that of the Council of Trent or of the "holy living" school of thought.[6] Whatever the abstract relationship of an ordered and secure society to the substance of the doctrine of justification, there was manifestly in seventeenth-century England a profound interaction of the two. Emphasis upon the free nature of grace and forgiveness tended to threaten the ordered structure of society, which led to modification of the doctrine itself in favour of "conditions" intended to guard against antinomianism, and also it led to a new emphasis upon the centrality of holy living.

Archbishop Ussher affords us an instructive example of how an atmosphere of stress and fear can affect the concern for soteriology. In 1656, in the midst of the "troubles", an anonymous writer entreated the Archbishop to explain his views on justification and sanctification "because I had formally heard him preach on these points things that seemed to make those mysteries more clearly intelligible to my poor capacity than anything I had heard from any other".[7] Ussher had been indeed deeply concerned in the 1630s to explicate such matters lucidly, but by 1656, in these "perilous times", concern for orthodox soteriology withered. He barely mentioned the matter about which he was interrogated, but launched immediately into dire predictions of an imminent apocalypse as the certain consequence of disturbing contemporary events.

Fear of antinomianism cannot, of course, be separated from the historical events which evoked it. The impact upon seventeenth-century theology of extra-theological events is indicated, for example, by the conference convened at the Duke of Buckingham's house to discuss Montague's works, which terminated in a request by five bishops for a royal injunction banning public discussion of specified controversial theological matters. That request was granted. Charles I and Archbishop Laud seem to have suppressed an explosion of religious controversy which had been seething under the surface for some time before the Long Parliament. It is probable that the religious unrest prevalent in sixteenth-century Europe was deferred in England by Tudor authority and did not erupt there until well after the advent of the Stuarts. Historical myopia (viewing the seventeenth century from a nineteenth or twentieth-century perspective) has led us to hold an inadequate appreciation of the tenuousness and precariousness with which people had then regarded the religious structure of society. The concept of tolerance, now so prominent, did not develop suddenly, and it was inconceivable in 1640 that different theological doctrines and polity should or could coexist in the same society.

> Even the sects who were themselves under oppression exclaimed against their rulers, not as being persecutors at all, but as persecuting those who professed the truth; and each sect, as it obtained the power to wield the secular weapon, esteemed it also a duty, as well as a privilege, not to bear the sword in vain.[8]

Episcopal, Presbyterian, Independent, and Roman Catholic divines (and also the Quakers and Anabaptists) preached distinct, often antagonistic gospels, frequently disagreeing even among themselves, and the resultant controversies excited a concern and alarm that is all too easily underestimated to-day. It is indeed easier to appreciate the precariousness of the social and political situation that developed in mid-seventeenth-century England than to grasp the disorder of theology. To a theologian nurtured in the seventeenth-century relationship between Church and State and the rôle of the Episcopacy within this concept, the events of the century must have been well-nigh traumatic. There was, at any rate, great alarm expressed by divines on all sides over the events which seemed to them to threaten the very foundations of society. Whatever its causes may have been, this alarm had profound and, on the whole, adverse effects upon Christian soteriology.

The paucity of Anglican criticism of the "holy living" teaching about a more lenient covenant and the "lowered market" not only indicates the strength of the trend but was also directly a factor in its growth. There was, to be sure, some contemporary objection to Jeremy Taylor, but it was characterized by a notable reticence. In a letter to Bishop Barlow, for example, Bishop Sanderson laments that "Dr Taylor is so peremptory and pertinacious of his error, as not to harken to the sober advices of his grave, reverend, and learned friends", and he urges Barlow not to name Taylor in reproving the error, "that there might be in these times of so much dislocation as little notice taken of differences amongst ourselves, as is possible . . .".[9]

Contrast this reception of Jeremy Taylor's work with that accorded the two works of Richard Montague some thirty years earlier. Though Montague's views were not nearly so vulnerable to criticism as Taylor's they elicited far more adverse response. Montague was even indicted before Parliament, and his works were the cause of a conference at the Duke of Buckingham's house of some half-dozen learned divines who solemnly deliberated upon their orthodoxy. Bishops Laud, Howson, and Buckeridge later wrote to Buckingham that some of the arguments Montague's accusers had made against him were indeed "such as are expressly the resolved doctrine of the Church of England, and these he is bound to maintain".[10] Following the Civil War, however, the situation so changed that Thorndike could publicly acknowledge that he had abandoned the doctrine of the Thirty-Nine Articles, and Taylor himself was able to advance flamboyant new doctrines without effective public opposition. This shift of attitude can in part be explained by reference to the remark of Sanderson that "in these times of so much dislocation as little notice [should be] taken of differences amongst ourselves as possible".

From a responsible theological perspective, as a matter of fact, the "holy living" doctrine of justification is actually much more vulnerable to criticism than was that of the Council of Trent (which was unanimously rejected by all Carolines). The "holy living" divines involved themselves in much the same difficulty about sin in the regenerate as did Trent, but they compounded confusion by requiring obedience before the grace of justification, an error Trent had carefully avoided. Even so, George Bull's theology represented a more extravagant departure from classical Anglicanism than that of any other member of the "holy living" school. While it evoked considerable criticism, it remains difficult to explain how so radical a departure would occur, and how it came to be so influential as it did.[11]

Bull was fortunate to have as his bishop a powerful and influential patron. Bishop Nicholson had suffered excessively during the Commonwealth, and was later appointed to the See of Gloucester. His patronage of Bull is surprising because he espoused very different theological positions. He was a close friend of Jeremy Taylor (having been associated with him in an educational enterprise during the Commonwealth), but in his sermons and catechism he expounded a view of the Gospel much closer to that of Davenant than to that of Bull. The latter informs us that the Bishop approved and encouraged the publication of the *Harmonia*, and, without doubt, it was published with Nicholson's consent. We are forced to conclude either that Nicholson had changed his views on justification, or that he had decided that different views should be taught about justification.

Two explanations have been given for the influence of Bull's doctrine of justification. Morris Fuller, in his *Life of Bishop Davenant*, suggests that Bull's work on justification gained prestige from his work on the *Nicene Faith*. The latter work, however, was not published until fifteen years after the *Harmonia*, and could not possibly have enhanced its reputation during the Caroline period. In fact, Bull had great difficulty in getting the Nicene work published, having been turned down by three publishers and only finally getting it to press through the influence of John Fell. Bull was not at the time the influential Bishop of St David's he was to become, but a relatively unknown priest just venturing upon the publication of his first work.

A second explanation for Bull's influence suggests that the flattering biography of him by his devoted pupil, Robert Nelson, enlarged his reputation. This may help to explain his fame in later days, but again it cannot account for his initial popularity since the biography was not written until the eighteenth century. Fear of antinomianism and reluctance on the part of the episcopacy to criticize Taylor, Thorndike, and Hammond during the Commonwealth may be construed as contributing factors to the growth of the "holy living" doctrine. Such considerations are, however, less applicable in the case of Bull who wrote, after all, during the reign of Charles II. Bull was criticized not only by Tully and Gataker, but by Bishop Morley in a pastoral letter, and by Dr Barlow in some lectures at Oxford. Later, as Bishop of Lincoln, Barlow wrote two private letters to a priest of his diocese strongly reiterating classical Anglican soteriology, but he was, in these letters, only implicitly critical of Bull. The fact that his letters were not published until after Barlow's death is another indication of the reticence of controversial discussion that developed among Anglicans. Neither lack of criticism nor fear of antinomianism, however, fully explains the growth of "holy living" moralism, especially as it proliferated towards the end of the seventeenth century.

SOME THEOLOGICAL OBSERVATIONS

More important than fear of antinomianism or paucity of criticism as negative contributions to the growth of the new soteriology was the absence of a viable systematic theology. There was no systematic theology that enjoyed a general acceptance. Confusion and disagreement were more characteristic of discussions about soteriology. Eschatological issues such as the doctrine of purgatory were disposed of, for the most part, merely by denouncing the Roman doctrine. It was an eschatological concern that moved Hammond to reject the notion that justification does not include and presuppose sanctification with the argument that, if justification came first and the justified died an instant later, "it must follow, either that the un-sanctified man is glorified, or the justified man is not glorified".[12] Denial of the Roman Catholic doctrine of purgatory excluded the possibility of growth in grace after death, and this, in turn, neces-sarily impoverished seventeenth-century soteriology.

Doctrines of grace in seventeenth-century England were more often than not either Calvinistic or downright heretical. Such Caro-lines as escaped the influence of Calvin seem to have escaped as well from any real concern for theology itself. To avoid charges of heresy or of Calvinism after the first quarter of the seventeenth century it was almost necessary to eschew theology altogether. Laud, Heylyn, and Cosin were not Calvinistic but, for the most part, they confined their attentions and their writings (not inconsiderable in volume) to practical matters, to specific questions like transubstantia-tion, or to catechetical writings on the creed. There was among all the Carolines not one systematic theologian. Those who ventured at all into substantive theological discussion expressed themselves mostly in the vocabulary and arguments of the prevalent Reforma-tion theology of nature and grace.

Controversies about substantive issues such as election and free will proved disturbing to many authorities. Another letter written to the Duke of Buckingham (eight months earlier than the one cited above) concerning Richard Montague and signed by Laud, An-drewes, Neile, Montaigne, and Buckeridge pleads, "that his Majesty . . . prohibit all parties . . . any further controverting of these questions by public preaching or writing . . .".[13] This was an "earnest" of the theological unrest that came with the Long Parlia-ment, and the efforts that were made to preserve a semblance of order by prohibiting public discussion and debate on controversial theology. Such a theological moratorium is indicative of the confu-sion about soteriology (specifically about the doctrines of grace and election) which rapidly spread, and of the absence of any effective theological response to the confusion. The conclusions to which the doctrines of grace and election were forced were denounced as dangerous or ignored as embarrassing. The negative and political approach to (or withdrawal from) the problem (however necessary

it may have been) certainly demonstrates powerfully the complete
lack at the time of any responsible alternative systematic theology.
Election, grace, and freedom proved annoying to the bishops in
1625, and to the Presbyterians and Independents in the 1640s and
1650s, and the same problems (which might have provided a theological context for discussion of the doctrines of justification and
sanctification) were actually, by the extremes to which they were
often carried, a source of anxiety, recrimination, and disrepute.

Even more important and basic was another deficiency which had
a most adverse effect upon the stewardship of the Gospel in the
seventeenth century. The conception of sin set forth by most theologians, especially after 1640, was one of *transgression*. Sin was
seldom described as a condition of *separation* (alienation) from which
transgressions flourish as symptoms. Bishop William Nicholson, contending against Pelagianism, speaks of the *transgressions* of un-
baptized infants rather than their *situation* or *condition* of sin.[14]
Hammond and Forbes discuss sin almost exclusively as if it constituted acts of transgression. Sin for Taylor is an avoidable act.[15] Sin
for Bull is breaking the law, disobeying a demand which could have
been obeyed. Even Davenant, discussing the sinful nature of concupiscence, stresses the transgressions which spring from concupiscence.

The distinction between *sin* as a separation and *sins* as expressions
of disobedience became increasingly rare as the century unfolded.
Since sin was considered by most as an action rather than as a
condition, imputation was all too often described as merely an
external reality. Imputation of Christ's righteousness became more
and more external to the justified person in the attempt to avoid any
internal (inherent) pretension of infused righteousness in the regenerate.[16] In contrast to earlier theologians such as Hooker, Donne,
and Downame (also George Walker and John Owen), there came to
be a general failure to conceive justification in terms of a new situation, a new being. Failure to appreciate the ontological nature of sin
precluded for most Carolines any ontological description of justification.

Coleridge points out that Taylor and his contemporaries so preoccupied themselves with the *phenomena* of sin that they lost sight of its *noumenous* origins.[17] Coleridge had studied the writings of Emmanuel Kant in Germany, and it might be assumed that it was from the German philosopher that he acquired these terms. It is, however, also possible (and particularly significant for this study) that he might have learned them from Richard Hooker. In a discussion of our new relationship with Christ Hooker remarks that "Christ is in us, saith Gregory Nazianzene, not κατὰ τὸ φαινόμενον but κατὰ τὸ νοούμενον".[18] Such a grasp of *noumenous* reality as Hooker displayed had largely vanished by mid-century.

The weakness of classical (orthodox) Anglican soteriology which led to its gradual demise as an element of Anglican theology under Charles II may well have been its lack of ontological dimensions, especially as related to the doctrine of "imputation of Christ's righteousness". Whatever its use in confuting the Tridentine doctrine of inherent righteousness, it remains that, at times, it led to the unhappy conclusion that justification is external to the regenerate. Emphasis upon sin as a *transgression* had a comparable effect upon the theology of the "holy living" divines. When they discussed justification as a property of the new covenant they explained it more as a method of overcoming transgressions than as a wholly new situation of being—as a new ontological condition.[19] Thus, with rare exceptions, inadequate understanding of the nature of sin issued inevitably in an inadequate understanding of the Gospel.

SPIRITUAL ENTROPY

Study of soteriology in seventeenth-century England provides an interesting historical illustration of what might be called "spiritual entropy" (the dissipation or "running-down" of energy), or the tendency of theological positions originally designed to be critical of pretension to become twisted or turned into the basis of another, more pernicious pretension. For instance, justification was originally conceived to be "by faith" in contrast to the pretension of soliciting the favour of God by virtue of (man's) works. But out of the same tradition over a period of time this article of faith became the foundation of a far more preposterous pretension. Faith itself became a work which by virtue of its righteousness as a (good) work merited justification.

Similarly, the doctrine of election (originally a humble affirmation of God's initiative) became, during this period, the basis of a presumptuous and obnoxious exclusiveness. The doctrine of "assurance" (intended to be a comforting confirmation of the love and forgiveness of God) was gradually corrupted into a doctrine of undoubted election for a select (and self-appointed) minority. The word "imputation" had been exercised as a witness against any presumption that righteousness within a person could satisfy the requirements God has established for righteousness. However, in time "imputation" came to mean, not the "imputation of Christ's righteousness", but the "imputation of faith", and faith was reconstrued to mean *our* "sincere endeavours" and *our* "evangelical" righteousness: thus, the imputation of *our* righteousness, not the imputation of Christ's righteousness, eventually became that by which we are justified.[20]

THE DISSOCIATION OF SENSIBILITY

There was a multi-dimensional and pervasive split of thought and passion in Western civilization that began in the sixteenth but reached its culmination in the seventeenth century. Paul Tillich describes it this way:

> The history of industrial society, the end of which we are experiencing, represents the history of the victory of the philosophy of the unconscious, irrational will. The symbolic name for the complete victory of the philosophy of consciousness is René Descartes; and the victory became complete even in religion, at the moment when Protestant theology became the ally of the Cartesian emphasis on man as pure consciousness on the one hand, and a mechanical process called body on the other hand.[21]

Blaise Pascal was the cultural embodiment of a blend of consciousness and unconsciousness that expired when Western civilization elected the contrary "rationalism" of his contemporary, René Descartes. This was indeed a "Cartesian Faux Pas" (though in a quite different sense from that intended by William Temple). Since Pascal neither culture nor the Church has grasped the totality (and therefore the Christianity) of the "grandeur and misery of man".

Professor Owen Chadwick has pointed out the wider context in which any particular judgement of the seventeenth-century split in soteriology must be grounded.

> The reaction against Calvinism was a European movement. Indeed it was a movement not confined to Protestantism, for the developments of the theology of the Counter-Reformation at the end of the sixteenth century and during the seventeenth often went beyond normal limits in emphasizing the power of the human will to salvation and the needs of the soul to co-operate with grace upon the roads to sanctification and to heaven. The perils of the Jesuit theology of grace in the seventeenth century are nearly as well known as the perils of their moral theology which Pascal portrayed in the Provincial Letters.[22]

T. S. Eliot, as was noted at the outset of this study, has pointed to a phenomenon in literature whereby the profound and pervasive philosophical, theological, and psychological separation manifested itself among seventeenth-century poets as a "dissociation of sensibility". Jeremy Taylor and George Bull obviously did not *cause* this development (any more than Milton and Dryden were *causes* of its exfoliation into poetry), but they were dynamic *symptoms* of it.

An effort to explain the unfortunate transition in exegesis of the Gospel from Richard Hooker to Richard Baxter would have to include at least these considerations: rampant fear of antinomianism, profound social and religious upheavals (postponed by Tudor authority) characteristic of the reign of the Stuarts (and the interregnum), paucity of criticism of the new soteriology as it began to proliferate, the influence of distortions of such related doctrines as election and grace, the absence of any viable alternative systematic theology, outright "spiritual entropy", and the pervasive schizophrenia in Western culture during the seventeenth century between thought and passion ("dissociation of sensibility") which infected not only literature and philosophy but also theology and religion. Whatever the causes, the seventeenth century bequeathed to the eighteenth century in England a soteriology which hopelessly alienated ethics and moral theology from their foundations in theological doctrine. What had been the typical synthesis of Anglican theology came to have no effective champion, and exegesis of the Gospel within the burgeoning moralism that afflicted the end of the century was full of awkward and debilitating consequences.

CONSEQUENCES
OF THE IMPOVERISHMENT OF
SOTERIOLOGICAL ORTHODOXY

Whatever the limitations of the Anglican position in the first part of the seventeenth century, its criticism of the Council of Trent has historical importance. Classical Anglicanism never objected to actual righteousness infused at justification; it recoiled only at the proclamation of such a doctrine as the formal cause of justification. It shuddered away from and shunned, prophetically, any teaching which, in effect, denied the possibility of a person being justified and a sinner at one and the same time. Father Victor White, Roman Catholic Dominican specialist on the work of C. G. Jung, describes well the limitations that the Council of Trent put upon pastoral and moral theology. He points out that conscious transgressions against established sanctions rarely are the cause of sickness, but rather it is unconscious tension and conflict which is ordinarily destructive to health and humanity.

> This idea of "unconscious sin" is often a difficult one for the moral theologian to grasp. Especially if he has been brought up in the traditions of post-Reformation Catholicism, he may find it particularly hard to square with his correct notions that mortal sin must be voluntary, performed with full knowledge and full consent. But it is a fact that the psyche is much less indulgent to unconscious breaches of its own laws and demands . . . and will revenge itself for their disregard. . . .[23]

Father White offers a poignant and enlightened example of the pastoral implications of post-Tridentine moral theology:

> We know of a young woman who had lived for some time with a married man, fully aware that what she was doing was morally wrong

in the eyes of her church and her parents, but with no psycho-
pathological symptoms. Her parents came to hear of the liaison,
brought strong pressure upon her to break it up, succeeded in doing
so, and in bringing her home to the parental roof. At once, obsessive
guilt took hold of her, and she became quite incapacitated for life.
Her sense of guilt was clearly to be attributed, not to her having lived
with her lover, but to her having left him and submitted weakly to
parental pressure and allowing herself to accept externally the parents'
moral judgement in spite of her own convictions. Whatever the
objective standards of right and wrong, she had "sinned psycho-
logically" in an infantile regression to dependence on the parents, in
which she felt she had abdicated her adult autonomy and responsi-
bilities.[24]

He appends this valuable observation:

> The exclusive emphasis of later theologians on "full knowledge and
> consent" can have the unfortunate result of putting a certain premium
> on unconsciousness, irresponsibility and infantilism.[25]

To escape the anathema of the Council of Trent, "unconscious
sin", in this context, must be put in inverted commas, and the
notion that "mortal sin must be voluntary, performed with full
knowledge and consent" must be considered "correct". However,
it was not only the classical Anglicans, but also the Saints Thomas
Aquinas, Bernard, and Augustine, who recognized that sin is also
in part unconscious and acts of sin may be committed in ignorance.

English Christianity after the Civil War, however, tended to share
with Trent a peculiar pastoral myopia suggesting that somehow
compulsion, surprises, passion, inadvertent and unconscious feelings
or even actions are morally less culpable or not even sin at all. The
consequence, of course, is that an unwholesome premium is placed
on ignorance, irresponsibility, and infantilism. Morality is deprived
of its roots, and is disastrously separated from orthodox Christian
dogma. This was the origin and the curse of the moralism which
now is ascendant in the West. It exhorts a power of freedom that
fallen man does not possess; it is a religion of control (called "self-
control") and not redemption, and it ends inevitably in despair
rather than in hope. The moral imperatives exacted of men are
predicated on a definition of sin as only wilful and deliberate,

thereby implying that the problem of sin is essentially superficial, a misconception that culminates in a false hope of self-justification.

The seriousness of this development is difficult to appraise nowadays because we are all afflicted with the consequences of the thing we seek to appraise. Eight or ten twentieth-century theologians have written books discussing Jeremy Taylor's theology, and not one of them has discerned its grave imperfections. The pastoral cruelty of the theology of Taylor (or of *The Whole Duty of Man*) is usually countenanced as a legitimate aspect of Christian teaching, or as a necessary corrective to antinomian inferences from the Gospel. What goes largely unnoticed is the radical distinction of the doctrine of the second half of the seventeenth century from that of the first half—and the loss of theological integrity that occurred. There was no lack of exhortations to good works and of denunciation of sin in the works of Hooker, Andrewes, Davenant, and Donne, and these continue throughout the century but without the corresponding emphasis on forgiveness and God's initiative. All is exhortation and denunciation in the public works of Taylor, Hammond, Bull, and in *The Whole Duty of Man*.

Contrast *Holy Living* and *Holy Dying* by Jeremy Taylor with *Disce Mori: Learn to Die* (1600) and *Disce Vivere: Learn to Live* (1602) by Christopher Sutton. Sutton rose to none of the majesty of Taylor's prose, but neither did he descend with Taylor to an exclusion of God's love from sinners.[26] Or, contrast Richard Hooker's treatment of despair with that found in *The Whole Duty of Man*. Hooker recognized that we cannot overcome sin, or more particularly despair, until we have first learned how to love. He was explicit that "fear worketh no man's inclination to repentance, till somewhat else have wrought in us love also".[27] The unknown author of *The Whole Duty of Man* did not manifest a comparable kerygmatic concern. Christianity's purpose, he said, is to produce righteousness, and the method is to persuade sinners of their own damnation and its nearness. The assumption is plain that the power of sin can be broken by the power of good will. No wonder, then, that, according to *The Whole Duty of Man*, the purpose of preaching is to "remind us of our duties".[28]

Typical modern discussions of the work of Jeremy Taylor evidence no dissatisfaction with the pastoral consequences of his rootless moralism.

> When he [Taylor] comes to deal with excessive grief for the inroads of death upon those whom we love he still calls for unquestioning faith in the goodness of God and he reinforces his religious advice with arguments drawn from the moralists of Greece and Rome to show that grief is not only wrong but unreasonable.[29]

Too few theologians since the age of Hooker and Donne have understood how extraneous and futile it is to tell a person in excessive grief that submission to his condition is sinful.

To understand the existential manifestations of grief or guilt it is helpful in our day to hearken to those who regularly encounter the results of moralistic theology. Gilbert Russell, a London psychiatrist, tells us of a woman whose history is, it seems to me, a parable of what resulted from the movement from orthodoxy to moralism in the seventeenth century.

> A woman in middle life consulted an analyst on account of fatigue, agitation, insomnia and depression, and an inability to get on with her job which amounted at last to breakdown. She was the daughter of a well-known professional man who, she said, was notorious for his marital infidelities. After many years of abuse and humiliation his wife, the patient's mother, broke down under the strain and was taken to hospital, where she stayed for many months. The daughter was at this time fourteen years old. While she and her father were living alone in the house (so her story went), he seduced her, and for the whole period of her mother's absence she slept in her father's bed. (This may have been fact or fantasy: in this connection, it matters little which.) Her mother returned in due course to her home and husband, but soon became worse and died. The girl's distress and misery were beyond description. It seemed to her that she could not forgive her father for such a betrayal. She was consumed by hate. She went to one confessor after another, seeking relief and pardon—a search that continued for the next thirty years. The advice she received from them all was in substance the same: it was not for her to pass judgment upon her father, outrageous though his conduct had certainly been; she must strive to forgive him, however impossible it seemed. In spite—or because—of this counsel, and determined efforts

to apply it, her anxiety increased. In the end she resolved to consult a psychiatrist. Asked if she had any dreams, she replied that one dream, which terrified her, recurred again and again. In it she and her father were walking together, each with a dog on a lead. She was making frantic attempts to get away from her father, but whenever she started to leave him he whistled to her dog, to which she was so much attached (by affection as well as the lead) that she could not abandon it; when the dog turned back to her father, she must needs go too.

The dream revealed in a moment what thirty years of spiritual counselling had not—that her problem was not to forgive a father she hated, but to forgive herself for still loving him. No pastoral help could avail until there was first laid bare the incestuous bond which held her. She was still in love with her father, and burdened with the guilt of that unnatural relationship. The dream showed what her real problem was, and psychotherapy helped her to deal with it. Until we are brought face to face with the actual cause of our symptoms and conflicts, on the level where they exist and not on the level where we expect to find them, we are in the hopeless position of a man exploring the roof for a burglar at work in the cellar.[30]

Russell's "case history" reminds us that there is a level of man's need not touched by much that has been called religion. Theologically, we have in large part lost touch with this deeper level since the time of classical Anglican theology. This woman's whole sense of duty (her "holy living") required that she control, suppress, and eradicate her sin without the consolation she might have derived from the reassurance of forgiveness by God while she was still in her sins. Had she been nurtured in the Christianity of John Donne's sermons, the devotional literature of Christopher Sutton, and the theology of Richard Hooker, there is every likelihood that she would never have become ill.

The theology of John Donne deserves more conscientious attention than it has so far received. He was not only an eloquent advocate for orthodox Anglicanism before it became corrupted by moralistic innovations, but he achieved a theological integrity unique even in that splendid age. While he was seldom quoted or referred to by contemporary theologians, his doctrinal respectability was none the less outstanding among his colleagues and admirable when compared with that of his successors.

Justification, according to Donne, is not finished "in one moment", nor is imputation merely some external intervention. A justified person is accepted as a new creature in Christ, and, as such, his inadequate righteousness is made wholly acceptable by the righteousness of Christ. This new relationship is not only the source of that grace which nurtures the imperfect, but is also the embryonic righteousness which will inform the regenerate. Because he understood clearly the relationship of grace and freedom, Donne did not become involved in the unfortunate freedom-denying positions which marred the works of some of his contemporaries. Nor did he stumble into the error of requiring as a condition of justification a righteousness that is only possible by the grace of justification. Donne's sermons elaborated a simple and effective criticism of the Tridentine formal cause of justification which was not inferior in theological content to that of Hooker, Hall, or Davenant. His insight that God will not save us without our participation led Donne to a vigorous exhortation of good works and holiness in sanctification. His consciousness of the severe and arduous demands of righteousness in the process of sanctification stands in marked contrast to the more lenient covenant doctrine of the "holy living" school.

Donne's apprehension of the power of sin, however, constrained him to stress that our wills are not able *to effect* but only *to accept* the gift of justification. Thus, the condition of sin must first be overcome by God's initiative in a free justification before our wills are enabled to perform the good works necessary for sanctification. Donne's theology of freedom was, in fact, the key to his doctrine of sanctification, and his theology of sin was the key to his doctrine of justification.

John Donne was consistent in describing sin as more than mere perverse acts or transgressions, an error of superficiality that came to prevail as the century rolled on. Sins, he argued, are symptoms and expressions of a much deeper *state* of sin, which is a situation of radical separation.

> Scarce any man considers the weight, the oppression of Originall sinne. No man can say, that an Akorn weighs as much as an Oak; yet in truth, there is an Oak in that Akorn: No man considers that

Originall sinne weighs as much as Actuall or Habituall, yet in truth, all our Actuall and Habituall sins are in Originall.[31]

This doctrine of sin coloured Donne's doctrine of justification in a profound and constructive way. Because sin is a situation of separation, justification, for Donne, is nothing less than a new reality, bridging that separation, and establishing a new being in Christ. Donne's soteriology, with its emphasis upon *being in Christ* (in a new ontological condition) was a blend of ethics and doctrine comparable in integrity to the blend of thought and passion that dignified his literature. A radical dissociation infected literature and theology in the next generation, and from it have flowed, to this very day, unfortunate consequences, rarely contested, for the whole Christian Church.

Appendix A

TRANSLATION OF PERTINENT PASSAGES OF
DECREES OF THE COUNCIL OF TRENT[1]

Session V, 5. If anyone denies that by the grace of our Lord Jesus Christ which is conferred in baptism, the guilt of original sin is remitted, or says that the whole of that which belongs to the essence of sin is not taken away, but says that it is only cancelled or not imputed let him be anathema. For in those who are born again God hates nothing, because *there is no condemnation to those who are truly buried together with Christ by baptism unto death, who walk not according to the flesh*, but, putting off the old man and putting on the new one who is created according to God, are made innocent, immaculate, pure, guiltless and beloved of God, *heirs indeed of God, joint heirs with Christ*; so that there is nothing whatever to hinder their entrance into heaven. But this holy council perceives and confesses that in the one baptized there remains concupiscence or an inclination to sin, which, since it is left for us to wrestle with, cannot injure those who do not acquiesce but resist manfully by the grace of Jesus Christ; indeed, he who shall have *striven lawfully shall be crowned*. This concupiscence, which the Apostle sometimes calls sin, the holy council declares the Catholic Church has never understood to be called sin in the sense that it is truly and properly sin in those born again, but in the sense that it is of sin and inclines to sin. But if anyone is of the contrary opinion, let him be anathema.

Session VI, chapter VII. The causes of this justification are: the final cause is the glory of God and of Christ and life everlasting; the efficient cause is the merciful God who washes and sanctifies gratuitously, signing and anointing with the holy Spirit of promise, who is the pledge of our inheritance; the meritorious cause is His most beloved only begotten, our Lord Jesus Christ, who, when we were enemies, for the exceeding charity wherewith he loved us, merited for us justification by His most holy passion on the wood of the cross and made satisfaction for us to God the Father; the instrumental cause is the sacrament of baptism, which is the sacrament of faith, without which no man was ever justified; finally, the single formal cause is the justice of God, not that by which He Himself is just, but that by which He makes us just, that namely with which we being endowed by Him, are renewed in the spirit of our mind, and not only are we reputed but we are truly called and are just, receiving justice within us, each one according to his own measure, which the Holy Ghost distributes to everyone as He wills, and according to each one's disposition and co-operation. For though no one can be just except he to whom the merits of the passion of our Lord Jesus Christ are communicated, yet this takes place in that justification of the sinner, when by the merit of the most holy passion, *the charity of God is poured forth by the Holy Ghost in the hearts* of those who are justified and inheres in them, whence man through Jesus Christ, in whom he is ingrafted, receives in that justification, together with the remission of sins, all these infused at the same time, namely, faith, hope, and charity. For faith, unless hope and charity be added to it, neither unites man perfectly with Christ nor makes him a living member of His body.

Appendix B

THE AUTHORSHIP OF
"CHRISTIAN CONSOLATIONS"

Considerable disagreement surrounds the question of the authorship of *Christian Consolations*. Anthony Wood, in the seventeenth century, listed it among Taylor's writings, and there was little hesitancy by Reginald Heber to include it in his edition of the collected works of Jeremy Taylor. Heber claimed that

> . . . the sentiments and piety appear in perfect unison with Bishop Taylor's known opinions; the style partakes of his merits and defects, and the weight of external evidence is such as can leave no reasonable doubt on the propriety of admitting them into the present collection.[1]

However, Charles Page Eden takes exception to this view, and in his revision of Heber's edition he excludes *Christian Consolations* on the ground that it was not written by Taylor. Eden explains in a footnote to his edition that *Christian Consolations* is by Bishop Hacket "as was suggested by the Reverend James Brogden, and is now proved beyond dispute. In the ensuing pages therefore of this memoir, no further mention is made of these treatises."[2]

On the other hand, George Gresley Perry in his article on John Hacket in the *Dictionary of National Biography* categorically denies that *Christian Consolations* was written by Hacket. Edmund Gosse, George Worley, and W. J. Brown in their respective biographies[3] omit the *Consolations* from Taylor's works but do not discuss the question of its authorship. John Wing's *Short Title Catalogue, 1641-1700*, lists *Christian Consolations* under Bishop Hacket with a cross reference to Taylor, but no reference is made to it under Taylor. *The Dictionary of Anonymous and Pseudonymous Literature*, edited by Halkett and Laing, continues to attribute this work to

Taylor. C. J. Stranks, in his recent biography of Taylor, agrees with
Eden that it is not Taylor's work and holds that it cannot be attributed to Taylor until some explanation is made for the theological
differences between the *Consolations* and Taylor's known works.[4]
Perhaps the earliest objection to listing this work as Taylor's was by
Alexander Knox in a letter addressed to Bishop Jebb of Limerick,
and dated 26 February 1825.

> To this, indeed to the entire prevalent theology of that tract, nothing
> can be more opposite, than the sermon preached in Christ Church,
> entitled "Fides Formata" . . . how he [Heber] could dream of the
> life of Taylor having thus closed, in the strangest theological, and in
> some sort moral contradiction, I can ill reconcile with the talents and
> judgement manifested so variously in Bishop Heber's work.[5]

Eden's argument and evidence for Hacket's authorship are
attached in longhand notes to a printed letter from Edward Churton
to Joshua Watson (London 1848) which is in the Bodleian Library.
Eden states that two of the three extant copies of the *Consolations*—
one in Trinity College library, Cambridge, the other owned by a
Mr H. H. Norris—have notes written on the fly-leaf attributing it to
Hacket. The Bodleian copy has "Jeremy Taylor, D.D." written
under the words on the title page, "By a late prelate". (Taylor died
in 1667, Hacket in 1670. *Christian Consolations* was published in
1671.) Eden claims that many passages in the *Consolations* are almost
identical with passages in Hacket's sermons. He lists several. The
other evidence is three fold: (1) The style, he claims, is altogether
different from that of Bishop Taylor. There are phrases in *Christian
Consolations* which are not "in sufficient good taste to have satisfied
the ear of Bishop Taylor". (2) The theology is manifestly inconsistent with that of Taylor's accepted writings, especially his sermon on
"Fides Formata". The belief that Romans 7 could be a description
of a regenerate person and the separation of regeneration from
baptism in the *Consolations* are diametrically opposed to Taylor's
theology. (3) The "topics and symptoms of character feeling" are
akin to Hacket's style and taste. The only evidence on the other
side, Eden claims, is the copy in the Bodleian with Taylor's name
written on the fly-leaf. Another piece of evidence for Eden's

position is a copy of *Christian Consolations* in Christ Church library, Oxford, with Hacket's name written on the title page. This copy is from the library of Archbishop William Wake (d. 1737), and Hacket's name is apparently written in the handwriting of the Archbishop.

However, as has been abundantly shown in chapter 4, the arguments that Eden and Knox offer on the grounds of the theology would also eliminate the prayers which Taylor unquestionably did write. The fact that *Christian Consolations* was written privately to a lady troubled with guilt with no intention of its being published would be consistent with Taylor's habit of saying quite different things privately from what he says from the pulpit. Furthermore, the *Consolations* contain Taylor's characteristic emphasis upon repentance and sincere endeavours. There is no theology in *Christian Consolations* that cannot be found in the accepted writings of Jeremy Taylor. It would seem that if one were to deny that Taylor wrote *Christian Consolations* it would have to be done on grounds other than those of theology.

If Hacket had written *Christian Consolations*, it is difficult to explain why it was not mentioned by Thomas Plume in his life of Hacket which was published four years after the *Consolations* and five years after Hacket's death. Plume's work manifests a remarkable knowledge of Hacket's life including such matters as the information that Hacket was the donor of several anonymous gifts. Plume discusses in detail Hacket's visitation articles, his sermons, and prints in full Hacket's address to the Long Parliament concerning the revenue of bishops. But there is no mention of *Christian Consolations*.

There does not seem to be sufficient evidence to be dogmatic about the authorship of this work. The evidence offered by Eden and Knox on the grounds of theology does not seem to be of any weight in view of the theology expressed in Taylor's prayers as is shown in chapter 4. It would appear likely, as a tentative suggestion, that Taylor did indeed write the work to a lady troubled with guilt in which he utilizes a few of John Hacket's illustrations. Since he had no intention of publishing it, he manifests the theology of his prayers without fear of antinomian interpretations.

Notes

CHAPTER 1

1. R. Hooker, *Of the Laws of Ecclesiastical Polity*, "A Sermon on the Certainty and Perpetuity of Faith in the Elect" (London, Dent, 1958), I, p. 3.
2. *Ecclesiastical Polity*, "A Learned Discourse of Justification" (Everyman edition), I, p. 17.
3. See Appendix A for quotation and translation of Council of Trent on justification.
4. Op. cit., p. 22.
5. Ibid., p. 21.
6. Ibid., p. 22.
7. *The Works of That Learned and Judicious Divine, Mr. Richard Hooker*: "Answer to Travers" (Oxford 1850), II, p. 684.
8. Ibid., II, p. 685.
9. Cf. "A Learned Discourse of Justification," op. cit., pp. 19, 20.
10. *The Works of That Learned and Judicious Divine, Mr. Richard Hooker*, II, p. 240.
11. *Ecclesiastical Polity*, VI, iii, 3.
12. Ibid., VI, iii, 3.
13. *Works*, Keble edition, Vol. III, Sermon III, pp. 609-10.
14. Ibid., Sermon IV, p. 692.
15. *Ecclesiastical Polity*, VI, v. 9.
16. Translated from the Latin by the Reverend Josiah Allport (London 1844).
17. *A Treatise on Justification*, I, p. 8.
18. Ibid., I, p. 231.
19. See Appendix A.
20. Bellarmine, *de Justif.*, lib. 2, cap. 16.
21. Davenant, *A Treatise on Justification*, I, pp. 164-5.
22. The Council of Trent, "De Peccato Originali", Session V.
23. Suarez, *Disputationes*, III, quaest. 69, art. 4.
24. Bellarmine, *de Amiss. Grat.*, lib. 5. cap. 9.

25. *"We teach that the evil root itself* is broken, bruised, and hewn in pieces; and moreover that another root of spiritual righteousness and holiness is implanted in the souls of the justified. This is much more than to be only *cut down* or *non-imputed*, let the Fathers of Trent and the Jesuits growl at us as they please". *A Treatise on Justification*, I, p. 17.

26. Ibid., I, p. 18.

27. Ibid., I, p. 227.

28. Ibid., I, p. 335.

29. Ibid., I, pp. 231-2.

30. Ibid., I, p. 160.

31. Ibid., I, p. 171.

32. Ibid., I, p. 296.

33. Ibid., I, p. 314.

34. Ibid., I, p. 315.

35. Ibid., The Preface, pp. xix-xx.

36. Ibid., I, p. 228.

37. Downame, *A Treatise of Justification* (London 1639), p. 15.

38. Ibid., p. 479.

39. Ibid., p. 1.

40. Ibid., p. 45.

41. Ibid., p. 6.

42. Op. cit., I, p. 170.

43. Op. cit., p. 2.

44. Ibid., p. 38.

45. *The Works of Joseph Hall* in 12 vols. (Oxford 1937-9), "The Old Religion", IX, p. 321.

46. *Works*, IX, p. 322.

47. *Works*, IX, p. 327.

48. *Works*, IX, p. 327.

49. *Works*, "No Peace with Rome", XI, p. 318.

50. *Works*, XI, p. 320.

51. *The Whole Works of the Most Rev. James Ussher*, D.D., Lord Archbishop of Armagh, and Primate of All Ireland, edited by Charles Richard Elrington, D.D. (Dublin 1829-64), Sermon XVII, XIII, p. 264.

52. *Works*, XIII. p. 250.

53. *Works*, XIII, p. 250.

54. *Works*, XIII, p. 251.

55. *Works*, XIII, p. 255.

56. *Works*, XIII, p. 256.

57. *Works*, XVI, p. 252.

58. *Works*, XVI, p. 253.

59. *Works*, XVI, p. 260.

60. *Works*, XIII, p. 260.

61. *Works*, IV, p. 257, *A Discourse of the Religion Anciently Professed by the Irish and British* (1631).

62. *Works*, Sermon XV, XIII, p. 239.

63. *Works*, XIII, p. 239.

64. *The Sermons of John Donne*, edited with Introductions and Critical Apparatus, by George R. Potter and Evelyn M. Simpson, Sermon III, II, p. 116 (Berkeley and Los Angeles 1953).

65. *The Sermons of John Donne*, Sermon VII, I, p. 287. See also Sermon VI, II, p. 149 and Sermon III, II.

66. Ibid., Sermon IV, II, p. 121.

67. *The Works of John Donne, Dean of St. Paul's, 1621-1631* with a Memoir of His Life by Henry Alford, M.A. (London 1839), I, p. 199. The quotations from the Alford edition may be found now in the Potter and Simpson edition also.

68. *The Sermons of John Donne*, Sermon VI, II, p. 160. See also Sermon III, II, p. 100.

69. Ibid., Sermon VII, I, p. 271. See also Sermon IX, I, p. 315.

70. Ibid., Sermon V, II, p. 143.

71. *The Works of John Donne*, Alford edition, V, p. 156.

72. *The Works*, IV, p. 111.

73. *The Sermons of John Donne*, I, p. 295.

74. There is a serious misunderstanding of justification and *prevenient grace* in a book on Donne's theology. The author states that Donne "laid great stress on the power of 'preventing grace' in saving us from committing those sins which we otherwise would have done" (Itrat Husain, *The Dogmatic and Mystical Theology of John Donne* (London 1938), p. 101). This misunderstanding distorts the author's discussion of Donne's soteriology.

75. *The Works of John Donne*, Sermon LIX, II, p. 518.

76. *The Works*, Sermon LIX, II, p. 518.

77. *The Sermons of John Donne*, Sermon XII, II, p. 264.

78. Ibid., Sermon V, II, p. 137.

79. Andrewes, Lancelot, *The Works*, The Library of Anglo-Catholic Theology, Sermon V, V, p. 166. (Hereafter abbreviated L.A.C.T.)

80. *The Works*, L.A.C.T., V, p. 124.

81. *The Works*, V, p. 114.

82. *The Works*, V, p. 118.

83. *The Works*, V, p. 116.

84. *The Works*, V, p. 556.

85. *The Works*, III, p. 340.

86. *The Works*, III, p. 102.

CHAPTER 2

1. The *Dictionary of National Biography* has the correct birth and death dates but claims he was forty-four years old when he died. It should be forty-nine. *D.N.B.* VII, Article, "William Forbes", p. 411.

2. *Forbes*, I, p. 17.

3. Ibid., p. 23.

4. Ibid., p. 165.

5. Ibid., p. 149.

6. Ibid., p. 269.

7. Ibid., pp. 317-19.

8. Ibid., p. 357.

9. Ibid., p. 447.

10. Ibid., p. 491.

11. Ibid., pp. 87, 89.

12. *Lectures on Justification* (London 1838).

13. Hagenback, *History of Doctrines*, III; p. 117; F. J. Hall, *Dogmatic Theology*, VIII, p. 260.

14. E. G. Selwyn, *The First Book of the Irenicum of John Forbes of Corse*, p. 7: "Dr William Forbes, who was the first holder of the See of Edinburgh (1634), represented a theological position scarcely distinguishable from that of Dr Pusey; and the perusal of his *Considerationes, etc.* led Dr Döllinger to say that he had never before realized how strong the case was for a Catholicism which was not Papal."

15. Op. cit., p. 17.

16. Ibid., p. 7.

17. Ibid., pp. 71, 73.

18. Ibid., p. 13.

19. Ibid., p. 85.

20. Ibid., p. 57.

21. Ibid., p. 165.

22. Ibid., p. 209.

23. Ibid., p. 175.

24. Ibid., p. 135.

25. Ibid., p. 129.

26. Ibid., p. 297.

27. Ibid., p. 149.

28. Ibid., p. 295.

29. Ibid., p. 135.

30. Ibid., p. 127.

31. Ibid., p. 127.

32. Ibid., p. 63.

33. Ibid., p. 27.

34. Ibid., p. 173.

35. See also pp. 175 and 297, as well as the entire second book.

36. *City of God*, lib. XIX, cap. 27.

37. Op. cit., pp. 217, 219.

38. Ibid.

39. Ibid., p. 25.

40. Session V.

41. Op. cit., p. 169.

42. Ibid., p. 221.

43. Ibid., pp. 391-3. See also p. 221.

44. Ibid., p. 223.

45. Ibid., p. 217.

46. Ibid., p. 59.

47. Ibid., p. 357 (italics mine).

48. Ibid., p. 317.

49. Ibid., p. 51.

50. *The Works of Thomas Jackson*, "Justifying Faith", III (Oxford 1844), p. 14.

51. *Works*, III, p. 287.

52. *Works*, III, p. 288.

53. *Works*, III, pp. 291-2.

54. *Works*, III, p. 357.

55. *Works*, III, p. 300.

56. *Works*, III, p. 297.

57. *Works*, "Commentaries on the Creed", X, p. 325.

58. *Works*, "Justifying Faith", III, p. 296.

59. *Works*, III, p. 301.

60. *Works*, III, pp. 301-2.

61. *Works*, III, p. 286.

62. *Works*, "Commentaries on the Creed", X, pp. 539-40.

63. *Works*, "Justifying Faith", III, pp. 321, 336-7.

64. *Works*, III, p. 297.

65. *Works*, III, p. 313.

66. *Works*, III, p. 13 (italics mine).

67. *Works*, III, p. 301.

68. *Works*, "Commentaries on the Creed", X, p. 583.

69. *Works*, "Justifying Faith", III, pp. 301-2.

70. *Works,* III, p. 318.

71. *Works,* III, p. 311.

72. *Works,* "Commentaries on the Creed", X, p. 541.

73. *Works,* "A Treatise", IX, p. 201.

74. *Works,* IX, p. 579.

75. *Works,* "Commentaries on the Creed", X, p. 325. See also: "Justifying Faith", III, pp. 366–7.

76. *Works,* "Justifying Faith", III, p. 368.

77. *Works,* III, p. 320.

78. *Works,* "Commentaries on the Creed", X, p. 581.

79. *Works,* "Justifying Faith", III, p. 312.

80. *Works,* III, pp. 320-1.

81. *Works,* III, p. 314.

82. *Works,* III, p. 320 (italics mine).

83. *Works,* III, p. 319.

84. *A Gagg for the Gospell? No: A New Gagg for an Old Goose* (London, 1624), pp. 142-3.

85. *Appello Caesarem* (London 1625), p. 144.

86. Ibid., p. 172.

87. Ibid., p. 199.

88. Ibid., p. 187.

89. *A Dangerous Plot . . .* (London, 1626), p. 8.

90. *Cosin's Works,* L.A.C.T., II, p. 49.

91. *Laud's Works,* L.A.C.T., VI (Part II), pp. 244-5.

92. *Cosin's Works,* L.A.C.T., IV, p. 468.

93. Chillingworth, *Religion of Protestants, A Safe Way to Salvation* (London 1845), p. 492. First published 1637.

94. Ibid., p. 493.

95. Ibid., p. 492.

CHAPTER 3

1. *The Whole Works of the Rt. Rev. Jeremy Taylor, D.D., with a Life of the Author and a Critical Examination of his Writings,* Reginald Heber (London 1828), VI, Sermon III "Fides Formata", p. 268. All references will be to the Heber edition.

2. *Works,* "Sermons", VI, p. 227.

3. *Works,* VI, p. 279.

4. *Works,* Sermon XXVI, "The Miracles of the Divine Mercy", VI, pp. 211-12.

5. *Works*, "A Letter to Bishop Warner", IX, pp. 378-9.

6. *Works*, Sermon II, "The Christian's Conquest Over the Body of Sin", VI, p. 247.

7. *Works*, VI, p. 258.

8. *Works*, VI, p. 259.

9. *Works*, VI, p. 255.

10. *Works*, "Holy Living", IV, p. 255.

11. *Works*, IV, p. 260.

12. *Works*, IV, p. 267.

13. *Works*, IV, p. 256.

14. *Works*, IV, p. 257.

15. *Works*, IV, p. 262.

16. *Works*, IV, p. 260.

17. *Works*, IV, p. 261.

18. *Works*, IV, p. 256.

19. *Works*, "The History of the Life and Death of the Holy Jesus", II, p. 412.

20. *Works*, "Unum Necessarium", VIII, pp. 317-18.

21. *Works*, "The History of the Life and Death of the Holy Jesus", II, p. 411.

22. *Works*, II, p. 415.

23. *Works*, II, pp. 396-7.

24. *Works*, Sermon V, "The Invalidity of a Late or Death-Bed Repentance", V, p. 493.

25. *Works*, "The History of the Life and Death of the Holy Jesus", II, p. 399.

26. *Works*, II, pp. 398-9.

27. *Works*, "Unum Necessarium", VIII, p. 315.

28. *Works*, VIII, p. 292.

29. *Works*, "Holy Dying", IV, p. 468.

30. *Works*, Sermon VII, "Of Godly Fear", V, p. 114.

31. *Works*, V, p. 475.

32. *Works*, "The Worthy Communicant", XV, p. 612.

33. *Works*, XV, p. 610.

34. *Works*, XV, p. 588.

35. *Works*, XV, p. 643.

36. *Works*, XV, p. 533.

37. *Works*, XV, p. 533.

38. *Works*, XV, p. 596.

39. *Works*, XV, p. 470.

40. *Works,* XV, p. 474.
41. *Works,* XV, p. 474.
42. *Works,* XV, p. 418.
43. *Works,* XV, p. 474.
44. *Works,* XV, p. 608.
45. *Works,* XV, p. 471.
46. *Works,* XV, p. 659.
47. *Works,* XV, p. 664.
48. *Works,* XV, pp. 425-62.
49. *Works,* XV, p. 471.
50. *Works,* XV, p. 539.
51. *Works,* XV, p. 587.
52. *Works,* XV, p. 518.
53. *Works,* XV, p. 610.
54. *Works,* XV, p. 586.
55. *Works,* XV, p. 627.
56. *Works,* Sermon XVI, "Of Growth in Sin", VI, p. 50.
57. *Works,* "Unum Necessarium", VIII, p. 514.
58. *Works,* Sermon IV, "The Return of Prayers", V, p. 65.
59. *Works,* V, p. 64.

CHAPTER 4

1. *Works,* "Holy Living", IV, pp. 284-6.
2. *Works,* IV, p. 260.
3. *Works,* IV, p. 276.
4. *Works,* IV, p. 292.
5. *Works,* IV, pp. 141-2.
6. *Works,* IV, p. 302.
7. *Works,* "Unum Necessarium", VIII, p. 532.
8. *Works,* "Holy Dying", IV, p. 485.
9. *Works,* IV, p. 382.
10. *Works,* IV, pp. 550-1.
11. *Works,* "Unum Necessarium", VIII, p. 417.
12. *Works,* "Holy Dying", IV, p. 552.
13. *Works,* "The Worthy Communicant", XV, pp. 665-6.
14. *Works,* XV, p. 497.
15. *Works,* XV, p. 497.
16. See Appendix B for question of authorship.

17. *Works,* "Christian Consolations", I, p. 125.
18. *Works,* I, p. 125.
19. *Works,* "Fides Formata", VI, p. 273.
20. *Works,* "Unum Necessarium", VIII, p. 513 (italics mine).
21. *Works,* "Christian Consolations", I, p. 93.
22. Cf. p. 4 above.
23. *Works,* "Unum Necessarium", VIII, p. 507.
24. *Works,* VIII, p. 508.
25. *Works,* VIII, p. 514.
26. *Works,* VIII, p. 530.
27. "Life of Jeremy Taylor", Heber, I, p. xlii.
28. A letter from Barlow to Walton, Walton's *Life of Dr. Sanderson* (London 1678).
29. A letter from Sanderson to Barlow; Tanner Papers lii, fo. 173.
30. *Thorndike's Works,* "The Covenant of Grace", L.A.C.T., III, Pt. II, p. 163.
31. *Works,* "Holy Dying", IV, p. 532.
32. *English Casuistical Divinity During the Seventeenth Century,* by Thomas Wood (London 1952), pp. 126-7.
33. *Works,* "Unum Necessarium", VIII, p. 514.
34. *Works,* "The Worthy Communicant", XV, p. 606.
35. *Works,* XV, p. 636.
36. *Works,* XV, p. 637.
37. *Works,* "Holy Dying", IV, pp. 428-9.
38. *Works,* IV, p. 433.
39. *Works,* IV, p. 369.
40. *Notes on English Divines* by Samuel Taylor Coleridge, edited by Derwent Coleridge, 2 vols. (London), I, p. 248.
41. Ibid., II, p. 38.
42. Ibid., I, p. 268.
43. Ibid., I, p. 278.
44. Ibid., I, pp. 274-5.
45. Ibid., I, p. 278.
46. Ibid., I, p. 268.
47. *An Exposition of the Apostles Creed* (London 1661), pp. 579-80.

CHAPTER 5

1. *Practical Catechism,* L.A.C.T., p. 78.
2. Ibid., p. 81.

3. Ibid., p. 78.

4. Ibid., p. 82.

5. Ibid., pp. 81-2.

6. Ibid., p. 82.

7. Ibid., p. 79.

8. Ibid., p. 79.

9. Ibid., p. 82.

10. *Hammond's Sermons*, Part I, L.A.C.T., p. 113.

11. Ibid., p. 115.

12. Ibid., p. 124.

13. *Practical Catechism*, L.A.C.T., p. 78.

14. *Hammond's Sermons*, L.A.C.T., Part I, pp. 113-14.

15. *Practical Catechism*, L.A.C.T., p. 79.

16. Ibid., p. 82.

17. *Hammond's Minor Theological Works*, "Of Fundamentals", L.A.C.T., p. 129.

18. Ibid., p. 126.

19. Ibid., p. 128.

20. *Hammond's Sermons*, Part I, "On the Necessity of the Christian's Cleansing", L.A.C.T., p. 115.

21. *Hammond's Minor Theological Works*, "Of Fundamentals", L.A.C.T., p. 170.

22. Ibid., "A Paraenesis", pp. 313, 311.

23. *A Brief Vindication . . .*, p. 9. *A View of Some Exceptions . . .*, p. 7.

24. *A Copy of Some Papers Past at Oxford . . .* (London 1650), p. 22.

25. Ibid., pp. 53-4.

26. Ibid., pp. 70, 72-3.

27. Ibid., p. 123.

28. Ibid.

29. Ibid., p. 124.

30. Ibid.

31. *Thorndike's Works*, "The Covenant of Grace", L.A.C.T., III, Pt. II, p. 592.

32. *Thorndike's Works*, "Just Weights and Measures", L.A.C.T., V, p. 144.

33. *Works*, V.

34. *Works*, "The Covenant of Grace", III, p. 9.

35. *Works*, III, p. 3.

36. *Thorndike's Works*, "Due Way of Composing the Differences on Foot, Preserving the Church", L.A.C.T., V, p. 35.

37. *Works*, V, p. 37.

38. *Works*, "Just Weights and Measures", V, p. 132.

39. *Thorndike's Works*, "Reformation in Church of England better than that of Council of Trent", L.A.C.T., V, p. 529.

40. *Works*, "The Covenant of Grace", III, pp. 592-3.

41. *Works*, III, pp. 593-4.

42. *Works*, III, p. 595.

43. *Works*, III, p. 595.

44. *Works*, III, p. 595.

45. *Works*, "Just Weights and Measures", V, p. 139.

46. *Works*, "The Covenant of Grace", III, p. 596.

47. *Works*, "Just Weights and Measures", V, p. 141.

48. *Works*, "The Covenant of Grace", III, p. 598.

49. *Works,* III, p. 598.

50. *Works*, III, p. 603.

51. *Works*, III, p. 652.

52. *Works*, III, p. 124.

53. *Works,* "Just Weights and Measures", V, p. 149.

54. *Works*, V, p. 137.

55. *Works*, V, p. 144.

56. *Works*, V, p. 142.

57. *Works*, V, p. 146.

58. *Works*, V, p. 148.

59. *Works*, "The Covenant of Grace", III, p. 595.

60. *Works*, III, p. 580.

61. *Works,* "Just Weights and Measures", V, p. 140.

62. *Works*, V, p. 136.

63. *Works*, V, pp. 142-3 (italics mine).

64. *Works*, V, p. 138 (italics mine).

65. *Works,* V, p. 153.

66. *Works*, "The Covenant of Grace", III, p. 580.

67. *Works*, "Just Weights and Measures", V, p. 145.

68. *Works*, V, p. 155.

69. *Works*, "Reformation Better than that of Council of Trent", V, p. 536.

70. *Works,* "The Covenant of Grace", III, p. 580.

71. *Works*, "Just Weights and Measures", V, p. 134.

72. *Works*, "The Covenant of Grace", III, p. 664.

73. *Works*, "Reformation Better than that of Council of Trent", V, pp. 536-7.

74. *Works*, "The Covenant of Grace", III, p. 663.

75. *Works*, III, p. 661.

76. *Works*, III, p. 571.

77. *Works*, "Reformation Better than that of Council of Trent", V, p. 536.

78. *Works*, "Just Weights and Measures", V, p. 552 (italics mine).

79. *Works*, "The Covenant of Grace", III, p. 661.

80. *Works*, III, p. 163.

81. *Works*, III, p. 99.

CHAPTER 6

1. George Bull, *Harmonia Apostolica*, L.A.C.T., Part I, pp. 14-15. The translation in the L.A.C.T. is based upon that of the Reverend Thomas Wilkinson in 1801. Bull's work on justification is divided into three parts, the *Harmonia Apostolica*, the *Examen Censurae*, and the *Apologia pro Harmonia*.

2. Ibid., p. 18.

3. Ibid., p. 32.

4. Ibid., p. 43.

5. Ibid., p. 57.

6. Ibid., p. 57.

7. Ibid., p. 58.

8. Ibid., p. 194.

9. Unlike the other critics, Truman explicitly agreed with Bull on the essential question that justifying faith must include the whole duty of a Christian.

10. Op. cit., *Harmonia Apostolica*, p. 22.

11. Ibid., p. 99.

12. Ibid., p. 8.

13. George Bull, *Examen Censurae*, L.A.C.T., pp. 38-9.

14. George Bull, *Apologia pro Harmonia*, L.A.C.T., p. 300.

15. Op. cit., *Examen Censurae*, p. 92.

16. Ibid.

17. Ibid., p. 219.

18. Ibid., p. 36.

19. Op. cit., *Harmonia Apostolica*, p. 15.

20. Ibid., p. 161.

21. Op. cit., *Examen Censurae*, p. 181.

22. Ibid., pp. 181-2.

23. Op. cit., *Harmonia Apostolica*, p. 195.

24. Op. cit., *Examen Censurae*, p. 171.

25. Op. cit., *Harmonia Apostolica*, p. 14.

26. Op. cit., *Examen Censurae*, p. 202.

27. Op. cit., *Harmonia Apostolica*, p. 14.

28. Ibid., pp. 54, 209; op. cit., *Examen Censurae*, pp. 59, 129, 131.

29. Op. cit., *Harmonia Apostolica*, p. 164.

30. Ibid., p. 148.

31. Op. cit., *Examen Censurae*, p. 103.

32. Op. cit., *Harmonia Apostolica*, p. 161.

33. Op. cit., *Examen Censurae*, p. 3.

34. Op. cit., *Apologia pro Harmonia*, p. 368.

35. Ibid., pp. 279-80.

36. Op. cit., *Harmonia Apostolica*, p. 214.

37. Davenant, *A Treatise on Justification*, p. 616.

38. Op. cit., *Harmonia Apostolica*, p. 30.

39. Op. cit., *Apologia pro Harmonia*, p. 288.

40. Op. cit., *Examen Censurae*, p. 72.

41. Op. cit., *Harmonia Apostolica*, p. 30.

42. Ibid., p. 39.

43. Ibid.

44. *Disp. Just.*, chapter 30, Thes. 1, Arg. 2.

45. See chapter 1 above.

46. Op. cit., *Harmonia Apostolica*, p. 99.

47. Ibid., p. 117.

48. Op. cit., *Examen Censurae*, p. 170.

49. Ibid.

50. Ibid., p. 182.

51. Ibid., p. 171.

52. Ibid., pp. 165-6.

53. Op. cit., *Harmonia Apostolica*, p. 21.

54. Ibid., p. 13.

55. Ibid., pp. 12-13.

56. Ibid., p. 209.

57. There is a grave error in the L.A.C.T. edition of Bull's works in regard to Bull's view of Bellarmine's doctrine. The page title over a long quotation from Bellarmine is entitled "Bellarmine's interpretation the true one" (*Examen Censurae*, p. 82). Actually, Bull is not here approving Bellarmine's argument, but is insisting that Gataker will be unable to answer either Bellarmine or the antinomians because of Gataker's interpretation of Romans 5.19. The same error occurs in the index under "Bellarmine".

58. Op. cit., *Apologia pro Harmonia*, pp. 258-9.

59. Op. cit., *Examen Censurae*, p. 74.

60. Ibid., p. 202 (italics mine).

61. Op. cit., *Apologia pro Harmonia*, p. 289.

62. Op. cit., *Harmonia Apostolica*, p. 122 (italics mine).

63. Op. cit., *Examen Censurae*, pp. 91-2.

64. Op. cit., *Harmonia Apostolica*, p. 29.

65. Op. cit., *Examen Censurae*, p. 23.

66. Ibid.

67. Op. cit., *Harmonia Apostolica*, p. 60.

68. Ibid., p. 43.

69. Op. cit., *Examen Censurae*, p. 222.

70. Op. cit., *Harmonia Apostolica*, p. 34 (verbo dicam, Quisquis e faece Romuli hanc hypothesin nude traditam acceperit . . . , Part I, VI, par. 2).

71. Ibid., p. 138.

72. Ibid., p. 58.

73. Tully, *Justificatio Paulina*, "Dissertatium . . . Rom. 7" (London 1674), p. 33.

74. Op. cit., *Apologia pro Harmonia*, p. 400.

75. Op. cit., *Harmonia Apostolica*, p. x.

CHAPTER 7

1. John Bramhall, *An Answer to M. de La Milletière*, L.A.C.T., I, p. 56.

2. Ibid., II, p. 220.

3. William Nicholson, *An Exposition of the Apostles' Creed Delivered in Several Sermons*, L.A.C.T. (London 1661), Sermon 22, Part II, p. 287. It is of historical interest to note that Nicholson was George Bull's Diocesan at the time of the publication of the *Harmonia*, and that it was to Nicholson that Charles Gataker sent his strictures upon Bull's doctrine.

4. Ibid.

5. Ibid., p. 286.

6. *Sermons by The Rt Rev. Rob't. Sanderson*, ed. by the Reverend P. Montgomery (London 1841), I, p. 543.

7. William Nicholson, *A Plain but Full Exposition of the Catechism of the Church of England*, L.A.C.T. (London 1686), p. 67.

8. See chapter 5 above.

9. Isaak Walton, *The Life of Dr Sanderson, Late Bishop of Lincoln*, 1st ed. (London 1676), p. 114.

10. *An Antidote Against Error . . .* , "To Which is Added": *The Way of Truth and Peace* or "A reconciliation of the holy Apostles . . . concerning Justification" by Charles Gataker, p. 86.

11. *Justificatio Paulina*, p. 3.

12. *Two Letters written by the Rt Rev. Dr Thomas Barlow* (London 1701), Tanner 729, preface.

13. Ibid., p. 133. See also pp. 80-1, 163.

14. Ibid., pp. 178-9.

15. Ibid., p. 125.

16. Ibid., p. 179.

17. Ibid., pp. 158-9.

18. Ibid., p. 164.

19. Ibid., p. 82.

20. Ibid. However, cf. Ussher's views on this matter in chapter 1 above.

21. Ibid., p. 62.

22. Ibid., p. 190.

23. Ibid., pp. 123-4.

24. Or "A plain Demonstration, that the induing with inward, real Righteousness (or true Holiness) was the ultimate End of our Saviour's coming into the World; and is the great Intention of his blessed Gospel" by Edward Fowler (London 1671).

25. Ibid., 4th ed., p. 190.

26. Ibid.

27. Ibid., p. 206.

28. Ibid., p. 218.

29. Bunyan, *A Defence of the Doctrine of Justification*, Preface: "From Prison, the 27 of the 12 month, 1671", p. 4.

30. *Dirt Wipt Off* (London 1672), Preface.

31. *The Design of Christianity*, 1st ed., p. 300 (italics supplied).

32. Ibid., p. 17.

33. *A Defence of the Doctrine of Justification*, p. 29.

34. Edward Stillingfleet, *Sermons Preached on Several Occasions to Which a Discourse is Annexted Concerning The True Reason of the Sufferings of Christ*, 2nd ed. (London 1673), p. 383.

35. Ibid., p. 261.

36. Ibid., p. 77.

37. William Beveridge, *On the 39 Articles*, L.A.C.T., VII, p. 292.

38. *The Theological Works of Isaac Barrow,* ed. Alex Napier, Sermon IV, V, pp. 159, 174.

39. *Works*, "The Doctrine of Universal Redemption", IV, p. 310.

40. *Works*, Sermon IV, V, p. 164.

41. *Works*, V, pp. 168-9.

42. *Works*, V, p. 162.

43. *Works*, V, p. 170.

44. *Works*, V, p. 179.

45. *Works*, V, p. 157.
46. *The Whole Duty of Man* (London 1806), pp. 4-5.
47. Ibid., p. 38.
48. Ibid., p. 45.
49. Ibid., p. 46.
50. Ibid., p. 47.
51. Ibid., p. 84.
52. Ibid., p. 53.
53. Ibid., p. 62.
54. Ibid., p. 37.
55. Ibid., p. 70.
56. Ibid.
57. Ibid., p. 55.
58. Ibid., p. 264.
59. Ibid., p. 265.

CHAPTER 8

1. See chapter 7 above.
2. Richard Baxter, *A Treatise of Justifying Righteousness* (London 1676), Book I, p. 22.
3. *The Practical Works of Richard Baxter*, by the Reverend William Orme, "Life of Richard Baxter" (London 1830), I, p. 448.
4. Ibid., "Short Meditation on Romans V, 1-5", XVIII, p. 503.
5. Richard Baxter, *Aphorisms on Justification* (London 1649), p. 60.
6. Richard Baxter, *A Treatise of Justifying Righteousness*, p. 161.
7. Ibid., p. 178.
8. *Aphorisms on Justification*, p. 70.
9. *A Treatise of Justifying Righteousness*, p. 88.
10. Ibid., pp. 129-30.
11. *Aphorisms on Justification*, p. 49.
12. *A Treatise of Justifying Righteousness*, p. 29.
13. Ibid., p. 35.
14. Ibid., p. 25.
15. *The Practical Works of Richard Baxter*, "The Christian Directory", VI, p. 522.
16. *The Practical Works of Richard Baxter*, "Life of Faith", XII, p. 306.
17. *A Treatise of Justifying Righteousness*, p. 163.
18. *The Practical Works of Richard Baxter*, "The Catechising of Families", XIX, p. 103.

19. Richard Baxter, *An Appeal to the Light* (London 1674), p. 3.

20. *A Treatise of Justifying Righteousness*, p. 170.

21. Ibid., p. 183.

22. Ibid., p. 10.

23. *An Appeal to the Light*, p. 2.

24. William Bradshaw, *A Treatise of Justification*, "Tending to prove that a Sinner is justified before God, onely by Christ's Righteousness imputed" (London 1615), pp. 87-8.

25. Op. cit., *A Treatise of Justifying Righteousness*, p. 157.

26. George Lawson, *Theo-Politica* (London 1659), p. 315.

27. Or "A Treatise of Justification wherein ye imputation of faith for righteousness (mentioned Romans 4.3-5) is explained" (London 1642).

28. Ibid., Section I, p. 57.

29. Ibid., p. 26.

30. Ibid., Section II, p. 99.

31. Ibid., pp. 3-4.

32. Ibid., p. 212.

33. George Walker, *A Defence of the True Sence* . . . (London 1641), p. 15.

34. Ibid., p. 22.

35. Ibid.

36. Ibid., p. 55.

37. Ibid., pp. 55-6.

38. William Eyre, *Vindiciae Justificationis Gratuitae* . . . (London 1654).

39. Ibid., p. 7.

40. John Eedes, *The Orthodox Doctrine* . . . (London 1654), p. 5.

41. Ibid., p. 56.

42. Ibid., p. 58.

43. Ibid., p. 62.

44. *Works of Joseph Hall*, IV, p. 60.

45. John Eaton, *The Honey-Combe of Free Justification* (London 1642), p. 87.

46. Ibid.

47. Ibid., pp. 475-6.

48. John Saltmarsh, *Free Grace* (London 1792), p. 163.

49. Ibid., p. 142.

50. Ibid., p. 161.

51. Ibid., p. 143.

52. Ibid., p. 8.

53. Ibid., p. 145.

54. Tobias Crisp, *Christ Alone Exalted* (London 1832), I, p. 36.

55. Ibid., p. 49.

56. Ibid., p. 91.

57. Ibid., pp. 34-5.

58. Ibid., II, p. 166.

59. Thomas Gataker, *Antinomianism Discovered* (London 1652), p. 4.

60. Ibid., p. 35.

61. Thomas Gataker, *An Antidote Against Error* (London 1670), p. 10.

62. Ibid., p. 16.

63. Ibid., pp. 37-8.

64. *The Works of John Owen*, D.D., "Arguments Against Universal Redemption", ed. Thomas Russell (London 1826), V, p. 374.

65. *Works*, "The Doctrine of Justification by Faith", XI, p. 258.

66. *Works*, XI, pp. 214-15.

67. *Works*, XI, p. 259.

68. *Works*, XI, p. 286.

69. *Works*, XI, p. 474.

CHAPTER 9

1. Barclay, *The Truth Triumphant Through Spiritual Warfare* (London 1692), p. 377.

2. Cf. p. 7 above.

3. Op. cit., *Considerations Modestae*, p. 223.

4. Cf. p. 142 above.

CHAPTER 10

1. A superb criticism of English Reformation soteriology can be found in G. W. H. Lampe's *Reconciliation in Christ*, Longmans, 1956.

2. Bishop Wand shows the radical dependence of Athanasius' position on his understanding of soteriology. "What moved Athanasius so strongly was the need to preserve the whole scheme of salvation" (*The Four Great Heresies*, London 1955, Mowbray, p. 47).

3. Cf. chapter 6 above.

4. P. 94 above.

5. Professor William Haller, in a recent work, *Liberty and Reformation in the Puritan Revolution* (New York 1955), is obviously under this impression. In speaking of John Walwyn's tutor he states that "John Preston, for example, Master of Emmanuel, would have denied the doctrine of free justification . . ." (p. 168). On the contrary, Preston was an exceedingly strong adherent of free justification as can be seen from his support of the charges against Richard Montague in 1625. See *Cosin's Works*, L.A.C.T.,

II, p. 36. Also, on p. 215, Haller states that the "army dominated by men who believed in free justification . . . was not likely to surrender its sword lightly to a parliament intolerant of such notions". The theology of Presbyterian divines was consistently one of "free justification" and instead of the Puritan revolution bringing this idea in as new, it was during this revolution that the new (for the seventeenth century) doctrine of a *non*-free justification arose.

6. One is tempted to speculate upon the relationship between the relatively ordered society of the ancient Roman world and St Paul's doctrine of justification. Perhaps only where the reality of law is quite strong does justification have much relevance. Is there any relationship between the content of St Paul's Epistles and the reality of which his adoption of Roman citizenship is a symbol?

7. A memorandum unsigned. MS. Cherry 19 9793 Bodleian Library.

8. Heber, *Life of Jeremy Taylor, D.D.*, Vol. I, p. xxvii (Heber edition).

9. A letter from Dr Sanderson to Dr Barlow, 28 September 1656, MS. Cherry 19 9793 Bodleian Library.

10. L.A.C.T., Part I, Vol. VI, p. 245.

11. The Reverend James Garbett, in the Bampton Lectures of 1842, argued that the decline in Anglican theology could be dated from the publication of Bull's *Harmonia*, but almost everyone else since the seventeenth century has been astonishingly uncritical of Bull's theology (*Bampton Lectures, 1842*, pp. 373-4).

12. *A Practical Catechism*, p. 82.

13. *Laud's Works*, L.A.C.T., VI (Part I), p. 249.

14. *An Exposition of the Apostles' Creed* (London 1661), pp. 579-80.

15. *Works*, "An Answer (2nd) to a Letter Touching Original Sin", IX, p. 395.

16. See Davenant, Hall, and Ussher in chapter 1 above; Barlow in chapter 7 above.

17. P. 94 above.

18. *The Works of That Learned and Judicious Divine Mr Richard Hooker*, II, p. 710.

19. See Taylor, Hammond, and Thorndike in chapters 3, 4, and 5 above; Bull in chapter 6 above.

20. See Thorndike, Taylor, Hammond, Baxter, Fowler, Goodwin, and Bull.

21. Paul Tillich, *Theology of Culture* (O.U.P., N.Y., 1959), p. 115.

22. Owen Chadwick, "Arminianism in England" in *Religion in Life* (Autumn 1960).

23. *Christian Essays in Psychiatry*, ed. P. Mairet (Philosophical Library, N.Y.: Camelot Press, London, 1956), p. 165.

24. Ibid., p. 164.

25. Ibid., p. 167.

26. P. 66 above.

27. P. 4 above.

28. Op. cit., p. 37.
29. C. J. Stranks, *Anglican Devotion* (London: S.C.M. Press: N.Y.: Seabury Press, 1961), p. 78.
30. *Christian Essays in Psychiatry*, pp. 128-9.
31. *The Sermons of John Donne*, Potter and Simpson edition, II, p. 121.

APPENDIX A

1. *Canons and Decrees of the Council of Trent*, tr. Reverend J. Schroeder, o.p. (London 1941), pp. 23, 33.

APPENDIX B

1. *The Whole Works of Jeremy Taylor*, ed. Heber, Vol. I, p. vii.
2. *The Whole Works of Jeremy Taylor*, ed. C. P. Eden and Alexander Taylor, 10 vols. (London 1850-9), Vol. I, p. vii.
3. Gosse, *Jeremy Taylor* (London 1904); Worley, *Jeremy Taylor* (London 1904); Brown, *Jeremy Taylor* (London 1925).
4. Stranks, *The Life and Writings of Jeremy Taylor* (London 1952).
5. Alexander Knox, *Correspondence between Bishop Jebb and Alexander Knox, Esq.*, ed. Forester (London 1826), Vol. II, p. 516.

Select Bibliography

Andrewes, Lancelot, *The Works*, L.A.C.T., 11 vols. (Oxford 1841-52).
—— "Sermons" (*Works*, Vols. III, V).
—— *"Responsio ad Apologiam Cardinalis Bellarmini"* (*Works*, Vol. XI).
Anonymous, *Animadversions upon a Sheet of Mr Baxter's entitled An Appeal to the Light Printed 1674* (Oxford 1675).
—— *A Dangerous Plot Discovered . . . Wherein is proved, that Mr Richard Montague . . . Laboureth to bring in the faith of Rome and Arminius* (London 1626).
Augustine, *Post Nicene Fathers*, "City of God". Edited by Philip Shaff. Book 17 (New York 1902).
Barrow, Isaac, *Theological Works. Sermons.* Edited by Alexander Napier. Vols. IV, V (Cambridge 1859).
Baxter, Richard, *The Practical Works with a Life of the Author and a Critical Examination of his Writings* by the Reverend William Orme, 23 vols. (London 1830).
—— "Christian Directory" (*Works*, Vol. VI).
—— "The Life of Faith" (*Works*, Vol. XII).
—— "Family Catechism" (*Works*, Vol. XIX).
—— *Aphorism of Justification* (London 1649).
—— *Letters between Mr Baxter and Mr Tombs concerning their Dispute* (London 1652).
—— *Confession of Faith; especially concerning the interest of repentance and sincere Obedience to Christ in our Justification and Salvation* (London 1655).
—— *Four Disputations of Justification* (London 1658).
—— *How Far Holinesse is the Design for Christianity* (London 1671).
—— *An Appeal to the Light* (London 1674).
—— *A Treatise of Justifying Righteousness.* "An Answer to Dr Tullies Angry Letter". "The Substance of Mr Cartwright's Exceptions Considered" (London 1675).
—— *A Defence of Christ and Free Grace* (London 1690).
Bellarmine, Robert, *de Controversiis.* Tomus Tertius (Ingolstadii 1586).
—— *"de Justif."*, lib. 2, cap. 16.

—— "de amiss. Grat.", lib. 5, cap. 6.

Beveridge, William, *The Theological Works*, L.A.C.T., 12 vols. (Oxford 1844-8).

—— "A Discourse upon the Thirty-nine Articles" (*Works*, Vol. VII), second edition.

—— "The Church Catechism Explained" (*Works*, Vol. VIII).

—— "Thesaurus Theologicus", (*Works*, Vols. IX, X).

Bradshaw, William, *A Treatise of Justification* (London 1615).

Bramhall, John, *Works*, L.A.C.T., Vols. I, II (Oxford 1850).

Bull, George, *The Works*, L.A.C.T.

—— *Harmonia Apostolica.*

—— *Examen Censurae.*

—— *Apologia pro Harmonia.*

Bunyan, John, *A Defence of the Doctrine of Justification* (1671).

Canones et Decreta Concilii Tridentini. Edited by A. L. Richter. Sessions IV, V, VI (Lipsia 1853).

Carleton, George, *An Examination of those things wherein the Author of the late Appeale holdeth the Doctrine of the Pelagians and Arminians to be the Doctrine of the Church of England* (London 1626).

Chillingworth, William, *Religion of Protestants, A Safe Way to Salvation* (London 1637).

Cosin, John, *Works*, L.A.C.T. (London 1868-70).

—— "The Sum and Substance of the Conference Concerning Mr Montague's Books, ... Febr. 11, 1625" (*Works*, Vol. II).

—— "Account of the Conferences with the Archbishop of Trapezond" (*Works*, Vol. IV).

Crisp, Tobias, *Christ Alone Exalted* (London 1690).

Davenant, John, *A Treatise on Justification or the "Disputatio de Justitia Habituali et Actuali".* Translated from the Latin by Josiah Allport, 2 vols. (London 1844).

Donne, John, *Sermons.* Edited with Introductions and Critical Apparatus by George R. Potter and Evelyn M. Simpson, 10 vols. (Berkeley and Los Angeles 1953).

—— *The Works.* Edited by Henry Alford, 6 vols. (London 1839).

Downame, George, *A Covenant of Grace* (Dublin 1631).

—— *A Treatise of Justification* (London 1639).

Downame, John, *A Treaties of the True Nature and Definition of Justifying Faith; together with a Defence of the same against the Answere of Mr Baxter* (Oxford 1635).

Eaton, John, *The Honey-Combe of Free Justification* (London 1642).

Eedes, John, *The Orthodox Doctrine concerning Justification Asserted and Vindicated* (London 1654).

Eyre, William, *Vindiciae Justificationis Gratuitae* (London 1654).

Field, Richard, *Of the Church*, 5 books (Cambridge 1852).

—— Appendix to Book III, Vol. II.

—— Book V, Vol. IV.

Forbes, William, *Considerationes Modestae et Pacificae*, L.A.C.T., 2 vols. (Oxford 1850).

—— *de Justificatione*, Vol. I.

Fowler, Edward, *The Design of Christianity* (London 1671)

—— *Dirt Wipt Off* (London 1672).

Gataker, Thomas, *Antinomianism Discovered* (London 1652).

—— *An Antidote Against Error* (London 1670).

Goodwin, John, *Imputatio Fidei* (London 1642).

Hacket, John, *A Century of Sermons* (London 1675).

Hagenback, *History of the Doctrines*, Vol. III (Edinburgh 1881).

Hall, F. J., *Dogmatic Theology*, Vol. VIII (New York 1920).

Hall, Joseph, *Collected Works*, 12 vols. (Oxford 1837).

—— "No Peace with Rome" (1611) (*Works*, Vol. XI).

—— "The Old Religion" (1628) (*Works*, Vol. IX).

Haller, William, *Liberty and Reformation in the Puritan Revolution* (New York 1955).

Hammond, Henry, *Works*, L.A.C.T. (Oxford 1847-9).

—— "The Sermons" (*Works*, Parts I, II).

—— "A Practical Catechism" (*Works*).

—— "The Miscellaneous Theological Works of Henry Hammond", third edition (*Works*).

—— *An Accordance of St Paul with St James* (Oxford 1665).

—— *A Brief Vindication of Three Passages in the Practical Catechism* (London 1648).

—— *A Copy of Some Papers Past at Oxford Betwixt the Author of the Practical Catechisme and Mr Cheynell* (London 1650).

Husain, Itrat, *The Dogmatic and Mystical Theology of John Donne* (London 1938).

Jackson, Thomas, *The Works*, 12 vols. (Oxford 1844).

—— "Justifying Faith" (*Works*, Vol. III).

—— "Commentary on the Creed" (*Works*, Vol. X).

—— "A Treatise" (*Works*, Vol. IX).

Laud, William, *A Relation of the Conference between William Laud and Mr Fisher the Jesuit*. Edited with an introduction and notes by C. H. Simpkinson (London 1901).

—— *The Works*, L.A.C.T. (Oxford 1857).

—— "Notes on Bellarmine" (*Works*, Vol. VI, Pt. II).

Lawson, George, *Theo-Politica* (London 1659).

Montague, Richard, *Appello Caesarem* (London 1625).

—— *A Gagg for the Gospel? No: a New Gagg for an Old Goose* (London 1624).

More and Cross, *Anglicanism* (London 1951).

Newman, John, *Lectures on Justification* (London 1837).

Nicholson, William, *The Works*, L.A.C.T. (Oxford 1854).

—— "An Exposition of the Apostles Creed Delivered in Several Sermons" (1661) (*Works*).

—— "A Plain but Full Exposition of the Catechism of the Church of England" (1684) (*Works*).

Owen, John, *The Works*. Edited by Thomas Russell (London 1826).

—— "The Doctrine of Justification by Faith" (*Works*, Vol. XI).

—— "Arguments Against Universal Redemption" (*Works*, Vol. V).

Prideaux, John, *Lectiones de Totidem Religionis Capitibus* (Oxford 1848).

—— "de Justificatione" (1620) (Lecture V).

Saltmarsh, John, *Free Grace* (London 1792).

Sanderson, Robert, *Sermons*. Edited by the Reverend P. Montgomery, 2 vols. (London 1841).

Selwyn, E. G., *The First Book of the Irenicum of John Forbes of Corse* (Cambridge 1923).

Stillingfleet, Edward, *Sermons Preached on Several Occasions to Which a Discourse is Annexed Concerning the True Reason of the Sufferings of Christ*, 2nd edition (London 1673).

Suarez, *Disputationes in tertiam partem*. III, quaest. 69 art. 4 (Moguntiae 1619).

Taylor, Jeremy, *The Whole Works with a Life of the Author and a Critical Examination of his Writing*. By Reginald Heber, 15 vols. (London 1828).

—— "Life of Jeremy Taylor" (*Works*, Vol. I).

—— "Christian Consolations", attributed to Taylor (*Works*, Vol. I).

—— "The History and the Life and Death of the Holy Jesus" (*Works*, Vol. II).

—— "The Rule and Exercises of Holy Living" (*Works*, Vol. IV).

—— "The Rule and Exercises of Holy Dying" (*Works*, Vol. IV).

—— "The Return of Prayers" (*Works*, Vol. V, Sermon IV).

—— "The Invalidity of a Late or Death-Bed Repentance" (*Works*, Vol. V, Sermon V).

—— "Of Godly Fear" (*Works*, Vol. V, Sermon VII).

—— "Of Growth in Sin" (*Works*, Vol. VI, Sermon XVI).

—— "The Christian's Conquest Over the Body of Sin" (*Works*, Vol. VI, Sermon II).

—— "The Miracle of the Divine Mercy" (*Works*, Vol. VI, Sermon XXVI).

—— *"Unum Necessarium"* (*Works*, Vol. VIII).

—— "Three Sermons Preached at Christ Church, Dublin" (*Works*, Vol. VI).

—— "A Letter to Bishop Warner" (*Works*, Vol. IX).

—— *"Ductor Dubitantium"* (*Works*, Vols. XII, XIII, XIV).

Thorndike, Herbert, *The Theological Works*, L.A.C.T. (Oxford 1844-1856).

—— "An Epilogue to the Tragedy of the Church of England".

—— "The Covenant of Grace" (1659) (*Works*, Vol. III, Pt. II).

—— "Just Weights and Measures" (1662) (*Works*, Vol. V).

—— "Reformation in the Church of England Better than that of the Council of Trent, 1670-72" (*Works*, Vol. V).

—— "Due Way of Composing the Differences on Foot, Preserving the Church" (*Works*, Vol. V).

Tombs, John, *Animadversions upon a Book of George Bull's which he hath Entitled the Apostolical Harmony* (London 1676).

Truman, Joseph, *An Endeavour to Rectify Some Prevailing Opinions* (London 1671).

Tully, Thomas, *Justificatio Paulina sine Operibus ex mente Ecclesiae Anglicanae Omniumque Reliquarum Quae Reformatae audient, asserta et illustrata contra nuperos Novatores* (Oxford 1674).

—— *A Letter to Mr Richard Baxter Occasioned by Several Injurious Reflexions of His upon a Treatise entitled "Justificatio Paulina"* (Oxford 1675).

Ussher, James, *The Whole Works*. Edited by C. R. Elrington, 17 vols. (Dublin 1864).

—— "A Discourse of the Religion Anciently Professed by the Irish and British" (*Works*, Vol. IV).

—— "Sermon XVII" (*Works*, Vol. XIII).

Walker, George, *A Defence of the True Sence . . . of Rom. 4. ver. 3.5.9.* (London 1641).

Walton, Isaak, *Life of Dr Sanderson* (London 1678).

Ward, Samuel, *Opera Nonnulla*. Edita a Setho Wardo (London 1658).

Wood, Thomas, *English Casuistical Divinity During the Seventeenth Century* (London 1952).

Works of King Charles I, Defender of the Faith, The (London 1662).

MANUSCRIPTS

Tanner Paper. A letter from Sanderson to Barlow, Vol. lii, fol. 173.

Two letters written by the Rt Rev. Thomas Barlow (London 1701), Tanner 729.

A Memorandum unsigned. MS. Cherry 19 9793 (Archbishop Ussher's view on justification).

Index